Advance Praise for

"What a jewel! An indispensible _____ _____ that can help us keep an inner ear open to the work of the spirit as we go about the everyday work of the outer world."

—Sarah Susanka, author of *The Not So Big Life*
and the Not So Big House series

"I love the simplicity of this book, but in its simplicity is so much power and knowledge—which is ours if we truly want it."

—Madisyn Taylor, founder of DailyOM and
author of *DailyOM: Learning to Live*
and *DailyOM: Inspirational Thoughts
for a Happy, Healthy, and Fulfilling Day*

"Debra Moffitt brings the noble and universal yearnings of the human soul down to earth, down to the ins and outs of daily life, down to practice."

—David Kundtz, author of
Quiet Mind: One-Minute Retreats from a Busy World

"Filled with daily practices that are easy to try and adapt into your lifestyle, Debra takes us on a life-altering journey to awaken our heart, mind, and soul."

—Kala Ambrose,
author, intuitive, wisdom teacher,
inspirational speaker, and host of the acclaimed
"Explore Your Spirit with Kala" radio show

"Debra Moffitt's simple and clear spiritual practices, which can apply to anybody regardless of their personal beliefs, are inspiring and non-intimidating. By incorporating them into your everyday life, you will certainly experience a greater sense of joy and inner peace."

—Mallika Chopra, founder of www.intent.com

"This inspiring book is an oasis in a stressed-out world. Debra is a gifted teacher who guides us to our sacred spaces and helps us connect with our spirit. I highly recommend it."

—Mary Alice Monroe, *New York Times* bestselling author of *The Butterfly's Daughter*

"The practices Moffitt offers are deceptively simple and easy. By using them repeatedly, you'll achieve profound results."

—Penney Peirce, author of *Frequency: The Power of Personal Vibration*

"Debra Moffitt has gleaned the essence of what truly matters in life and has given you simple, yet profound, pearls of wisdom. These practices can transform your life!"

—Denise Linn, author of *Sacred Space* and *Feng Shui for the Soul*

"Debra Moffitt offers us much wisdom from the world's spiritual traditions. She weaves it beautifully from her own life story and interlaces it with poetry and prose from the masters."

—Carolyn Rivers, founder and director of The Sophia Institute

Awake
in the
world

About the Author

Debra Moffitt is an author and teacher devoted to nurturing the spiritual in everyday life. She leads workshops on spiritual practices at the Sophia Institute and other venues in the U.S. and Europe. Her mind/body/spirit articles, essays and stories appear in publications around the globe and were broadcast by BBC World Services Radio. She has spent over fifteen years practicing meditation, working with dreams and doing spiritual practices. Read her blogs at Intent.com and www.debramoffitt.wordpress. com. Visit her online at www.debramoffitt.com and www. awakeintheworld.com.

Awake in the world

108 Practices to Live a Divinely Inspired Life

DEBRA MOFFITT

Llewellyn Publications
Woodbury, Minnesota

First Edition
First Printing, 2011

Cover design by Ellen Lawson
Cover image © iStockphoto.com/Elena Ray

Llewellyn is a registered trademark of Llewellyn Worldwide Ltd.

Library of Congress Cataloging-in-Publication Data
Moffitt, Debra, 1961–
  Awake in the world: 108 practices to live a divinely inspired life /
Debra Moffitt.—1st ed.
      p. cm.
  Includes bibliographical references.
  ISBN 978-0-7387-2722-6
1. Spiritual life—Miscellanea. 2. Success   Miscellanea. I. Title.
  BF1999.M725 2011
  204'.4--dc22

                                      2010054165

Llewellyn Worldwide Ltd. does not participate in, endorse, or have any authority or responsibility concerning private business transactions between our authors and the public.
  All mail addressed to the author is forwarded but the publisher cannot, unless specifically instructed by the author, give out an address or phone number.
  Any Internet references contained in this work are current at publication time, but the publisher cannot guarantee that a specific location will continue to be maintained. Please refer to the publisher's website for links to authors' websites and other sources.

Llewellyn Publications
A Division of Llewellyn Worldwide Ltd.
2143 Wooddale Drive
Woodbury, MN 55125-2989
www.llewellyn.com

Printed in the United States of America

Contents

Introduction

A few years ago, my successful, materialistic life unraveled one thread at a time. I fell ill, my French husband moved out, and I lost my high-paying executive job. It was the best thing that ever happened to me. Up until then, it seemed I'd been doing everything by the book—working hard, making money, creating a solid marriage, and living a jet-set life with a dream job that required international travel. I lived in a sea-view apartment in Antibes on the French Riviera, surrounded with beautiful things, and I thought life would continue forever more or less the same. But God had other plans. All of these things would disappear over the next years until almost nothing of my old life remained. The shattering and death of the familiar and comfortable world opened the door for a deeper, more vibrant and joyful experience of life. But it didn't feel like it at the time. I felt mostly scared, confused, and hurt and didn't know where to turn to find something enduring.

Inside, I felt world-weary and sick of all the material pursuits that led to more and more desires and discontent. The more money I earned, the more I wanted, and the farther happiness seemed out of reach. My soul cried out, *Is this it? Is this all there is? Will I ever be at peace?* This crisis opened the door to my wandering in search of meaning. I traveled to Virginia Beach and the Association for Research and Enlightenment, Buddhist retreats in France, and an ashram in India. In my yearning for answers, I attended Tibetan rituals and Catholic masses, explored sacred texts from the Bible to the Vedas, and learned that truth is truth regardless of the source. It resonates with an inner knowing and recognition.

At the time I flinched at the word "God." It had come to mean an entity separate and apart, like the image of Michelangelo's Adam reaching out to a bearded image of God on the ceiling of the Sistine Chapel. Some of the people I'd grown up with held a view of God as a being separate and apart and threatening punishment and passing judgment. Their God lived in a narrow, exclusive world with rigid laws and admitted only a select few. I rejected this idea, but kept my eyes and heart open to help me understand something that I suspected was far more expansive. Something told me that if God is omniscient and omnipresent, that his presence must be no farther away than my own heart and breath—and must be everywhere.

On my search, I observed Catholics in Antibes who saw divinity in the graceful gilded statue of Mother Mary. They lovingly carried it down from the Chapel of the Garoupe on the Cap d'Antibes to the cathedral in the old town for a celebration. Their reverence and piety moved me as I watched the fishermen dressed in blue and white uniforms walk barefooted down the sharp stone "path of the cross," carrying her on a simple platform on their shoulders. In the Camargue of southern France, the Roma—gypsy people—traveled from across Europe to converge on Saintes Maries-de-la-Mer to worship the Black Sarah of Kali. I joined the procession to see Sarah, dressed in her beautiful robes in the claustrophobic vault of the cathedral where her splendid obsidian face glowed in the light of hundreds of candles. Followers touched her feet and their lips moved in silent prayer for healing and guidance.

In Bangkok, I heard the greeting *Namaste* for the first time from a smiling woman at the airport. I later learned it means "I bow to God within you." I watched from my hotel window as the Buddhists carried daily offerings of mangos and pigs' heads to the shrine on the street corner by the mall, and their prayers seemed to waft upward like the smoke of the incense. In discourses from a Tibetan lama, I heard no mention of God or anything separate or distinct from nature, but his teaching pointed to that thing which cannot be understood by the mind. In India, the notion of God became so vast that it encompassed everything—the deities in the trees, Kali, the Goddess with a necklace of human heads; the five-headed Gayatri; elegant *Saraswati*, money in the form of Goddess Lakshmi, Brahman, the Indivisible Supreme Absolute, and in Sanskrit, *"sath, chith, ananda"*—being, consciousness, bliss. As a guest in an Indian household, even I was the embodiment of God and served with kindness and reverence.

And finally I experienced God in nature high in the Swiss Alps. I listened to a small bird and a surge of love flooded my heart; the barriers broke between what I had imagined to be "me" and the bird. In an instant, we merged and I felt its heart beating as it/we/I sang a joyous song until my frightened mind jerked me back into my little self. Later, the same happened with human hearts as I felt them breaking, perceived their fears, and shared the joys of friends and strangers as my own. In this state of being, all simply "is" and all hearts beat as one. God is all of this. I am that essence that reaches beyond words—constant integrated awareness. As one teacher said, "I am God. You are God too only you have not realized it yet." In India this is sometimes referred to as realizing the "One without a second." It's a profound experience that leaves no space for separation or division. This is what "God" refers to in the practices that follow.

What I found on the journey was not new, but it brought solace and a profound sense of acceptance and peace. Most wisdom traditions believe that hard times serve to move us inward and bring us into deeper contact with our spirits. Without the crises, we may continue comfortable and asleep. The trials break us open and the light that enters falls on the seeds of love and peace inherent in human nature, and they can start to grow. The challenges we face are opportunities for awakening and learning. They're there to help us.

This book is the result of those many years of searching and practicing what I garnered from teachers and sacred texts. The exercises have lit the way for seekers for millennia and continue to help us today. They help us embrace the challenges and use them as opportunities to grow. The wisdom in the practices reminds us of our vast inner resources, and that the best place to look for answers is within our own hearts. They connect us to each other and help us overcome the fears and anxieties that plague us in difficult times.

Inspired by many spiritual traditions and wise teachers, these 108 practices provide anchors for the mind and spirit during tough challenges. They require effort, but when used, they build inner strength, improve character, and tighten your relationship with God in whatever form or name you choose. They help to integrate the sacred of the heart with the profane of everyday life, which we cannot avoid. They can enrich your spiritual connection and help you bear the natural hardships of life with fortitude and patient perseverance. Above all, cultivating them will help you rediscover joy.

What are spiritual practices, and why 108? Spiritual practices promote awareness of the divine in and all around you. They subdue the ego, tame the wild mind, and encourage focus on the essential and eternal. We may think that outside of Sunday worship or sitting in *puja* (a place of worship) in a Hindu temple, a cathedral, or a mosque, integrating the deep experience of the sacred in daily life seems virtually impossible. But each moment of each day offers rich opportunities to strengthen faith, expand awareness, and love more. The number 108 represents spiritual fulfillment, and this is the ultimate aim of the practices.

The Buddhists say we have 108 desires to transcend to merge with the Buddha nature; some Japanese temples have 108 steps to climb before reaching the altar. The number 108 is most used in relation to *japa malas*, the 108 sacred prayer beads used by Hindus, Buddhists, some Japanese priests, and Jains. A Sikh equivalent in the form of beads or a knotted rope also uses 108 knots to anchor the mind. Fingering each bead on the strand while reciting a mantra or prayer to the end symbolizes the completion of a cycle.

My favorite interpretation of 108 describes the *1* as symbolic of the God-Self, Oneness, and merging with Love. The *0* represents the emptiness necessary to be in union with

God. The *8* is perceived as the sign for infinity, which links us to our true nature as infinite, peaceful, and blissful beings. The spiritual practices help to clean, purify, and empty the heaviness and obstacles that stand between us and the gems of peace and joy waiting inside us.

Some *malas*, or prayer beads, are made up of *navaratana*, nine precious gems that protect and balance body, mind, and spirit. The practices here are organized into nine gems with the aim of doing the same. They include self-discovery, heart opening, peace of mind, relationships and sharing, purification, discovering God at work and in the world, inner transformation, and cultivating Oneness. It divides neatly into twelve exercises per section.

These 108 practices will assist you in making life spiritual seven days a week. They will anchor your spirit through encouraging you to watch your speech, mend your mind, and feed your soul with beauty, sacred thoughts, and images. The exercises will enrich your spirit regardless of your faith or religious tradition and give more meaning to your life by transforming it into a walk with the divine. Many of these practices come from ancient traditions and have been renewed and renovated for today's fast pace. All of them point to deeper self-understanding. These simple, non-sectarian tools will give you the opportunity to become more deeply aware of the interconnectedness of all life. They especially act as refuges in troubled times, helping you to stay focused on the inner life. Most of the exercises require no special tools and take place within you. They will help you to make your world a better place simply by encouraging you to be more present, aware, and peaceful.

Choose any single one and practice it for a moment, a day, or a week. Come back to it again and again and let it expand. If you cultivate any of these practices and sincerely yearn for a connection with Spirit, then you will learn and grow. The practices are like seeds—your effort is the earth, and divine grace is the light that makes them grow. Plant some seeds and watch yourself expand in new and unexpected ways. Ultimately, these practices can help you open your heart and mind until the barriers fall away and move you into a deeper sense of Oneness with all of life.

How to Use the Practices

Find a practice that appeals to you and set the intention to explore it by actually doing it throughout the day. Be bold and go for something that challenges you. If you choose a practice like "Catch Dreams" or "Merge in Silence" as your focus, read about it, and then hold it in your awareness and put it into action at every opportunity. While the practices may appear simple, they require conscious effort. It helps to take the work to heart and set a discipline. Explore how it broadens your awareness and at the end of the day examine how you feel. Are you satisfied with yourself? What would you like to improve? Would you like to repeat it tomorrow or move to another practice? Take stock of yourself gently; don't beat yourself up. Spiritual work is like cutting and shaping an exquisite, priceless diamond. It takes slow and careful exertion to achieve the brilliance of perfection. The work can't be rushed.

If you balk at the use of the word "God," replace it with the name that rings true to your heart—Higher Power, Everywhere Spirit, Christ-consciousness, Love, or any other name. Childhood memories or concepts used by others to judge and demean may have interfered with and denied your divine Self-expression. Our minds can lock us into limited ideas of an experience that is far more vast and incomprehensible. Choose the word or name that works for you—one that expresses the all-inclusive, mystical wisdom and power—know that the word you choose can only point to that which defies description and encompasses everything.

In spiritual practice, the perspective shifts from "out there" to "in here," and from trying to change others to focusing on self-transformation and what happens in the mind, emotions, and heart. Remember that spiritual practices are like laundry. It's never done once and for all. It comes back again and again. The laundry might be less dirty the next time around, but it will still come back. The practices here are not one-shot activities that you succeed at in one day and then graduate onto the next. They require effort and perseverance.

As you work with them, your understanding will grow and the same practice will reveal deeper levels. Little by little, these tools will help you transform and grow you into a more tolerant, kindhearted human being. The work moves you into a more conscious union with the divine. Turning everyday life into a conscious, spiritual practice will make it a worthwhile and purposeful existence. It may be challenging in the beginning, but in the end it will bring you a quiet bliss.

Initiating a spirit-focused life is much like giving birth to a new baby; you may need to nurture and protect it before exposing it to others. Unless you're in a community of like-minded family and friends who are also engaged with you, it will help you to keep spiritual pursuits as your private joy. If you publicize your practices to people who are not interested in spiritual matters, then you may open yourself to jeers and sneers instead of the hoped-for support. The tests may be tougher, or the ego may puff up rather than diminish. Exposed to hostile and unfriendly forces too early in its new life, your spiritual baby may die an early death. Most of the practices listed here can be done without anyone realizing your aim. Let others discover the subtle transformations in you over time. You'll find there's no separation between the material and spiritual, between the sacred and profane. All intermingles. What makes life spiritual is your chosen perspective and intentions.

Setting goals in the spiritual life may move the focus away from the divine Self and back to the small, separate "you" that thinks it can achieve nirvana or enlightenment by getting somewhere else. The *atma*, or God-realized Self, is whole and present in you now. It's not necessary to go out and seek it anywhere. It's wherever you are right now. But to connect with it requires both individual effort and grace. Practices help to break away the barriers, open the doors, and make this treasure hidden in your innermost room conscious.

When you set a discipline, you will begin to cultivate awareness and move the mind into the presence of the divine. It's essential to realize that the little "you" is not the doer and transformer of your experience. That essence which makes your heart beat and your pulse quicken without any effort on your part also initiates the process of transformation and makes it happen. The practices help you to awaken and merge with it.

One final note: In the beginning when one fully commits to living life from the inside out, from the spiritual Self first, the changes seem difficult. An Indian saying proclaims that spiritual life is bitter in the beginning and sweet in the end, while material life is sweet in the beginning and bitter in the end. There's no quick fix. It requires hard work to gain spiritual treasures like peace, but it's the only kind of work that will bring lasting satisfaction. Hang in there and make the effort. You'll gain a deep sense of contentment and joy as you become more even-minded and less affected by the world's inevitable ups and downs. It's well worth it.

Occasional experiences that enter the realm of the mystical arrive like little gifts, but they can also become distractions as seekers yearn for them rather than the daily experience of Oneness. These esoteric experiences, like a cool breath, scents of flowers, seeing colors, or perceiving energies appear through the mind and senses, but they're not the end in themselves. On the contrary, they shouldn't lead to a sense of feeling special or separate. To identify with the One in all things and dissolve the sense of borders created by body identification and ego is the greatest gift. Dreams, meditation, chanting, and prayer are a few pathways to realizing the Oneness that unites us all in breath and heart. They're not the end in themselves. Stay on the path and stick to the yearning for liberation from desires and ego. Be practical and balanced, and your wisdom heart will light and guide your way.

I

Self-Discovery

1

Circle to the Center with a Labyrinth

Labyrinths provide great mini-retreats from the frantic rush, and offer meditation in movement for those who find it hard to sit still. Unlike a maze that leads to confusing dead ends, a labyrinth sets a single, unobstructed path that circles inward to the center. Labyrinths can be found in public parks, universities, churches, and hospital courtyards. The American Psychological Association, headquartered in Washington DC, created one in its green rooftop meditation garden for employees and the community.

The John Hopkins Bayview Medical Center built a fifty-two square foot outdoor labyrinth for patients, surgeons, students, and faculty. One hospital uses its courtyard labyrinth for hospice patients and created an annual celebration of remembrance to honor families and their deceased loved ones. An officiant guides participants to release the grief of their losses through a ceremony that includes a walk inward to let go of pain, and the walk out from the center pays tribute to the departed.

While there's no specific way to walk labyrinths, experienced walkers suggest beginning at the threshold with a pause and slowly entering on the inward path with the intention to release anxiety, worry, and fear. The path sometimes may appear to go straight to the center before weaving back out near the outer rim, but finally it leads to the core. At the heart of it, pause. Anchor in the center of your being. Open up to receive and be present. Some people leave a physical object behind as a symbol of letting go of an obstacle or attachment. On the return path contemplate an action plan, renew, and reenergize for your reentry into the world. Walking one may take from fifteen to twenty-five minutes. Walkers say labyrinths provide an alternative to sitting meditation and a place where they find solutions to problems, feel soothed, and become more creative.

Some historians believe that walking labyrinths, like the one in Chartres Cathedral in France, represented a symbolic pilgrimage to the Holy Land, while today's walkers use them as a pilgrimage to the sacred Self. Ancient labyrinths are found across the globe from Crete to Java and are made from a variety of materials including stone, sand, turf, and pottery. Some labyrinth lovers also make them using canvas, pebbles, or even string for quick, easy setup. A labyrinth may be found near you by checking www.labyrinthlocator.com.

If you don't have time to go out, but still want the benefits of a left-right brain balance and a mini-pilgrimage, order a wooden desk-sized version of a labyrinth and let your fingers do the walking on the path, or print out a copy of the Chartres Cathedral labyrinth and trace it meditatively with a pen. An anonymous visitor to the APA labyrinth left her reflections about the benefits she gained in the outdoor waterproof journal: "In the midst of working, going to school for my doctorate, helping raise a six-year-old, planning a wedding, and trying to stay sane, the labyrinth gave me twenty minutes to focus on one thing I've forgotten lately—myself."

2

Transform Yourself through Ritual

Rituals have been a vital part of man's spiritual quest since the beginning of time. Rituals relating to solstice, equinox, religious beliefs, births, coming of age, marriages, deaths, and building dwellings all helped to deepen meaning and provide insight into the purpose of these life-changing moments. The word "ritual" derives from an Indo-European root that means "to fit together." According to Barbara Biziou, author of *The Joy of Ritual*, "Engaging in a ritual allows your mind to expand, your mood to change, and your spirits to rise." While Thomas Moore wrote in *Care for the Soul*, wrote that rituals are "any actions that speak to the soul and the deep imagination."

In Europe rituals with roots in ancient traditions continue to play out in the piazzas and public squares. In Locarno, Switzerland, around mid-January, bands of children and adults group together and march around the town banging tin cans with sticks to chase away winter. In Zurich, the ritual takes place in March and includes burning an effigy of "old man winter" in the form of a *papier-mâché* snow man. Whether the weather changes or not, the air feels lighter and the antics bring people worn down by the long dreary days to smile a little and turn their minds toward spring. Banging the pots literally seems to clear the air and break up heavy thoughts and dreary sentiments that hang around weighing everyone down.

In the south of France, the *Fête de Saint Jean* (Festival of Saint John) coincides with the summer solstice. Residents erect logs for huge bonfires on the open squares and light a blazing fire. When the flames die down to a manageable height, the more adventurous people line up to jump over it. While this event may correlate to ancient pagan summer rites to thank and worship the sun and its fire (and was later co-opted as a saint's day by the Catholic church), today it plays a role in bringing communities together and helping people build courage and confidence as they leap over the flames. The circle of people who crowd around the fire gain a sense of unity reminiscent of early tribal gatherings.

The scientific mind often denigrates these acts as meaningless and unimportant. It denies that rituals have any impact on the human psyche. In reality, rituals weave together the various levels of consciousness. In India, breaking a coconut at the shrine of Ganesha, the elephant god who removes obstacles, represents sacrificing the ego for the higher good. In the Christian tradition, taking communion of the wafer and wine symbolizes integrating the Christ-consciousness and becoming more Christ-like—compassionate, tolerant, and loving. Rituals can make conscious the innate desires to elevate the mind to the spirit. They can be used to let go of obstacles and attachments, honor relationships, and mark the passages into various stages of life. Some people also participate in ritual blessings of their animals by priests as a way to honor and love them.

Croning has become a popular contemporary ritual with women at menopause. Women around the world have begun to gather in private ceremonies to honor this new phase of their womanhood as they move out of childbearing age into the age of wisdom and feminine power. In the croning ceremony, a woman who's no longer of reproductive age helps other women to embrace this new stage of life and move comfortably into the freedoms it brings.

Creating Your Rituals

When I wanted to make the career transition from the corporate world to the writing life, I used a ritual to help me gain courage to make this scary step. Despite frequent business travel, I hated flying. I told myself that if I could face my fears and parachute out of a plane, I could also make a leap of faith and move out of the corporate life to write. The jump required getting strapped to a guide and plunging from 14,000 feet. It seemed to me one of the most terrifying things I could do and still survive. I did it as a symbolic leap of faith, survived the exhilarating experience, and two months later the company phased out my job and offered me the opportunity to take a new position in another division or break my existing contract with compensation. The jump gave me the courage to take the money and run. It magically opened doors to the creative life in unexpected ways. Parachuting as a ritual signaled to the universe that I was ready and willing to take the next step and grow. When I made the steps, all the pieces came together.

Simple rituals can also be very transformative. When I traveled to Egypt, I took a trip up the Nile on a paddle-wheel boat from Aswan. I decided it was time to release all of my attachments to the old role of business executive, which I'd just left, and fully embrace the writing life. While standing alone in my small cabin on the boat, I stood near the porthole and swept my hands from my feet to my head and imagined collecting all of the suits, briefcases, reports, and everything related to my business career and dumping it out the window into the Nile. A sense of relief flooded in.

But it can be difficult to change from the comfortable and familiar to the new and unfamiliar. A few days after I returned home to Antibes, I awoke in a panic. In a dream I was back on that same boat tugging frantically at a thick rope. At the end of it, deep in the Nile I saw a dead business woman wearing a suit. I worked hard to pull her up and revive her. But the captain stood beside me on the deck looking calm and collected. "Help me," I pleaded. "Help me pull her back up. I've got to save her."

He stood with his arms crossed placidly and said, "Leave her. She's dead." When I awoke with my heart pounding, I recalled the ritual and the business woman I'd left in the Nile. The simple ceremony, using only imagination and no props, spoke deeply to my psyche, which revived it through symbolic images in my dream. The day before the dream, I'd been struggling and worrying about money and wondering if I should go back into business rather than write. The answer here came with a resounding, "No."

If you would like to create a ritual around your work, the loss of a friend, a new marriage, a new home, or a changing role, first take a moment to go inside and reflect. Don't seek mentally, but hold the intent in your heart while you're sitting for a designated period. Next note any impressions or ideas at the end of the fifteen or twenty minutes of silent contemplation. If you find it hard to sit, try walking in a park or find a labyrinth. Cultivate a playful, imaginative frame of mind. You may want to research history and cultures to discover different approaches to a given ceremony. Write out and collage or draw your ritual as you imagine it and then try it out in a trial run. Do it with all of your heart and devotion to the divine. If you repeat the ritual on a regular basis, keep the awareness focused on the present movement and words. Don't let them become automatic and devoid of feeling. Performed with faith, rituals will transform your heart and mind, as well as the space and the environment around you.

Rituals may be as simple as starting or ending the day with a prayer or a conscious intent. What kinds of rituals would you like to explore and create? Consider the rituals that bring meaning to your life and examine how you would consciously like to use them to enhance your spiritual life. You may want to consider ways to ritually start or end your work period, begin a meal, inaugurate a new home (some people do a sort of christening of new building sites), and honor relationships or mark their dissolution.

You can also transform the energy of a place through ritual and prayer. Places where crimes and accidents have occurred may be in particular need of the transforming energies of rituals. Hospitals and assisted living communities also can benefit from them. A group of friends might perform a circle of light ritual at a local airport to bring in light to travelers. This is done by joining hands and imagining a ray of light filling the circle and spreading out to the entire building, landing strips, and out to the city. Use your imagination for whatever ritual you choose and invite in goodness and guidance.

3

Make a Pilgrimage

Pilgrimages once sent seekers walking and sailing thousands of miles to shrines and holy temples. Taking a sacred journey remains popular today as seekers yearn to be in the presence of relics of saints or visit holy places like Lourdes, Jerusalem, Rome, Lhasa, Cairo, or Mecca to imbibe sacred feelings. In Europe, many people have renewed ancient pilgrimage routes through France and Switzerland, walking hundreds of miles over the Pyrenees Mountains on the Way of Saint James to reach the Cathedral of Santiago de Compostela in Spain. Shrines to the saints, cathedrals, and hostels dot this footpath, which pilgrims have walked since the Middle Ages. The pilgrimage takes seekers into the presence of the holy relics of James, Jesus's beloved apostle who, according to tradition, is interred in the cathedral.

Though many of today's walkers claim not to be religious pilgrims, they find this step out of their ordinary world an invitation to contemplate the spiritual path and commune with their personal sense of the sacred. Katia, a lawyer and an agnostic, took to the path of Saint James during a period of midlife transition. On her walk, she met and made new friends, but she also passed long periods in solitude seeing no fellow travelers. When she lost her way or found herself farther from a hostel at dusk than expected, she would often meet kind women who offered a ride. One day while walking in a particularly isolated and remote area on the Way of Saint James, she felt deeply moved by a benevolent presence walking with her, but said she saw nobody. Yet she knew and felt deeply that she did not walk alone. The walk didn't bring a lightening burst of transformation, but rather slowly built her trust in the divine and synchronicity. She returned home knowing that it was time to change careers and she began to train as a therapist.

A pilgrimage is a conscious journey to bring the sacred more fully into life. It requires setting an intention and moving into contemplation on the life journey whether it's to a sacred site or simply to work. Mythologist Joseph Campbell wrote of the structure of the journey as described in myth and story through the ages. The hero moves through a process of separation, initiation, and return. She travels out of her ordinary, familiar world into a new adventure of self-discovery to return home more complete and whole. Some aspect of the old self must die for her to become complete and reborn into a new role and a more unified Self.

Understanding the steps of the journey can also help us to know what stage of life's expedition we're on. The first stage is the ordinary world. In this place where we're comfortable and familiar, we begin to feel dissatisfied and become aware of a problem. We receive a call to adventure, a call to change our lives that may manifest in a desire to take a pilgrimage or go on retreat, but often we refuse the call and try to remain entrenched in our usual, familiar, and often painful existence. Those around us may also put up obstacles to our change and warn of dire consequences if we try. Finally, a guide or mentor may nudge us to take the first step over the threshold out into the new, unfamiliar world. Think of this not only in mythological terms like Odysseus setting out on an adventure, but consider changing jobs or moving to another state or country as the beginning of your adventure or journey. On a spiritual journey, it may mean testing new boundaries and exploring new terrain.

Tests, allies, enemies, and obstacles become part of the scenery and help us strengthen our resolve to continue and move to new levels of self-discovery, self-confidence, and self-doubt. As in most stories and journeys, there's an ultimate test or battle where inner demons and doubts meet up with the power of the spirit. If the hero is successful, she conquers her inner demons, which often manifest in some external force like a harsh spouse or a tough boss. She returns with an elixir or gem of wisdom to share with her community. This may be a real item, self-knowledge, or experience that she can share with others. There is also a death of old roles, attitudes, or habits, and a rebirth into the new Self, new attitudes, and roles. This loose description of the journey can be explored more deeply in Joseph Campbell's work *The Hero with a Thousand Faces,* or in Christopher Vogler's work *The Writer's Journey*.

Contemplate your spiritual path and where you are. Have you started the journey? Are you daring enough to cross over the threshold out of and away from your ordinary, familiar world? Joseph Campbell wrote, "That step, the heroic first step of the journey, is out of, or over the edge of, your boundaries, and it often must be taken before you know that you will be supported." Do you feel the need to take that first step toward change?

Rainer Maria Rilke, mystical poet and author, wrote, "There is only one journey. Going inside yourself." Consider the pilgrimage as an inner journey. How far have you dared to travel on this sacred inner path?

If you cannot go on a pilgrimage, turn the day into one. The word "journey" derives from the French word for day, *une journée*. It refers to the time traveled between sunrise and sunset. Set the intention to discover the divine presence through the journey of your daily life. Awaken with renewed excitement and anticipation of seeking the sacred in all surrounding you from morning until night. See with renewed eyes as you walk out to a park, a place in nature, an inner courtyard, or some other place you discover where you feel yourself in the presence of the divine. Contemplate your steps, breath, and heartbeat, and feel God. Imagine the benevolent divine presence walking with you to support you on this journey. Turning each day into a pilgrimage transforms life into a spiritual hero or heroine's journey and uplifts the mind to the sacred.

On the Way of Saint James, the scallop shell became a symbol for having made the voyage and returned home safely. The shells were found on the seashore not far from the Cathedral of Santiago de Compostela and pilgrims who returned to the interiors of Europe took home these shells as souvenirs and to signal to others they'd arrived at the destination. Inspired by this practice, you may want to find a symbol for your journey. It needs only to hold significance for you. What will it be?

4

Grow Your Secret Garden

In the Middle Ages and into the Renaissance, Europeans built secret gardens as refuges from the madness, chaos, and disease of the time. Inside the protected walls, medicinal herbs, exquisite roses, and trees grew. Fountains gurgled in the silent center, and people took refuge there for safety. These secret gardens were considered spaces for healing and spiritual communion and a place to escape from plague, war, and confusion. Initially they symbolized sacred feminine spaces often associated with Mother Mary. These gardens continue to remain profoundly engraved in European culture and often people will suggest exploring something in your *jardin secret* in France. Or in Italy they might advise you to keep an idea to reflect on in the quiet of your *giardino segreto*. Over time, the meaning has changed from a physical place to a symbolic one inside oneself. As a universal symbol, the garden also appears as a powerful place to commune with the gods in Chinese lore as well as in many other cultures.

The secret garden symbolizes the sacred, protected garden of paradise within us. Take a moment to rediscover and explore your secret garden. Find an inner courtyard, a meditation room, a library corner, or a place at home where you can retreat into your personal inner sanctum for a few minutes. Enter into a reverie or a brief meditation. You may want to use some serene background music without words to transport you. Imagine yourself walking down a path toward your secret garden. Take in the view, the path, and when you see the garden gate, find the key in your pocket. Open the gate and enter. Walk around and explore this place. What does it look like? What colors and scents do you perceive? Spend some time discovering your refuge. This is your secret, sacred space, a creative place to renew yourself. When you're ready to leave, return to the gate, cross the threshold, and walk again into the ordinary world.

After the visit, make a drawing or collage of your secret garden or find an image that reflects it. Keep the image in view to remind you of this beautiful place where you feel at peace. Put pen to paper and write about your experience in this sacred space. Both the images and the writing will anchor the experience and help you return to it later on. In a rough encounter, in the heat of a disagreement, or in the heart of the noisy city, recall this place and let the natural peace resurface. You don't need to take a long trip to a retreat. It's right there inside of you, easily accessible, and you can return again and again when you remember it. Watch your inner garden grow and transform. It may even begin to show up in your dreams as flowers spring up, trees bud or die, pests and serpents enter, and weeds grow.

By taking a real break in the middle of the day and moving inward rather than chatting with colleagues or having lunch at your desk or usual place, it's possible to reenergize. Seek out a place where you can enter into a reverie and revisit this sacred interior. You'll be renewed for a better second half of the day. Enjoy the quiet and calm you discover inside your garden. It's better than a spa and often as good as a healing massage. Revitalize in your private inner sanctuary and watch how it blossoms and grows as you cultivate it with spiritual practices.

Grow a Garden

If you're lucky enough to have some space, get your hands dirty, plant some seeds, and watch your garden grow. If you only have an indoor area, try potting herbs, aloe, or other plants. Planting and growing trees, flowers, vegetables, and fruits outdoors or in can be a rewarding practice and a nice parallel to cultivating your inner garden.

5

Catch Dreams

Picture a vast university that contains all the knowledge and wisdom available from the beginning of time and extends into eternity. Libraries extend in all directions filled with sage texts and videos on every subject from what's wrong with your computer to the mystical properties of the universe. It's also possible to access an archive of past events and peek into the future. In this place you can find answers for many of life's big questions. Would you like to visit? This place is inside of you, and dreams open doors and give access to this knowledge and wisdom.

Dreams unveil a deeper part of human experience. From early indigenous cultures down through history, humanity's unending fascination with dreams continues to grow. Dream temples in Egypt invited those seeking direction and answers to come pray for dreams and sleep inside the temple. Priests interpreted the symbols and scenes on waking. But dreams are not only relegated to ancient cultures. Contemporary writers, scientists, mystics, and business executives have all relied on dreams to help them be more creative and find solutions to challenging problems. Mary Shelley dreamed *Frankenstein* before writing the book. Stephen King dreamed the setup of his book *Misery*. Elias Howe dreamed the solution to a problem that stood in the way of creating the modern sewing machine, and Dr. Jonas Salk used dreams to spur his imagination to help find cures.

Dreams also influenced many religious traditions. In the Bible, they foretold disasters and the birth of Jesus. They warned the pharaoh about future periods of bounty followed by famine, and they communicated to Joseph, Mary's husband, about what course of action to follow. Mohammed, the founder of Islam, related a series of dreams called "The Night Journeys" as a profound element of his spiritual experience, and the Babylonian Talmud contains many references to dreams and divination.

Freud related dreams to desire and sex while the Swiss analyst, Carl Jung, studied dreams as a step toward self-realization. Jung's work encouraged individuals to become whole through using dream work to understand other perspectives of ourselves and balance the masculine and feminine energies. He viewed dreams as a way to shine light on the "shadow," or darker side of human nature, and make a step toward self-understanding.

Following dreams means more than simply chasing aspirations and desires. Dreams that emerge from sleep can provide insight into our nature and the world. While they may reveal hidden desires, they can also contain messages from the soul. At their best, dreams give guidance and information that help to heal, protect, warn of challenges, and indicate changes that need to be made in behavior and lifestyle. Dreams reveal intuitive information that includes everything from what you should (or shouldn't) eat to right decisions about relationships, jobs, and creative projects. By taking a few minutes to write down dreams first thing in the morning (or whenever they occur during the night), you may find solutions to problems, gain knowledge of future events, better understand how to cope with a difficult relationship, find a better course of action, and save a great deal of time later on.

If you would like to begin exploring this vast untapped resource, catch your dreams by keeping paper and pen or a recorder by the bed and record the scenes, words, or feelings immediately when waking. Keep physical movement to a minimum until the dream is captured or it may slip away as the dream consciousness fades into waking awareness. Before going to sleep, make the suggestion to yourself to recall your dreams. You can also seed dreams and ask for a solution to a particular problem by simply requesting help before going to bed. Say a prayer of protection and request that the divine may accompany you into your sleep and bring the messages you need.

Some people meet a threshold guardian in initial dreams. The guardian may warn of dangers in exploring this new territory. One dreamer's husband appeared in a dream scene and forbade her from opening the closet doors to this world. He felt threatened by change and he represented a side of herself (probably the ego) warning her not to alter herself in any way and especially not to explore what he perceived as dangerous territory because he wanted to maintain his power. Dare to face the guardian and move past him to reach the jewels inside you.

Not all dreams are valuable. Some dreams may be gibberish, brought on by bad food, too much media, or medications. The most precious dreams come from the teacher within us. This teacher knows us intimately and shows us the truth about ourselves with the intention of helping us grow. She has access to many levels of consciousness and offers guidance and counsel on all areas of life from the material to the spiritual. But sometimes this teacher takes on the role of trickster to test and play. The trickster may give you a dream foretelling that you will win a million dollars. This is more likely an example of ego desire rather than an actual dream of premonition.

Other dreams open up profound contact with God. These dreams leave us in awe, often bathed in light or tears of joy, and a deep sense of peace. They can also predict events as simple as a friend stopping by later in the day and as big and complex as a stock market crash. By working with your dreams, you'll begin to know which ones come from a source inspired by the spirit, how to interpret your dream symbols, and how to respond to their guidance.

In dreams, the soul speaks in the language of symbols. Just like any other language, we need to make the effort to learn what our symbols mean and interpret them so they can be used to enrich our lives. There is no single one-size-fits-all answer for a symbol's meaning. No symbol dictionary will have the answers, though they may provide clues as to what they've meant in some cultures and historically. Be very wary of any dream guides that give a single, absolute definition for specific images, animals, insects, or places.

Explore your personal language of symbols by making collages, drawings, or collecting images from magazines that connect with your dream scenes. Note the characteristics and qualities of the animals, plants, insects, birds, machines, and people who appear. Are they slow sloths or busy bees? What qualities or weaknesses do the people show? Is Uncle Bill renowned for being lazy? Did your old classmate, Jackie, make a point of smoothing over differences and helping people out? Make note in your dream journal and you may want to create a dream symbol dictionary to help you define and explore what your images and scenes mean.

Become aware of archetypes like the mother, the father, the harlot, the baby, and the mentor. Getting to know the qualities or weaknesses associated with each will help you to identify the roles and characters played out in dream scenes. The settings within dreams can also reveal clues to their meanings. Kitchens may be related to cooking something up, such as new creative projects, a product, or art. An office or factory may relate to work life, and classroom scenes could indicate there's something to learn or you're entering a learning phase. Consider also the sayings that relate to the images. Getting into bed with someone in a dream may represent partnering with them in a business relationship or merging with and taking in the qualities of the person you're in bed with rather than a sexual tryst.

Watch the interplay between the levels of your mind and daily activities as the unconscious begins to become conscious. In a series of dreams where serpents appeared, I understood that they represented energy and how I used it. I often saw snakes in unusual places during my waking activities as well. Of course they appeared on the French pharmacy signs as the caduceus—the two snakes winding around a staff—and a powerful symbol of health and vitality. More directly, one slithered across a sidewalk in an unusual place and another perched on top of a hedge. On another day when I awoke with a warning snake dream, I nearly stepped on a viper during a hike in the Alps. It marked a very real reminder to not abuse the energy as I'd done the day before. On another occasion, a water snake slithered to shore on Lake Lugano, a symbol to me of the energy becoming spiritualized. All of these incidents connected dreams and internal work with vitality, health, and the powerful *kundalini* energy—the vital energy lodged at the base of the spine that brings spiritual awakening when it rises.

To deepen work with dreams, write them down as soon as you wake up and reread them before going to sleep again. Work to interpret what they mean to you. Very often they will reveal if you're aligned with your highest aspirations. Defining guiding values will help with this. Interpreting dreams requires a great deal of courage, honesty, and inner strength because it asks that we face the realities of who we are in our entirety. We know people and ourselves by our actions, and we also are subject to the universal law of "like attracts like." Identifying the qualities that our friends and people in dreams mirror back to us—both weak and strong—brings a great deal of humility. Dreams are not meant to condemn or judge the self or others. They are given to us as aids and guides on our journey. Act on the dream guidance you receive when appropriate. Dreams are there to help you and put you in touch with your Inner Teacher, the higher, wiser part of you.

Some Tools

Native Americans used dream catchers as a type of protective amulet placed above or near the bed to capture nightmares and prevent evil from entering dreams. According to the Native Languages of the Americas organization, the

Ojibwa (Chippewa) tribe originated the practice, which spread to other tribes, including Cherokee, Navajo, and Lakota. The Ojibwa made round or tear-shaped wooden hoops usually wound with sinews or thread; the interior resembles a woven spider's web with feathers dangling from the bottom. The dream catchers can be found in Native American arts and crafts shops and on many Indian reservations. Using one may give you more courage to open this door to your inner self.

You may feel inspired to create a dream journal to help you to remember the basics. Make room at the top for a title to identify each dream. Record the events in present tense and leave some space for sketching and collage. You may also want to leave an area in the back to list common symbols that appear—use your imagination to define them. Adding encouraging and inspirational quotes among the pages may help keep you motivated.

In ancient Egypt, priests invited initiates who desired dream guidance to enter a dream temple to aid them in dreaming. You may want to imagine your bedroom as a dream temple. Purify it by saying a prayer to call in light, love, and protection while you sleep. A simple prayer, like the Our Father from Christian traditions, repeated three times to attune body, mind, and spirit, or one of your own creation will do. You may wish to make a symbolic offering of flowers, incense, stones, or a poem to your Inner Teacher and place it on your altar or bedside. Whatever you're inspired to offer with reverence and devotion will be right.

Keep your notebook, pen, and possibly a small night light or candle by the bed to record dreams if you wake up at night. As you fall asleep, imagine entering into the heart of your dream temple. If you awaken with dreams at various stages of the night, make the effort to write them down immediately. Review them the next day and hold the images and scenes in your heart to contemplate over the coming days. Ask your inner guide to help you to identify the meanings and understand your personal symbols. Review them before falling asleep the next night. Pray for understanding and conscientiously work to discover your personal language of the soul. This work is not a goal to achieve and cross off of a to-do list, but is best approached with patience as an ongoing learning process that continues to unfold over a lifetime. It's one of the most exciting adventures you can take into the final frontier—the one inside of you.

6

Create Sacred Space

"A shrine is a little place for magic, or for converse with divinity," writes Joseph Campbell in his book *Primitive Mythology*, which explores sacred spaces in various cultures across time. His intriguing definition invites in the mystical by creating a place apart from the mundane. The word "altar" means "to elevate or raise up." Originally intended for sacrifice or making offerings to God, altars provide a space to symbolically sacrifice ego desires and elevate the mind to the divine. Throughout history, sacred spaces have appeared in homes, workplaces, groves, and forests, as well as organized religious spaces. Today they're experiencing a revival in houses, gardens, and offices. One can manifest as an elaborately designed area or be as simple as a shelf or the corner of a desk.

At an altar you can turn your mind to God, regain calm, and remember the passing nature of the events that challenge and trouble you. It can become a place to find peace, healing, and forgiveness. Use your altar on a regular basis to unify your body, mind, and spirit. Sacred space, such as an altar, speaks to the elevation of the spirit. Joseph Campbell called it a "place for creative incubation." He wrote,

"At first you might find that nothing happens there, but if you have a sacred place and use it, something eventually will happen. Your sacred space is where you find yourself again and again."

Think of this sacred space as the altar of your heart where you can unburden yourself to God and leave behind cares and worries. The more you use it, the greater its positive charge will be. Like ancient cathedrals, temples, and ruins, the prayers and power of devotion that have gathered over time lend an air of peace to the environment. It can be a place to come "home."

Build an Altar

While God is everywhere, creating an altar helps focus the mind. To create an altar at home, in your work space, or in an appropriate place, collect sacred objects and images. Contemplate what "sacred" means to you and select items that reflect your personal view. These may include feathers, stones, photos, statues, or whatever moves you to embrace and focus on God. Take a few minutes over a period of days to design and realize your sacred space. When it is finished, let your spirit revel in the place you've created. You may wish to consecrate it with prayer and invite the presence of God to fill it.

If it's at home, if possible choose a place where you will not be disturbed by phones, television, noise from the household, or movement in a nearby passageway. One woman redesigned and renovated an attic space specifically for meditation practice. It sat beneath the roof and its open round window created the perfect space for gaining a higher perspective. Some people create a personal sacred space at the office or in their work area as a reminder of what's essential to them throughout the day.

A low table covered with a beautiful brocade or silk cloth may be perfect for some while others may choose a desk-level space. Include images and objects on it that evoke a response to the sacred within you. A candle creates a nice central focus and activates the space with the element of fire; stones like quartz, amethyst, or pebbles from a beach or mountain may remind you of communing with nature. Invite light and love by asking in prayer that your space be purified.

Using your altar for mediation, contemplation, and as a space for spiritual reading and writing will make it holy; if it is saved solely for your practice, the place will begin to resonate with the stillness of ancient cathedrals and churches. A Buddhist lama kept an elaborate, multi-tiered altar with images and photos of all of his revered teachers and parents. Covered with silk embroidered fabric, it became a beautiful repository of memory and gratitude to those dear to him. On it stood several candles and sticks of burning incense in special holders to collect the falling ash.

For your own altar, reflect on the places that have felt sacred to you. If you're inspired by churches or if the scent of incense burning in a Catholic cathedral sends you immediately into the sanctum sanctorum of your soul, you may wish to find that type of incense. Some like to include elements of fire, water in a small bowl, fresh flowers as offering to the divine, and even food. Asian restaurants often have an altar with food offerings to deities. Use the altar frequently and well. Enjoy this place. Each time you see it, let your mind turn to the divine and remind you of your soul's purpose.

7

Collage a Bridge to Your Soul

Sometimes we maintain distant relationships with our spirits and need to build a bridge to the soul in much the same way we would put energy into building a new road or developing a relationship with a new friend. The soul speaks in the language of symbols. It talks in images and through dreams and visions or by drawing our attention to some object or animal that may intensely attract or repel us. By working with images you can begin to develop a deeper relationship to the soul and its intuitive, feminine language and balance it with the more masculine, analytical mind.

One good way to begin this is to work with pictures and images through collage. Used by artists and in crafts for one hundred years or more, collage is an art form that invites play. The word comes from the French word *coller* and means simply "to glue." I like collage because it becomes a meditative, light, childlike way to experiment with images and doesn't require any particular artistic ability. Start by collecting a pile of magazines that you're willing to cut up. You may find them in recycling areas, or ask friends to contribute. Put on some music that appeals to you. (I prefer music with no words to keep it "right-brained," which is more creative and loose, rather than "left-brained," which is more word oriented.)

Gather scissors, glue or rubber cement (which lets you slide images around or remove them easily for adjustments), colored pens, and some blank paper. If you'd like to work in a big format, buy some large sheets at an arts and crafts store or use a sheet of newspaper and cover it over. Five-by-seven-inch index cards or even playing cards can make great backgrounds to hold your small creations. Large rolls of white paper give flexibility to create big scenes or storyboards; you may choose to cut out circles, triangles, or whatever form pleases you.

Leisurely begin to peruse the magazines. You may have an idea or scene in mind when you begin, or you may discover the scene as you go. Tear out images, colors, words, and shapes that attract your attention. Let the focus of your eyes and face relax. You may wish to start with meditation and invite in light. Let your eyes and hands play as they wander through the magazines in search of adventures. Try to stick to images rather than words, and don't let them encroach on this playtime; save any articles you'd like to read for later. In this space of exploration and discovery, collect your images and glue them onto one of the formats you choose. Keep some colored pencils, markers, and crayons around to add touches of flair and draw in additions. It's also fun to add ribbons, dried flowers, and other items that may appeal.

If you have scenes or objects from dreams that you're particularly fascinated with, making a collage to manifest the images in a conscious way will help you to work with and understand them. Once your scenes come together, take a moment to commune with the image you've created. Grab pen and notebook and start a dialogue to deepen your understanding of them. Ask the image questions that you would like to explore. You may want to change hands (using the nondominant hand) for the symbol's response. You might also change positions or chairs as you assume the role of yourself as the asker followed by the role of the symbol or scene that responds.

In a recent series of dreams, I looked hugely pregnant. One day while standing in the shower I noticed my body felt achy and swollen as if reflecting this dream image. While I knew I was not pregnant, I decided to explore this curious symbol more. I drew and collaged a pregnant woman and then started a dialogue with my belly.

Me [to my belly]: You're so taut and huge. What do you hold?

Belly: I hold your future.

Me: What does it look like?

Belly: It looks rosy and pink, all aglow. Pretty as a button. It'll be marked with bawling sometimes, but mostly you'll be happy with your new children.

Me: How can I help ease the birthing pains?

Belly: Relax and enjoy the growth. The rest happens of its own volition. Give birth to a new life.

I'd not expected my dream belly to be so articulate and reveal such things. This is a fun part of the process. As a child I'd often said I'd give birth to books rather than babies. I was writing this book when the dreams occurred and I was symbolically very pregnant with it. I later found an image of a pregnant Madonna to keep in my office.

You can repeat this process as often as you like to build the picture dictionary of your soul's lingo. It's ideal to stay in a playful frame of mind and not seek to accomplish a goal. Remember how you played as a child and time could pass so quickly as you created a play world? Returning to this playful place will help you to connect and deepen the relationship with your spirit.

8

Build Self-Confidence

"At the center of your being you have the answer; you know who you are, and you know what you want."
—Lao Tzu

When the world shifts dramatically, a relationship falls apart, a job disappears, and there seems to be no one around to turn to, faith in your inner Self becomes essential to survival. The word "confidence" is derived from two Latin words, *con fidentia* (*con fiducia* in Italian), which literally means "with faith." Developing faith in the Self— one's inner capacity and strength—can be done easily by identifying with God and knowing that you and God are One. This sense of faith comes from effort, listening to conscience, grace, and knowing that divine energy animates and inspires the heart. Putting faith in outer things engenders fear and insecurity. None of the things outside of us endure, but Self-confidence is like a mountain that stands solid and enduring in rough winds and turbulent times.

Steps for Building Esteem and Self-Confidence

Self-confidence is required to accomplish any task. Work to identify with the divine. Develop the faith that the Great Spirit is above, below, beside, all around, and in you. It can be heard through the inner voice that speaks with a quiet, soft demeanor. It can be easily ignored, missed, or yelled over by other mental chatter. Some people call this voice the conscience. Some people feel it as a chord of rightness that resonates throughout the body, mind, and spirit as if a note of truth has been struck and reverberates within them on every level with a resounding "YES! That's it!" This inner voice is the sound of your wisdom. It empowers you and helps you to build Self-confidence. But when the mind chatters so much, how do we know which voice is the right one to follow? Here are some keys:

1) Become conscious of your desires and know your guiding values. Your better angel or conscience will nudge you to align with these higher aims.

2) Be practical! As you grow on the spiritual journey, examine your experiences and use them wisely.

3) Follow a regular meditation practice that focuses on listening to the spiritual heart.

Meditate on these questions:

1) Does the inner voice separate you from your highest spiritual aspiration or move you deeper into harmony with it?

2) Does it bring together good thoughts, good words, and right actions into one unified whole?

3) Does your inner voice suggest you harm yourself or others? Unless you're acting in self-defense, it is not the voice of your wise Self. Love protects and promotes peace and nonviolence.

4) Does your inner voice guide you to be more kind, loving, patient, and selfless?

5) Does it help you to become conscious of your inner motives?

6) Does it make you more tolerant?

Through listening, practice, and observation you will become aware of the subtle differences between the chattering mind full of wants and the still small voice of your spirit. The mind is an instrument of arrogance and the soul acts with humility. Holding this reflection, do your actions and choices reflect the mind's attitude or the soul's higher purpose?

Self-confidence means putting trust in the part of you that is divine and eternal, and knowing that the divine guiding hand is moving the strings that make you dance. It means identifying with the sacred and the spiritual. The material world will never give permanent satisfaction. Life will be a continual ride of pleasure between two pains. By adjusting your focus and anchoring your faith not in the world, but in your Self—the unchanging, eternal spirit that pervades all—you will be well prepared to weather the storms. Live in the awareness of the divine presence within and all around you. It animates every heart and soul and will never fail you.

9

Make a Spiritual Retreat

A spiritual retreat is a way to step back from the world and just focus on where you are, where you come from, and where you're going. It gives an opportunity to reflect on life's purpose and do inner housekeeping. The word "retreat" comes from the French word *retirer*, and means "to move away from," or "to pull away from." In a very literal sense, retreats offer an opportunity to pull away from the concerns of the world and just be with yourself. Very often a retreat will include periods of meditation, silence, spiritual teachings, and nature walks. They may take place at a monastery; Buddhist, Christian, or other spiritual centers; or they may be entirely of your own making at a place by a lake or the sea or some other place where you find natural, undisturbed calm. A retreat may be alone or with others who hold the same intention. The focus ideally remains on cultivating the connection with your divine Self.

Retreats allow for time away from secular responsibilities and duties related to family and work. They make room for contemplation of the spirit and give a chance to reconnect with God. They also serve as opportunities to observe oneself, listen to the inner workings of the soul, and watch the mind. Often retreats allow for time and space to clear out inner garbage and return to a place of serenity.

Without connections to outside demands, including telephone and Internet, the daily rhythm can turn to interior silence. Each retreat will vary. Some retreat centers focus on meditation practices while others may unfurl in total silence. Some will combine spiritual teachings and group discussions with service activities like kitchen, yard, and gardening work. The quiet environment at retreats may make us more acutely aware of inner mental chatter and magnify our fears and weaknesses. Contrasted with the stillness, the mental chatter can sound loud and distracting. We may become conscious of our criticism and judgment of ourselves and others. Dawning awareness of these traits presents an opportunity to observe, accept, and begin to transform. The silence can also provide moments to identify our qualities and gain self-esteem that comes from an inner, immutable source.

The choice of where to take a retreat will depend on your spiritual tradition and need. Some Catholic monasteries allow non-Catholics to spend time in contemplation within their walls. They often allow visitors to participate in services and hear their chants. Even if one is not Catholic, being in a sacred environment where others devote their lives to the experience of God inspires the spirit to soar. Many Christian groups also organize retreats. Buddhist retreats can be found around the world and some Indian ashrams also open their doors for retreat seekers. Steeped in spiritual traditions, these sacred places can inspire a change in heart and bring healing. Sai Baba's Indian ashram, Prashanthi Nilayam, or "The Abode of Infinite Peace," receives visitors from around the world and welcomes people of all faiths and backgrounds. "A Muslim should go away a better Muslim. A Christian should go away a better Christian," says Sai Baba. Beds and meals cost little, and no charge is ever made for teachings.

Retreats at or Near Home

If you're not able to afford the time and cost of taking a retreat, schedule a day out in nature or organize to housesit for friends while they're away. Moving out of the usual home/work environment is essential to opening up the experience of retreat. At home the daily chores and demands continue to pull one back into the world. The aim of a retreat is instead to take an opportunity to step out and away from these daily activities to gain perspective. Set aside a time to escape from busyness. Stop "doing" and rest in quiet contemplation. Retreat centers and chapels or sacred spaces reserved for contemplation in these centers can help you to move into a sense of peace and connection with spirit.

10

Learn Your Soul's Language

Symbols are the language of the soul. They point to deeper meanings and contain emotional power when we're open to them and pay attention. When we're cut off from symbolic sight, we remove ourselves from a vital, creative source of information. When we attune to the energy of symbols, we can use them to find solutions to problems and understand ourselves and the world in profound ways. Perceiving with symbolic sight means keying into the images that communicate in subtle ways. For example, a bird on a park bench or a gold pen on a table may draw attention and somehow relate to your activities during the day.

Learning the language of symbols isn't unlike learning another language. It requires practice. Symbol dictionaries can help you to understand potential meanings of a bee or a cat, but understanding exactly what a particular symbol means for you demands effort. Symbols have a fluid quality. They transform in meaning as we grow and change through life experiences and often this is reflected through the way a symbol appears. For example, a tree in blossom communicates something much different than a dying tree. One may relate to a period of flowering while the other may be a warning.

Symbols may be personal or universal. Personal ones speak uniquely to your individual experience, while universal ones may communicate across cultures and be understood in similar ways by people across the globe. In *Star Wars*, symbolic characters Luke Skywalker and Darth Vader resonated with people around the world. Skywalker was associated with the good hero struggling to overcome the evil influence of Vader, Skywalker's father. Houses may be universal symbols for protection and safety, and around the world marriage generally signifies union between opposites. On the other hand, a peach pit might be a personal symbol for illness because it relates to cancer-stricken Uncle Ned who left partially eaten peaches around the house when he was dying.

Symbols grow and contract as we go through periods of blossoming and change. They may reflect our inner state, reveal our deeper feelings, and help us weave together the fragmented pieces of our self into a rich, beautiful tapestry that integrates both darkness and light. Learn to see with symbolic sight. Most of the time we take things literally, but seeing symbolically means seeing beyond the superficial and daring to delve into the depths. Hearing a hawk cry or seeing one circle in the sky at a significant moment may mean to watch for the signs. A purse as a symbol may represent your wealth. A baby may attract your attention and represent giving birth to a new project or a new part of yourself.

Paying attention to symbols also means coming face to face with personal demons and angels. Through symbolic sight, an inner, miraculous play is set in motion that transcends and balances out the strong emphasis on the rational, concrete perspective of the masculine mind. This rational side relies on analysis, reason, and deduction. The feminine side integrates and embraces intuition, spontaneous knowing, and insight. Cultivating a symbolic view extends beyond dreams and can begin to enter into career, relationships, and every aspect of life. Pay particular attention to experiences that hold strong emotional charge. Some scenes that you live through can be seen symbolically—and hold hidden messages that ask to be deciphered.

Developing Symbolic Sight

When the Berlin Wall fell in 1989, its demise reverberated around the world. Why? This symbol of containment, oppression, and repression was torn apart piece by piece by crowds of unyielding people no longer threatened by the guards in turrets or the mines set in the "no man's land" that separated what was once a unified country. Tearing down the wall represented not only the failure of repression, but it also tore down barriers within the human psyche.

Ever consider why terrorists sought the destruction of the World Trade Center? It represented the United States as a worldwide financial power even more than the White House or the Pentagon. Destroying it and watching it crumble financially and shut down Wall Street for days sent a message to the rest of the world that the United States was weak, vulnerable, and would crumble if it kept its focus on money. The destruction of this symbol of financial power was meant to mark a shift in power. For citizens within the country, it united people around national symbols like the flag, a symbol of unity; the eagle, a symbol of freedom; and the Statue of Liberty, a powerful image of liberty and the welcoming nature of America.

To begin to practice symbolic sight, be alert and see what images attract your attention and contain emotional power. Is it a pen, telephone, school bus, airplane, or something at a restaurant? Make a note and write down what the symbol might mean for you. Watch to see if it pops up again over the next days and weeks. Look around and be aware of what symbols stand out today. One way to begin to do this is to collect images that speak to your soul and move you—even if the movement is one of fear. By becoming conscious of the image that creates this reaction you can explore more deeply what's beneath the surface of your feelings.

You can enhance understanding symbols by working with dreams and searching for their meaning. The soul often takes advantage of this mental downtime—when the rational, ego-protective self is asleep—to stir up images that awaken us to inner feelings and outer realities. The scenes very frequently relate to events that took place during the day and will let you know if you did the right thing or not. Very often sleep is a time when the conscience can speak loud and clear. It's a good idea to listen, because the messages will likely be in your best interest.

If scenes seem too wacky or wild, then try to relate to one image or one piece of it. In a recent dream I entered a kitchen and found the counter tops chin high. I needed to reach into some deep blue cabinets, but I felt like a child standing on tiptoe and unable to get to the good stuff. When I awoke, I knew it related directly to my work. To write well, I needed to reach into the higher part of my inner Self, but I felt too small to attain it. When I sat down in meditation, I revisited the dream image and found the solution to the problem. I grew! I took a deep breath and allowed myself to expand and I literally and quickly grew up in the inner image. I could easily reach all that I needed to complete the writing over the next weeks.

Sometimes it's fun to act out symbolic scenes as well. By working with imagination in this way, life becomes a playful, joyful process. You may also want to pay attention to the songs or phrases running through your head at certain times. They may clue you in to symbolic views and help you to understand a situation or how you feel. When approached with symbolic sight, life suddenly takes on profound meaning. Make an effort to learn the language of your soul and understand its messages. It not only turns life into an adventure, it will also help you to grow! With a child's attitude of play you'll figure out the significance through drawing on the guidance and wisdom of your heart. If you feel a need for some additional guidance on dream analysis, a Jungian analyst may be of help.

One way to play with dream images is through creative play with cards. I love to make symbol cards to help me understand images. If you'd like to play with this, start with a standard deck of playing cards. On a sheet of paper, create a window the size of the card by tracing around a card and cutting it out to create an open area the size of the card. You can then go through magazines and use the "window" to determine the size of images, trace around them, and cut them out. Glue them on the cards with rubber cement and in no time you'll have a deck of symbols to play with.

In workshops I place the cards around the room and people collect one or two cards that they feel attracted to in a deeply emotional way. I ask them to engage in dialogue with the image and ask it what it wants to communicate as if it's alive or sentient. If the image is troubling, like a serpent, and they can't face the creature, then I suggest they talk to the gardener, or someone else in an imaginative scene that includes the serpent, and let that character speak about its qualities and what it's trying to communicate with them. In Jungian circles (where followers are inspired by the work of Carl Jung), this is called active imagination—where the soul Self takes over and communicates with us through play, images, and words.

11

Explore Your Spirit
through a Vision Quest

A vision quest is the Native American version of a retreat, but it's often more physically demanding. True to its name, the one who goes out into the forest or onto a mountain top seeks a vision of guidance from the Great Spirit. The seeker creates a sacred circle around her, drawing it with corn meal, stones, or something similar. Prior to the days of the quest, she may prepare by holding a question or a yearning at heart. Some people enter into the quest by fasting during the duration. The seeker may take along a talisman or items of significance. This may be an image, a blanket, a feather, or something that speaks to the questing individual. It's a good idea to determine in advance the amount of time to dedicate to the quest. Given the rigorous nature of the quest that leads people into the wilderness under challenging conditions, it's often helpful and may even be necessary to be accompanied by an experienced guide.

The quest is preceded by a symbolic purification and often completed by a similar rite. In a traditional American Indian quest this may include a sweat lodge, which is a circular hut covered with canvas or hides that encloses hot stones and may be equated with the maternal womb. The seeker would enter the lodge before making the trek out as a way of offering the purest self to the Great Spirit, which she may encounter on her venture.

The quest can be done at home by creating a sacred circle and determining a time to remain in it while yearning and praying for a vision of guidance and assistance. When practicing a vision quest, find a place and time where you will not be disturbed by outside influences. Ideally no one will be able to interrupt you during the designated period; this may be an hour, four, eight, or more. Consider what your heart yearns to know. Make preparations by bringing a notebook, images, photos, or other things you feel will be useful to have at hand.

At the time of the quest, prepare with a shower or bath as a rite of purification. This may include using a few drops of essential oils that elevate and stimulate, such as lavender or eucalyptus. You may wish to recite mantras or pray. Picture anything that may separate you from your vision washing away down the drain leaving you free to receive. Create your sacred circle with stones or corn meal spreading them out at a large enough circumference for you to move around comfortably inside the circle, but still near enough to give you a sense of being in the center.

Remain inside the circle, a symbol of wholeness, during the time that you designate in advance. Leave only to go to the bathroom or take care of necessities. Ideally, eliminate eating for the chosen time and focus solely on the Great Spirit. When your designated time draws to an end, note any insights or impressions that arise. A vision may arrive in a powerful, overt way, but it may also be very subtle and barely perceptible. Sometimes the quest is also part of a learning and self-observation process. At the end, offer the quest to your image of the divine and return to your world with wisdom and insights. Carry the realizations into your daily life and apply the insights that lead you in the direction of your highest aims and values.

12

Discover Crystals for Beauty, Calming, and Healing

Crystals, quartz, amethyst gemstones, and diamonds have incited desire in human hearts from the beginning of time. Created in heat and pressure, these gems embody beauty formed through powerful forces of nature. When brought to light out of the dark heart of the world, the play of sunlight falling through the facets of theses stones attracts the eye and inspires the spirit. Their various colors correspond to the colors of the chakras. They're found in all colors of the spectrum and can bring soothing influences to body, mind, and spirit. Clear diamonds are believed to bring clarity to the mind, while violet amethysts emanate soothing properties.

Some areas, like the Swiss Alps where quartz crystals can be found in abundance, seem to vibrate with the powerful energies of these stones. In Asia, the *navratana*, or nine gem necklaces derived from Vedic astrology, use different precious stones that correspond with the planets for balancing their influences and harmonizing the body, mind, and spirit. They include pearl, diamond, blue and yellow sapphires, red coral, emerald, hessonite, and tiger's eye or chrysoberyl. The nine stones are often mounted in a circular-shaped pendant and worn as a talisman.

The healing power of gems and crystals first appeared to me in a dream. I'd not considered them as more than decoration and I didn't have any particular desires to wear them. But one morning I awoke with this: *I see a round faceted stone that's violet and I know it's an amethyst. A voice tells me, "This will be beneficial for you."* Perplexed by the idea and dubious that any stone could help a body, I nevertheless had decided to work with my dreams and went in search of the gem of the approximate size and shape I'd seen in the dream. Unlike many dreams, I recognized this one to be literal rather than symbolic and I acted on its guidance.

That night I went to bed wearing the ring I'd found. In that in-between state just before sleep takes over, a tingling energy arose from the stone and filled my arm, neck, chest, and body with soothing vibrations. I felt surprised that a seemingly simple stone might give off such comfort to soothe the nerves. I still wear the ring years later and have added a necklace of amethysts as well. To learn more, I began to research the esoteric power of crystals and found Edgar Cayce's work referred to properties of some stones for healing and soothing.

Azurite, a deep blue stone, is said to aid some people in meditation, but it will affect each individual differently. I found the vibrations too intense and distracting. Lapis lazuli may contribute to spiritual Self-confidence. Its deep blue color may help an individual attune to the spirit on higher levels. Deep ocean blue is often associated with high spirituality and expansiveness. Rubies, given their deep red hue, may aid in keeping a body grounded. I find the blue obsidian's watery appearance very beautiful, but its strong vibration makes it uncomfortable to wear. It's a volcanic glass formed by molten, red-hot lava.

Rose quartz feels appropriate for helping open the spiritual heart, which I associate with the pink tone. Amethyst is my stone of preference because it helps soothe sensitive nerves that are often overwrought or working hard to adjust to the energies that come in through meditation. I love to keep the raw, uncut, unpolished amethyst crystals by the bed and also on my altar. Pearls also can have a soothing effect. Pearls result from the secretion that forms around a grain of sand that irritates the interior of the oyster. I associate pearls with the creative process, particularly in relation to writing and the arts.

Choosing Your Soul Stone

The best way to decide what, if any, gems would be helpful to you is to consider their colors and properties, where they came from, and where you are in your spiritual growth. If you feel a need to be more connected to the heart and caring, perhaps green-colored stones like malachite or emerald will aide. One Indian teacher gives diamonds to some of his students and refers to them as "die-minds." Diamonds have two essential qualities: clarity and brilliance. They may serve in aiding mental clarity and quieting the chattering, muddled mind.

If you'd like to learn more, Judy Hall's book *The Encyclopedia of Crystals* is a comprehensive starting point. I also encourage you to trust your hands and use them to scan stones and sense how different crystals make you feel. Hold the gems and stones before buying them. Relax and see if your body, mind, and spirit respond. Unpolished stones sometimes are preferable. Experiment by buying small stones first. There's no need to make a big investment. Because stones may lose their energy or pick up unwanted vibes with use, it's ideal to cleanse them by placing them in salt water and then recharge them in sunlight.

II

Heart Opening

13

Grieve Losses and Heal Your Heart

In today's fast paced world, we rarely take time out to digest feelings related to loss. We quickly rush to the next thing to patch over the unease and fill up the empty space; but unattended, the wounds beneath the surface fester. Facing loss and coping with it takes time and awareness of the process. When a loved one, a job, a house, or a relationship is lost, it usually hurts. Allow yourself time to grieve it. Don't bury the hurt and pretend it's not there. Don't wallow in it either. Rushing into another relationship head on to replace what's missing without bringing closure may simply result in more pain and loss. Face the feelings. Let them surface and let go. Tears can be very healing at this time and the emotions that arise are part of the process of mending the wounds. In this way, loss can bring lessons and soften the heart.

Elisabeth Kübler-Ross, MD, author of *On Death and Dying*, studied the stages of dying in terminally ill patients. When patients learned of their illness, they experienced a process of grief that is common among most all people who experience loss. They moved through stages of denial and anger. They attempted bargaining with doctors to revise the diagnosis and some negotiated with God. When the illness remained, they went through a phase of depression and finally arrived at acceptance. While losing a mate or job is not as deep or severe as losing the body, these stages of how we cope emotionally apply also to how we experience the loss of jobs, homes, and most anything we value.

By being conscious of this process, it's easier to understand the feelings, let them arise, and accept them. Often loss and transitions move us into better places, though it may not feel like it at the time they occur. It's very difficult to comprehend the purpose of misery and pain, yet what if it's meant to break us open and draw us deeper into an experience of our divine Self? If life remained smooth and even and if we were perpetually content, would we ever look inside or seek out the sacred for answers? Would we ever seek a deeper purpose?

Job, from the Bible's Old Testament, possessed a loving family, great wealth, social status, and good health. In a short time, Job lost all and found his body covered with boils. His friends thought he must have done something to offend God. They encouraged him to curse the God he adored and turn his back. God reproached them. "Where were you when I laid the earth's foundations?" he said. Job endured the suffering, and through work and grace, he regained his health, a bigger family, and an even greater fortune.

How can we know and understand life's mysteries? Release the need to know the answers and judge. Accept that all happens for a reason beyond our limited capacity of comprehension. Acceptance means acknowledging something consciously, looking at it, and then making the effort to let go through an inner process, a ritual, journaling, or sharing it with a confidant. Letting go of pain associated with loss reflects an inner attitude. In the cycle of nature, caterpillars leave behind their caterpillar lives, surround themselves in cocoons, and emerge as butterflies. Trees that appear dead in winter burst out in glorious greenery in the spring, only to lose their spectacular dress again in the fall. Movements and change are natural in the ebb and flow of life. Nothing except the spirit Self will remain forever. Using a focus on breathing, meditation, a mantra, or some other method, move deep within and identify with this eternal, unchanging solid core. Cultivate the spirit and know that the fruits it brings will remain as treasures that can't be lost or stolen.

If the losses still trouble you, create a personal ceremony to honor that which is past, accept the current state of life, and welcome in the new. Symbolically acknowledge the grief and release the pain associated with it. You may do this by giving away things related to the loss, writing about it, or putting photos and mementos in a special box to honor what's lost. Other rituals or ceremonies may include the planting of trees or a garden to commemorate the loss. If the loss relates to death of a child in the family, organizations like KinderMourn can provide solace and support, and help to honor the loved one while shoring up a family's courage to move forward. For more on grief, you may wish to visit the Elisabeth Kübler-Ross (EKR) Foundation website. EKR Foundation recommends that no big changes or decisions be taken during the first year after the death of a close loved one.

Breakups and divorce also require time for transition. Sometimes a ritual of release can help to let go of a difficult relationship and make the change easier. Though intellectual, Western culture often denigrates rituals as meaningless, but they are powerful tools to help in transitions and mending broken hearts. Rituals can help to heal the wounds and move the psyche into a place of deep peace; they can fortify the spirit and affirm that you're ready to move into a new stage of life.

Divorce and breakups can result in wounds and fears that close doors to the heart. My favorite ritual to help ease the transition into the single life or clear the space for a new partner brings in the element of fire. Fire burns away the old, destroys pain, and makes way for the new to grow. The phoenix, a mystical bird of antiquity, died consumed in its own flames and was reborn from the ashes. The fire ritual can be done in a safe place like on a sandy beach or at an outdoor fireplace or fire pit where there's no risk of embers popping to create a hazard. I like the beach with the sound of wind and waves to accompany the ceremony.

To begin, say a prayer of protection and call in light to surround and envelop you and support your intent to release, honor the other, and heal the heart. Prepare matches and the symbolic items you'd like to use to dissolve the ties that represented your relationship. Only one or two symbolic objects like a letter or some photos will be enough. Take a candle with a steady flame (possibly protected in a jar) and let the items catch fire and burn until only ash remains. A prayer of release or a song may accompany the burning, along with a sincere desire to let go of any chains that bind. It's said that chords of attachment grow up between partners as they become connected. Consciously envision the chords that have grown between you and the ex-partner and let them dissolve and burn away in the flames along with the other items. If possible, recall some aspect of the relationship to be grateful for and consider what you have learned.

Once the objects disintegrate, return the ashes to the sea, river, or water source or bury them. This resembles how families often return the cinders of their loved ones to the waters and earth after a cremation or funeral service. It's essential to hold in heart the idea of letting go of attachment and bonds to the ex-mate, spouse, lover, or friend and also wish them well. Consciously dissolving the chains that bind you to the ex-partner will allow the mending to begin.

Once the ritual is completed, ask for help in curing the pain. Picture any wounds as bandaged and healing quickly. You may also be inspired to create your own ritual uniquely adapted to your situation. "When one door of happiness closes, another one opens," wrote Helen Keller. "But often we look so long at the closed door that we do not see the one that has been opened for us." May your wounds heal and grace descend as life lessons are learned that will open new doors to a more peaceful life. Look toward the open door now. There's much more to come.

14

Talk to a Psychic

Most everyone wants to know about the future, but I feared it. While working full-time as an international business executive for a French company, I only believed in what I could touch, see, smell, hear, and rationally understand, calculate, and control. Anything "psychic" terrified me and I ran away from my dreams and intuitions. But once I left that square-walled corporate environment and began to explore the broader world of the soul, I also began to meet psychics. This opened my mind to a whole new world of possibility. What does psychic mean? It comes from the word "psyche," which means simply "of the soul."

My first experience with a psychic came unexpectedly in Egypt when a tour guide took me to an exquisite perfume shop near the Great Pyramid of Giza. Inside, sunlight fell on elegant wood carved shelves that held hundreds of hand-blown bottles of essences and perfumes. Along the edges of a large open-roomed shop were built-in seats with thick cushions and exquisite oriental carpets filled the center of the room. Jamal, the perfumer, greeted me and escorted me into an area off of the main room. He offered sweet hibiscus tea and cool water in the custom of Egyptian hospitality.

As I sat uncomfortably in front of him, he began to reveal what he knew of my life—that I had no children and I was separated. I'd also experienced some traumas that he described. My rational business mind nearly exploded as it tried to comprehend how this man who I'd just met knew so much about me. I went away reeling from the shock and couldn't make the pieces add up rationally. He provided the proof that these abilities exist. He also perceived a very challenging problem I was facing and he gently coaxed me to work on it. I never saw him again, but he left an indelible impression and his selfless and loving help remains imprinted in my memory.

Later on the same trip I met "the Champion," a local sage who literally lived at the base of the Great Pyramid in a mud hut. He too had eyes that saw beyond the material world and could read people like most read books. Finally, the experience that blew away all doubt involved a lovely psychic in Virginia Beach, Barbara Harriman. Barbara did not advertise. She kept her practice low key and charged very little money for her service—and she was very accurate. She not only helped with health issues, she also gave me hope for a future that I could not then see as I wallowed in a dark night of the soul steeped in deep confusion.

Her selflessness, nonjudgmental attitude, humility, and lack of any need of recognition confirmed her deep connection and devotion to divinity. Over the years until her death, we kept in touch and I called on her to confirm intuitive feelings and help with health issues. Though I was single at the time and worried I might not remarry, she assured me of a man in my future and described my future husband with specifics. Much of what she's said has come to pass. When I asked how it works, she said "There's no separation. No time. All's One." I believe this is how she experienced life, from a perspective of Oneness. Others, often called medical intuitives, are particularly gifted at helping to identify and suggest ways to heal health issues.

Those who move into deep communion with the soul may have psychic experiences that seem to transcend usual human understanding. Yogis, saints, hermits, and people who renounce the material world have often been endowed with what many consider supernatural abilities to read minds, perceive the future, or see auras. In some cultures, a local astrologer or wise old man or woman will still predict the future of a new born child. Across Europe, gypsies wandering through towns and cities propose palm readings in parking lots and at café tables. While some psychics may be pranksters or tricksters, others truly have gifts of inner vision and can know your heart, hear your thoughts, and perceive glimpses of your past and future. These abilities are not only limited to those who have taken religious vows or made spiritual commitments, and some people may be downright scoundrels about this and abuse their real and imagined powers of perception.

Setting Aims

If you consult a psychic, pay attention to your inner spirit and understand your motives. What do you hope to get out of this? What do you want to know? Check with other people who may have consulted the psychic you would like to contact and learn about their experiences. Look for certain signs that confirm the psychic aligns with divinity. Is she humble? Does she judge others? Does she seek to work with the divine to selflessly serve others? Does she encourage you to pay attention to your own inner voice and grow? If she tries to develop a relationship of dependence and take your spiritual self-sufficiency, then she's not working in your best interest. When you find a psychic you can trust, take the plunge, experiment, and enjoy. Once you start keying into psychics you may also want to develop your own intuitive and psychic abilities.

15

Develop Your Psychic Tools

Everyone is psychic. Remember, the word "psyche" means "of the soul" and comes from the Greek word for "breath." In Greek mythology, the goddess Psyche was a personification of the soul or spirit who was pursued by Eros, the god of love. When love and soul unite, these abilities may grow. What we often intend when using the word "psychic" today relates to knowing people's hearts and minds and perceiving glimpses of the past and future. While the Western mind embraces knowledge that comes through science and technology, it often sneers at psychic abilities. But when we deny subtle impressions that arrive in inexplicable ways, we limit our knowing and lose a considerable portion of our ability to understand. Tuning into the subtle information of the psychic world helps us to live a more complete and full existence.

Almost everyone has had hunches or intuitive experiences where they knew something would happen before it actually took place. Ever have a hunch that you shouldn't go someplace or engage in something and then find that "gut" feeling verified by an accident or other incident? These are psychic experiences. By noting them, how the information arrives for you, the sensations you experience, and what happens, you can begin to fine tune your psychic abilities.

With effort and careful attention, the information from the psyche or soul level becomes more readily available and we learn how to "read" it. It comes in different ways for everyone. When seeking to develop it combines with a sincere spiritual practice and an urge to use the information to grow and serve others, then the possibilities become potent with energy. You can learn what's literally going on behind the scenes and in people's hearts, note warnings that will protect you and others, and find solutions to challenges in relationships and creative projects. Some psychics even use their abilities to assist police investigators and solve crimes.

Developing psychic ability is a creative process. Combined with play and a light touch, it can help you to tune into the subtle. Psychic information is all around us constantly. It is very subtle in much the same way a scent of rose or jasmine is subtle, but present. Part of the challenge in the beginning is to thoroughly know yourself. Know your fears, your likes and dislikes, and what you avoid and what attracts you. The better you know yourself, the easier it will be to separate real psychic information from your own mental and emotional noise. One psychic has said that if she is very tired and emotionally challenged, she is worthless in reading people and situations.

Enhance your development with prayer and meditation and clean out the negative emotions and attachments that can get in the way. A first step in developing intuitive and psychic ability is concentration and relaxation. A regular meditation practice helps. It also helps to cultivate the feminine quality of being receptive to energy and information rather than trying to go out and grasp or seek it. Like listening, it's akin to a state of being attentive where the sound simply moves into you without needing to go out and get it, similar to a radio receiver picking up a frequency. The information is simply there, and by staying centered and making space, it will arise spontaneously. The mind needs to be concentrated in one-pointed attention in much the same way it focuses while driving. A good way to actively develop this is through the *Jyothi* or light meditation exercise from ancient India. (See section: Lighten Up with the *Jyothi* Meditation.) Some people like to test for psychic ability through use of the Zener cards developed specifically for this aim.

Like most other skills, psychic development takes practice and some people will be more receptive to certain things than others. Psychometry is the practice of using one's hands to feel the energies in things like a hand writing sample, an object worn by someone, or a map. Using your hand, it's possible to scan a list of doctors, lawyers, or workshops, for example, to help identify which one will suit you best. Auras, the light energies around a body, reveal things about individuals. Many practices exist for learning to see auras.

A good practice to start with is to sit outside on a sunny day, relax on a lounge chair or the grass, and look into the blue sky to see the vitality in the air. NASA scientist and author, Barbara Ann Brennan, conducts workshops on the human energy field. She refers to this vitality as "orgone." It makes squiggly patterns and may appear as tiny points of white light and sometimes has a black spot. The points dart around and appear and disappear. Being out in nature also offers a good opportunity to experiment with seeing auras or energy fields around the edges of leaves, plants, and trees. It works best if the eyes remain relaxed and very loosely focused rather than searching hard for the phenomenon. Brennan describes this universal energy field in detail in her ground-breaking book, *Hands of Light*.

One of the biggest lessons I've learned about psychic abilities is to pay attention to details. Details include not only the colors someone wears and the sound of her voice, but also pertain to the subtle details. Someone may appear picture perfect and the setting may, for all physical appearances, look good, but if feelings of anxiety and dark or disharmonious images pop in or you pick up on something unusually discordant, don't push it away and ignore it as meaningless. Try to make distinctions between your inner feelings, like hope or fear, and what's going on in the environment; your inner feelings may interfere and cloud perceptions. When you come to know your own feelings, you can begin to distinguish the difference between your anxieties and desires and information coming from outside sources.

I returned to a South of France mountain retreat where I sometimes took refuge from Riviera tourists. On this visit, I perceived a disturbing red all around this usually peaceful place, which I typically associated with greens and blues. On a walk in a wooded area, semi-permanent campers had moved in and trashed it with debris. Two young men seemed particularly out of place in this spiritual setting. One of them appeared flat and one-dimensional, as though he had no aura. I dreamed that night that the two men could be dangerous and I packed up and left at dawn. Despite the spiritual setting where the center was founded and guided by a respected monk, not everyone there had elevated intentions.

Pay attention to how you best receive information. Subtle images may pop in. You may be more kinetic and sensitive to vibration, or you may hear quiet, yet powerful words in the area of your spiritual heart. Dreams can also provide a doorway into psychic ability. Take note of your psychic experiences. Anchor them in a journal. Pay attention to when, how, and in what way they come to you. What is your frame of mind when it pops in? Psychic information is there to help and protect us. Start to play with it and learn your pathways into this realm.

16

Use Sacred Art to Open the Heart

Images of God from Michelangelo's Sistine Chapel to the familiar icons that decorated medieval and Renaissance Europe's cathedrals depict visions of saints, Mother Mary, and Jesus with expressions of beatitude and compassion. The artists hoped to inspire and move those who viewed the art to have elevated thoughts. Many of the people at the time these works were created were illiterate and relied on images to communicate with their souls. In Thailand, India, Switzerland, Italy, and France, shrines still dot the roadsides. They are inevitably decorated with art—images meant to communicate beatitude, joy, devotion, miracles—and even display fear of death and evil. The messages they bear often cut through mind stuff and go straight to the heart.

In Val d'Osola, a narrow mountain valley in Switzerland's Tessin, stone shrines along the path date from the 1600s. One of them shows Mother Mary in the enclosed, protected part of the shrine under the stone roof. But on the outside wall, closest to the passerby, stands a skeleton with a scythe. In words above its head the skeleton says, "What you are is what I was. What I am is what you will be." It's believed to date from the time of the plague when the doors to this valley were literally closed to keep out foreigners who might carry the pestilence. The mocking, sharp talking skeleton serves as a reminder of the passing nature of physical life, while Mary stands inside wearing her blue robe, looking peacefully up at a dove, unharmed, and fearless. The images speak to the heart. The shrine communicates that the physical world fades but keeping the face turned to the skies or spirit will help the heart stay at peace.

Statues of the Buddha inspire a deep sense of calm appreciation for the absolute, untroubled countenance of the enlightened one. *Tankas*, or Buddhist tapestries, often depict the Bodhisattvas reincarnating over and over out of compassion to serve and save humanity from despair. Tankas may also represent the opening of the heart with rays of light emanating from a body or illustrate the chakras. Ten-headed demons show up in Thailand's temples—reminders of the power of sensual desires to destroy a good life.

Contemporary artists, like Russian painter Nicolas Roerich, communicate spiritual experience and visions in brilliant color with auras and divine light. Roerich, inspired by the Himalayan Mountains, opened his heart to many spiritual forms of the divine and painted Saint Nicholas, Saint Francis of Assisi, the Buddha, angels, and Mohammed. His openness to different religions came through in his art and also inspires those who view it to ascend to new heights like the white-capped mountains he sometimes portrayed.

Beautiful nature and animal photos can achieve the same effect. Find some image that touches your spirit and keep it in a sacred space. Let it connect you with the beauty and splendor of the divine. Some faiths consider seeing God in images, icons, and statues is a sacrilege. But God is omnipresent, omniscient, and the essential in all things. The images are soul tools to help connect with God. We feel their power in cathedrals that have been constructed with stained glass windows, vaulted ceilings, gilded statues, and ornate altars. White marble angels bigger than life soar out of stone and their wings lift them into the sky bringing a sense of elevation and awe-inspiring trepidation.

Find Sacred Art That Speaks to Your Heart

Images connect the inner and outer worlds of our being and act like a bridge to the Self. Sometimes the images we choose can only be understood after long periods of reflection. In the Catholic churches in Europe, Jesus stands in life-sized form carved out of wood or marble. He wears long, flowing robes; has soft, gentle eyes; and in his chest is a flaming fist-shaped heart. This image of his heart on fire remains a powerful, mystical symbol that continues to fill me with awe and inspiration. Though my mind cannot fully grasp the meaning, my heart understands it and feels moved. What sacred images attract you?

If you feel inspired, begin to explore sacred art from contemporary artists like Roerich to icons from the devoted artists of the medieval and Renaissance periods. Are you attracted to Native American art and images or Celtic crosses? Keep the images in your sacred space and in sight during regular periods of meditation and contemplation. If you feel inclined to draw or paint, create images that speak to you and support you. Sacred images foster and feed the spirit, and at their best, they can deepen your understanding and lead you deeper inside.

17

Animal Blessings: Love and Care for Furry and Feathered Friends

In Europe on Saint Francis of Assisi's feast day, lines of animals, including horses, donkeys, cows, and other beloved creatures, stand in front of churches and wait to be blessed by priests during special services of gratitude. This day, usually around October 4th, marks a special occasion to remember, recognize, and honor four-footed, feathered, and finned friends. This ritual probably started sometime in the twelfth century and was inspired by Saint Francis's reverence for nature and love of animals.

Saint Francis's legendary love for animals spread around the world. It's said that he preached to birds and fish and helped animals on many occasions during his lifetime. Francis traveled on the road, and when he saw flocks of birds in a tree he joyfully ran toward them. When they didn't fly away he preached the word of God. In his discourse, he asked his "brother birds" to praise and love God and ended his discourse by touching them on the head and blessing them. Legend holds that a wild rabbit was

Saint Francis's only companion during his forty-day fast for Lent.

Saint Francis created the first nativity scene to include live animals, a tradition that remains common in some countries at Christmastime. He loved and revered animals so much that he nearly petitioned the emperor to declare an amnesty for animals on Christmas Day. Animals, according to his petition, would not be captured or killed that day of the year. They would be feted and fed grains and wheat along the roadsides to allow them to share in the Christmas celebrations. Today, Saint Francis is the patron saint of animals and is often depicted in statue form with a bird on his shoulder.

The Bible says, "But ask the animals and they will teach you; the birds of the air, and they will tell you. Ask the plants of the earth and they will teach you; and the fishes will declare to you." (Job 12: 7–8.) Many traditions have sought to learn from animals and nature. If we patiently watch, we learn teamwork from heron couples that work diligently to build nests and feed a family. Mother bears teach us about nurturing and protection as they defend their cubs, and dogs display loyalty and obedience.

Create an Animal Blessing Ceremony at Home

No need to wait for the next feast day of Saint Francis to celebrate your love of animals and gratitude for your pets.

Design your own ceremony, keeping some basic ideas in mind. Search for some sacred texts and poems about animals or write out an homage. If you invite other friends and family to bring their pets, respect the natural affinity (or animosity) between certain creatures; some cats and dogs need to be kept apart. You may wish to sing, include a prayer, and write out a benediction drawing attention to particular moments that you (and the others) may feel grateful for. If some pets cannot attend or if they've passed on, bring a photo of them to include.

Nineteenth-century Russian writer Fyodor Dostoyevsky wrote, "Love the animals, love the plants, love everything. If you love everything, you will perceive the divine mystery in things. Once you perceive it, you will begin to comprehend it better every day. And you will come at last to love the whole world with an all-embracing love." Remember to extend your love and compassion to animals like chickens, cows, ducks, turkeys, fish, and pigs, which are sometimes considered only as food.

This lovely incantation from a Buddhist text might end your ceremony. "Whatever breathing beings there may be—frail or firm, long or big, short or small, seen or unseen, dwelling near or far, existing or yet seeking to exist—may all creatures be of a blissful heart."

18

Be Grateful for Obstacles and Tests

A spiritual student desperately yearned to experience enlightenment and merge with God. He visited his teacher and the teacher sent him to a cave to meditate for six months. "When you return I will give you what you ask, if you've made progress," the teacher said.

The student traveled to the cave, endured six months of taming his mind and returned proudly to his teacher. "I'm ready to receive enlightenment," the student said.

"Go down to the river, wash yourself and put on this white robe," the teacher said.

When the student departed for his ritual cleansing, the teacher called to the sweeper woman to collect all of the trash and dust she had gathered during the work day and dump it on his student when he returned. The student ambled in with a proud smile and as he walked up the path to greet his master again, the sweeper woman covered him in trash. The student erupted in a rage. "What the ... did you do that for?" He cursed, grasped her throat, and threatened her. The teacher intervened and the student remembered his aim and felt deeply embarrassed at his loss of equanimity. "I guess I didn't treat her well or act with self-control," the student said sheepishly.

"Go to the mountain top for two years," the teacher instructed the student.

The student marched off, did his two years of meditation, and returned. "I've learned levitation and transcended the seven circles of hell," the student said.

"Do you still yearn for God?" the teacher asked.

"Yes, yes," the eager student said. The teacher handed him a white robe and sent him again to the river for a bath. Three sweepers cleaned the path and the teacher gathered them together and instructed them to collect their morning's garbage and dump it on his student. The student returned feeling content with himself and his achievements. He smiled full of pride at the master, but when the trash flew at him from all directions the student again erupted in anger. He swore and began to strike a blow at one of the sweepers when he caught himself and stopped. The student again remembered his spiritual practices and folded his shoulders forward in shame.

"Go back to the mountain again," the teacher said. "Stay for ten years. Learn to master yourself."

The student departed with a heavy heart. When he returned the master repeated the scene—sending his student to wash in the river and return in his white robe. This time, ten sweepers with pails of dust and garbage awaited him. When the student appeared, they covered him in dust and trash and soiled his white robe. But this time he paused and bowed in front of each sweeper and said, "Thank you. You are my teacher. Thank you. You are my teacher."

Though we might wish to confine spiritual practices to retreats in mountains and forests, the real tests occur in daily life. Spiritual life cannot be separated from everyday living. Every day offers opportunities to put spiritual precepts and values into practice. Each day gives us tests to prove to ourselves we truly understand and fully integrate the wisdom and humility it brings. Teachers appear in the form of spiritual beings, but also in the form of neighbors, bosses, colleagues, and enemies. While they may not be dumping physical trash on you, there may be plenty of verbal and emotional garbage. Consider the student and his humble attitude of realization. Consider Jesus and his compassion as crowds attacked and crucified him. Become aware of the teachers and the challenging situations in your life that are trying to teach you something and give you a meaningful message.

Take a moment to sit down and contemplate these difficult situations: Are you having challenges at home, in your marriage, or family? What about at work or school? Picture these scenes from the perspective of the spectator or witness. What do you observe about your actions and reactions? What would you like to change? Remember you cannot change others, but you do have power to change your own attitudes and actions.

When we make decisions to change and move in a new direction, the world and our environment may put up obstacles and test our determination. Be thankful. These same tests will challenge you and prepare you for bigger things to come. Think of them as a preparation and a way of helping you to build courage and confidence. If you have to do a small presentation to twenty colleagues or a room filled with family at a wedding reception, embrace it, and accept it. Face your fears and you may even enjoy it. The experience may prepare you for bigger and better things to come, like speaking to a group of 500.

Even the most challenging events can help us grow. Illness, loss of a loved one, or separation and divorce can all move us into periods of asking questions about what happened. If we reflect and find our role in the events and see how we contributed to the outcome, it becomes an opportunity to learn and grow.

19

Conquer Fear with the Antidote of Love

By the time Alexander the Great invaded India, he had conquered many great lands and felt convinced that he would conquer the world. He entered the country with his vast armies that had already decimated tribes and peoples in Europe and Asia and some parts of India. But legends recount that he arrived in India and came upon a man, likely a *saddhu*, an ascetic, sitting in the middle of the road. Alexander announced his greatness. "I am Alexander the Great. I've conquered many lands and people fall at my feet. Hear this and tremble," he said. The saddhu sat peacefully, undisturbed in a state of *samadhi*, a state of enlightened bliss, and remained totally unmoved by the boastful display.

"If you do not move I will cut off your head," Alexander said. He unsheathed his sword to amplify the threat.

The man opened his eyes and smiled serenely. "You cannot kill me. I am *atma*." The ascetic identified so with the atma, or the immortal soul, that he knew his body was only a dress that would fall away in time and he experienced no fear.

Alexander stood there unnerved by this man, the likes of whom he'd never seen before. "If all of the peoples in this country are like this, then we do not stand a chance," he said. "They're a formidable and fearless people in this region." He turned and left the place leaving the man unharmed.

The level of fearlessness attained by this ascetic comes from plugging into the inner source of life. Putting faith only in material things engenders fear and insecurity. None of the possessions, relationships, bodies, or anything of the world will endure eternally. Only Love lasts. Love conquers fear. "If a man places a gulf between himself and God, this gulf will bring fear. But if a man finds the support of the Invisible and Ineffable, he is free from fear," say the Upanishads. Reread the phrase replacing "God" with "Love": "If you place a gulf between yourself and Love, this abyss will bring fear. But if you find the Invisible and Ineffable through Love, you are freed from fear."

Fear is an obstacle to growth. It's a left over from past pains and instincts, and often hangs around waiting to invade when it's least wanted and needed. Fear diminishes the heart and makes it burn with dread. I once suffered terrible fears—fear of the dark, fear of ridicule, fear of what I didn't know, fear of the future, fear of people, fear of failure, and fear of contact and intimacy. The fears, like bricks, built a wall around my heart and kept me separated from my inner Self and from the divine in others. It's hard to find happiness and peace with fear as a constant companion. It left me perpetually unsettled and ill at ease. I felt hyper-vigilant and ready to kick in the adrenaline pumping fight or flight mode at any instant.

How does one shatter overwhelming fear of everything in life? What was I actually afraid of? I considered the possibilities. The worst fears invaded when I sat in a plane as it was taking off. Tears sometimes welled up because I felt unable to control what might happen and I knew that my heart was not right. If I died then and there, I would be separated from divine Love. My life would be wasted and lost to something grander that I was meant to explore and hadn't yet discovered. I feared death, but more than death, I feared separation from something bigger, more meaningful, and more important than what I perceived at that point in my life. And worse, I felt I wasn't doing anything to take me in the direction of discovering and exploring this greater thing of life, which turned out to be the journey of the spirit.

Fear crept in at night when light faded. What demons lurked there in the shadows just beyond the beam of electric light? What murderer? What destroyer? In retrospect, the murderer I feared at the time was my rational, materialistic mind that cut me off from my soul and pretended it did not exist. But once the mind grasps the power of the spirit and its immortality, and detaches from identifying itself with the body, it soars and no fear can invade.

Through love, grace, and doing what your conscience knows is right, it can be conquered.

If fear invades your day, make an extra effort to feel the energy of love flow through you. If it feels impossible, then pray. A woman trapped during a high-jacking of a plane in Asia prayed for help. As she sat trembling in her seat and armed, hooded men stormed the cabin, she heard a response well up through her heart, "Send love." She felt terrified, helpless, and anxious. "I can't. I can't love these people. Send love through me. Use me as your instrument," she prayed. Many of the passengers escaped unharmed including the woman who prayed to the divine.

20

The Darkness to Light Chant

The darkness to light chant touches on our highest aspirations as spiritual seekers.

> Lead me from the unreal to the Real.
> Lead me from darkness to light.
> Lead me from death to immortality.

It is often chanted in Sanskrit to retain its original sense and power:

> *Asato ma sad gamaya*
> *Tamaso ma jyotir gamaya*
> *Mrtyor ma amritam gamaya*
>
> —From the Brhadaranyaka Upanishad

This prayer from the Upanishads guides the seeker from understanding she is the limited body, mind, and intellect to understanding that she is, was, and always will be eternal, absolute, blissful consciousness. One who uses this prayer transcends praying for things because she knows that more homes, clothing, cars, and mates will not fulfill the deep yearning of her soul for Self-realization.

Sages say that ultimate reality is *sat-cith-ananda*: being, pure consciousness, and bliss. Darkness and light refer to ignorance and knowledge. Ignorance, like darkness, obscures true understanding. And in the same way that the only remedy for darkness is light, the only remedy for ignorance is knowledge. This knowledge in the prayer is the knowledge of one's true nature. We believe ourselves to be limited by the body, time, and death; however, in truth, we are not limited or bound by these things—never have been, and never will be.

The prayer stating, "lead me from death to immortality," does not request to live endless years in heaven or on earth. It is a prayer to the divine Teacher for help in realizing the truth as described in the *Bhagavad Gita*, that, "I was never born, nor can ever die, as I am not the body, mind, and intellect, but the eternal, blissful consciousness that serves as the substratum of all creation."

Sprititual teacher Amma says, "We don't need to transform our self into our self. Nor do we need to travel to it. We are it. The journey is a journey of knowledge. It is a journey from what we misunderstand to be our self to what truly is our self. What the mantra really means is 'Lead me to the understanding that I am not the limited body, mind, and intellect, but am, was, and always will be that eternal, absolute, blissful consciousness that serves as their substratum.'"

21

Sing from the Heart

Music speaks to the soul. "The aim and final end of all music should be none other than the glory of God and the refreshment of the soul," wrote composer Johann Sebastian Bach. Devotional singing can uplift the mind and heal the heart. Used across the globe in religious gatherings, spiritual meetings, and community settings, singing can bring the soul to soar in ecstasy. When combined with love, it serves to elevate, regulate breathing, soothe nerves, chase away depression, and create a profound sense of unity for people that chant together.

Since ancient times, using the human voice raised in song has helped to uplift the spirit and ward off base sentiments. Jewish songs, Negro spirituals, Gregorian chants, and gospels are a few of the many forms that devotional songs take. In ancient Indian tradition *kirtan*, or devotional singing, takes the form of a call and response accompanied by a humming harmonium and *tabla*, or Indian drums. As in Gregorian chants, the words consist usually of a holy name, and the songs progress from slow to a faster rhythm and move the singers into an elevated meditative state through repetition and uplifting music.

Contemporary singers of *kirtan* in America, like Krishna Das, share the experience of song from this Hindu tradition, but without adhering to a religion. Others, like Rabbi Kirtan, have adapted the form of call and response to Jewish songs like "Sheme Israel." This form of devotional music makes singing accessible to many people, including those who feel they cannot sing or hesitate to participate. The overall effect brings the mind to merge in the soothing vibrations and produces a relaxation response. The combination of a fuller breath combined with the mind focusing on the words shifts one away from the usual mental chatter. Singing can also move you into a state of flow and awareness, which is much like the joy of writing, running, or creating something new.

Even a contemporary love song can be suffused with devotion when the intent shifts the meaning of the words from romantic love to the divine. When a group of children sang "My Heart Will Go On" from the film *Titanic* at the feet of their spiritual teacher at a celebration, the sweet voices and hearts sang of God as the object of affection in the song and moved the meaning to a higher level. Singing in groups unites hearts and moves one beyond the surface agitations of the mind. The vibrations of the sound purify the environment and raise the mind while helping to soften and open the door of the heart.

Many of us feel blocked about singing. Our idea of perfection prevents the first effort. If you feel inspired, join a group that practices kirtan, or you could also join a choir. Some worship services include singing. At home, take a song you love or learn a new one and sing it as a devotion to God within and around you. A chant or song like "*Da Pacem Domine*" (Latin for "Give Us Peace, God"), "*Antara Jyothi Namo*" (Sanskrit for "Salutations to the Light Within"), "Ave Maria," "*Om Mani Padme Hum*" (Buddhist chant with a literal translation of "Om, Jewel in the Lotus"), "I Offer Myself to Thee," or even a contemporary rock song will do. If you'd like to hear a sample of meditative chants and learn them, try the soothing Taizé chants, which can be heard and downloaded for free at the Taizé Community website: www.taize.fr/en.

"Where there is devotional music, God is always at hand with his gracious presence," wrote Bach.

22

Join the Rhythm of the Universal Heart with Drumming

"Native American drums beat to the rhythm of the universal heart," says Tony, a full-blooded Navajo. As a traditional drum maker and drum circle leader teaching people about Native American ways, he brings people back in touch with the rhythm of their own heartbeats. He's passionate about drumming as a way to relax the mind and he shares this passion at the community drumming circle at the Eiteljorg Musem of American Indians and Western Art. His practice, combined with prayer, expresses kinship with all living things. "I was taught a long time ago to try to feel the heartbeat of everything in the entire world—trees, stars, grass, fish, birds, skies," Tony says. The drum beat takes us back to the sound of the hearts of our mothers when we were in the womb and ultimately connects us to our Mother Earth.

In his gatherings, Tony seats people in a circle and combines drumming and the sharing of spiritual insights to bring people into a focused, clear-headed place. He also makes his own drums and teaches others how by using a maple wood hoop frame and elk or buffalo hide. The round hoop of the frame stands for wholeness. He says the drum beat echoes the heartbeat of the whole universe, and focusing on this expansive Oneness can help people to heal. "Drumming vibrates throughout the body. It releases angst, anxiety, and stress," he says. "It puts people in a different space and allows them not to think for a little while and can open up a different path."

Tony and other Native Americans willing to share their wisdom at museums, powwows, and private teachings can guide you to make your own drum and teach you how to use it. Many areas across the country hold regular drumming circles where people gather to play and share. You may wish to create your own group and learn about the deeper meaning of drumming through direct experience, research, and reading. Part of the bliss of drumming or playing any instrument comes with losing oneself in the rhythms and sounds. The mind relaxes and merges in the flow of the music. Seek to learn the subtleties of your instrument. Be grateful to it and enjoy the play.

Learn to Play a Native American Drum or Instrument

Many of us have been put off of playing music and think it's only something to learn in early years. While learning as a child certainly makes it easier, many instruments, like the Native American drum and flute, are easy to play. Explore the instruments and music that currently appeal to you and dare to play. What would you like to try?

Pick up your chosen instrument and begin to experiment. Playing music can help you relax attune to soothing vibrations and improve concentration by learning to read and follow notes. If you're not a virtuoso or feel you lack musical talent, a Native American flute or drum may offer a good introduction. Almost anyone can pick up either of these two instruments and improvise. Recorders or English flutes also require little investment and are easy to learn. As you play, imagine yourself a flute through which God's breath blows. If you prefer a drum, imagine God beating the rhythm of your heart. Know that as the instrument plays for you, so you play out your life as an instrument of God. You may wish to join a group or find a teacher to instruct you in the fine points.

23

Rest

Become a human "being" and not just a human "doing." Stop and take a break. Busyness is often another form of laziness, a way of avoiding the inner view of one's soul rooms. Thomas Merton, Trappist monk and world renowned author, wrote:

> Some of us need to discover that we will not begin to live more fully until we have the courage to do and see and taste and experience much less than usual. ... And for a man who has let himself be drawn completely out of himself by his activity, nothing is more difficult than to sit still and rest, doing nothing at all. The very act of resting is the hardest and most courageous act he can perform.

Restful Place

Schedule a time to rest. Don't clean, pick up the phone, watch television, or go on the Internet. Find a way to rest your mind and enter into peacefulness. Stop "doing" and move into your state of human "being." Rest or repose, when done right, becomes a way to reenergize the spirit and revitalize the body. The mind, when it is constantly active, can wear one down and drain energy simply by its constant, unceasing activity. Through repetition of the divine name, sitting by a gurgling brook, or watching the sunset over the sea, the mind can find stillness and rest in the moment. Swimming, fishing, hiking, contemplative knitting, sewing, and cooking—doing something manual in a contemplative way—can also be very restful. Sometimes taking a warm bath is a good way to rest. Where do you find your rest? Schedule a regular time for this in your life.

24

Make Yourself Bigger

A group of students complained about a fellow student who seemed stubborn and difficult. They felt the difficult student put up obstacles to creating a peaceful environment and they asked the teacher to do something. The teacher stood by the chalk board and drew a line. "How do you make this line smaller without touching it?" he said. The complaining students reflected but ventured no answers. After a pause he drew a second, longer line above it. "Make yourself bigger," he said.

Applying this teaching is a good way to cope with difficult colleagues, challenging family members, and friends. Instead of touching them with words or action, simply make yourself bigger. If you're unsure about how to do this, ask the God within you and listen intently in silence for an answer. Ask God to speak and act through you. You will gain Self-confidence and create a more peaceful environment.

During the challenging time of the American Civil War, President Lincoln had many critics. One of the more harsh ones was the new governor of New York. Instead of scolding or criticizing the governor in return, Lincoln wrote a wise letter to him that extended friendship:

> You and I are substantially strangers and I write this that we might become better acquainted. I am the head of a nation which is in great peril; and you are at the head of the greatest State of that nation. . . . In the performance of my duty, the co-operation of your State, as that of others in fact is indispensable. This alone is a sufficient reason why I should wish to be at a good understanding with you. Please write me at least as long a letter as this—of course saying in it, just what you think fit.

In response, Governor Seymour sent his brother to Washington to convey his assurances of loyal support. Lincoln's wisdom and his ability to transcend his ego and perceive the bigger picture made him an expansive and unifying force that kept a troubled nation together.

Both the teacher and the president used different methods to deal with their challenges, but both expanded and went beyond their limits to accommodate. How can you make yourself bigger today?

III

Peace of Mind

25

One-Minute Mind Training

At age fifteen, I found myself bent over in agony. The family doctor sent me for x-rays and the diagnosis came back as a duodenal ulcer. He warned that given the size of the wound in my stomach, it could turn into a bleeding ulcer, and he prescribed antacid and strong sedatives to calm my nerves. (Ulcer medications weren't yet available.) The tranquilizers disturbed my concentration and studies, and I hated the feeling of floating a foot above the ground. I threw them away and decided to meditate instead.

Each night I sat silently alone in my room, eyes closed, and determined to be calm and peaceful. I knew that my strained mind had caused the illness and I knew intuitively that training it to be silent with a disciplined practice would cure it. By the time the next appointment rolled around about six weeks later, the x-rays showed the ulcer had completely disappeared and it has never returned. A similar event happened when I was about thirty-five and another doctor diagnosed a golf ball–sized cyst that required surgery. Using visualization and meditation, the cyst disappeared. This is one of many reasons that I highly recommend learning to train the mind.

Like an athlete who trains for a marathon, a human being must train the mind. Even just one minute in focused concentration will help to calm the mind before the morning rush and allow for a pause in the hectic heart of the day. At night it will give a moment to reflect and recollect. In this quiet place, open the doors to receiving a solution to a problem or insight into a relationship. Without attitudes of seeking or expectation and by totally letting go of the preoccupation, answers and realizations may arise unforced and outside of any self-willing. In this state of receiving without grasping, miracles can happen.

Mind training is a practical, helpful tool that contributes directly to quality of life. With patience and regular practice, it helps to defragment us and bring the mind home. The first step requires a practice of concentration. Most people cannot jump straight into meditation. The mind initially needs an anchor or a focal point; two easy tools are repetition of a divine name and focus on a form. Sitting silently and concentrating the mind on either the chosen name or form mark a preliminary step toward meditation. With practice, the one minute will expand to several minutes and the mind will move into a stage of contemplation. Ultimately it moves into meditation and carries us to merge in God.

Often we imagine that we are the mind and identify ourselves with it. In meditation, glimpses may arise of being outside of the mind, and we can perceive it as an instrument that measures and deciphers information from the five senses. The mind's constant chatter affirms its existence, but by looking for the spaces between the words and expanding them, the natural quiet of our deeper nature grows and the mind eventually ceases in awe at the vast peace beneath the monologue.

Mind training will enhance concentration. If you practice it regularly, your tennis or golf game will show progress as your reflexes and reaction times improve. You will open paths to insightful resolutions to troubles, and creative ideas will pop in without any effort. Through meditation you can draw closer to the divine. If you continue the practice, you will naturally expand the time spent in this quiet place. One learns meditation by doing it. Begin by focusing on a beautiful object or an image sacred to you. If the mind wanders, treat it like a small child and bring it gently back to the object. It will wander again. Bring it back again. Treat your mind with kindness. Be firm but gentle.

Silent Sitting for One Minute

Sit quietly in a place that you plan to return to every day at the same time. Surround yourself with a prayer of protection. Schedule one minute to begin this practice of concentration. Find an image, a candle flame, or a beautiful flower, and bring the eyes to gently focus on it. It doesn't matter if you chose to sit on the floor with legs crossed or in a straight back chair, but keep the back straight.

It's best to start small and work up to longer periods like an athlete in training. Set your timer for one minute and let the mind remain fixed on the point you've chosen. At first the mind may resist. It may say, "Why bother with this when I have so many things plaguing me right now. This is waste of time." But don't listen. This will become the most constructive time you spend during the day. Observe the frustration and let it float past. Soon it will subside. Emotions will arise like clouds. Don't float away with them. Simply observe their rising and let them continue by on a breeze.

The internal monologue of the chattering mind will become apparent. Step back on the river bank and let the river of words flow by with the current like sticks or leaves floating down stream. Watch them go past, but don't follow them. Stay on the river bank. If the mind wanders away from the object of your concentration, then when you become aware of it, carefully and gently bring it back to your object of adoration. Continue this for one minute. Extend the time to three minutes, then five minutes, and you'll gradually want to add more. It's a gentle training. Begin to watch for the spaces between the words in the internal chatter. Expand the spaces of silence and begin to master your mind.

The discipline of entering into the silence of meditation will equip you to deal with the rest of the challenges. It provides an opportunity to get to know the functioning of your mind so that you can begin to control the thoughts and emotions rather than let them control you. It also opens a space of receptivity where it's possible to hear the voice of your wisdom heart with its guidance and direction. With practice and effort, even in one minute increments, the mind will yield. It will become the student and an instrument to use in constructive and careful ways.

Cushions, Bells, and Timers

While meditation can be done with nothing except yourself, for those who like the physical tools and find them helpful, plenty abound. Some teachers, particularly in the Buddhist tradition, use *tingsha* (or hand cymbals), singing bowls, or a clear ringing bell to mark the beginning and end of the meditation period. The bell rings out one clear note cutting through the mental chatter. The bowl is also a nice symbol of emptying oneself and becoming a vessel to receive.

If you prefer floor cushions over straight-backed chairs, they take various forms and come in organic fabrics and fills. I personally like the crescent-shaped cushions or the back support floor chairs to keep the back straight. Timers can range from travel alarm clock style to an iPhone app available from Insight Meditation Center. The center also makes it possible to set a timer that begins and ends with a bell tone from your computer.

26

Anchor the Mind
with *Malas* and Rosaries

If you have a wild-child mind that leaps about from shopping spree, to office, to the next meal, and you want to anchor it during meditation, *malas* and rosaries come to the rescue. The mala (a strand or garland of 108 beads used by Hindus and Buddhists) or a strand of rosary beads help keep the mind focused. Malas, often made of sandalwood beads, are strung together loosely and held between the index finger and thumb. In traditional practice, the index finger represents the individual. It slides a bead forward toward the thumb with each repetition of the name of God, the word "Om," or a mantra. The thumb represents God. The act becomes deeply significant of the individual moving consciously towards the divine with each movement and repetition.

The mala beads belong to an ancient tradition and function to keep the mind present. Sandalwood, from which the beads are traditionally made, is a tree symbolic of sacrifice. It gives off its lovely, soft fragrance even for the ax man who chops it down. This practice of using the mala aims to purify the mind by keeping it filled with sacred thoughts. Teachers say that repetition of the name of God when performed with devotion leads to sacrifice of the ego and liberation. It keeps negativity at bay and helps one get through difficult periods as well as good ones.

The rosary functions in a similar way to the mala. Inspired by malas, Jesuits who had traveled to the East brought this practice back with them. The word "rosary" comes from Latin, and means "rose garden" or "garland of roses." Associated with the Roman Catholic faith, the linked beads correspond to the individual's recitation of the name or prayer—from the Our Father, to the Hail Mary—and contemplation on the holy mysteries.

One doesn't need to be a Hindu, Catholic, or Buddhist to use these tools. The rosary or the mala can be used by anyone with the aim of maintaining a spiritual focus and a need to secure the mind. The practice calms and anchors the mind in the moment, deity, name, prayer, or sound that is most alluring. It's useful to help calm the worried mind, particularly during times of stress. Some people keep a rosary at hand to help them confront fears.

Using the beads is a beautiful way to keep the focus on the spirit. We come to resemble that which we think upon and the images we hold in our mind. By moving one bead forward with each repetition of the prayer, name, or word, the mind will be elevated and the spirit nourished. This can be done on an airplane, in a waiting room, during a break at home, in the office, or in private. Don't worry about what others will say or think. Use the beads to keep the mind turned inward toward the refuge of the divine in the heart. If done with love and devotion, this practice may also benefit the atmosphere and people around and bring in calming vibrations.

Make Your Mala or Rosary

You may want to create your own mala or rosary. Materials can be found at bead shops or on the Internet. Choose the stones, glass, or wood that appeals to you. Find a string and decide on the number of beads you wish to include. If you decide on 108, then string them together, make a knot, and add in the 109th bead, which is not counted but helps to keep track of the cycles. Keep the strand loose enough between the beads to let them slide a little. On the end, you may wish to add a tassel, a cross, or a symbol that connects you with the divine. As you string the beads, chant your prayer or mantra and weave in the good energy that will help sustain you through your future practice.

27

Conquer Your Enemies

In life, we sometimes imagine that enemies abound in the world around us. They may take the form of people and outer forces, but in reality they are nothing more than reflections of the inner enemies that haunt us in the form of anger, lust, greed, envy, jealousy, and hatred. These enemies sap our strength, battle within us, and drive us to self-destruction. Through meditation, self-inquiry, and observation, the enemies become apparent and we gain the strength and courage to face them. Perceiving them is a difficult task. They hide in the shadows away from our conscious awareness until we seek them out and face them. Sometimes simply shining a light on them is enough to make them flee, but often it requires a more determined effort to discover them.

Take a moment to turn on the light within and become aware of any enemies lurking in the shadows. Do this through light meditation (see the section Lighten Up with the *Jyothi* Meditation), quiet contemplation, and self-inquiry. Anger emerges from frustrated desires. The antidote for anger and hatred is love. Combat jealousy and envy with compassion and happiness for the success and good fortune of others. Lust can be overcome by raising the energy and focus to your heart level and letting it expand. Conquer greed by sharing and volunteering to help others. Become self-aware. Turn on the light inside your inner rooms and become conscious of the enemies living there, then make an effort to chase them out. Which of these is your worst enemy? How will you transform its energy into something positive? What allies will help you reform?

Some Native American traditions perceive enemies with gratitude because the obstacles they create will make us stronger and prepare us for bigger challenges ahead. A Cherokee elder instructed his grandson on the spiritual warrior's approach to these lurking enemies. "Inside of me a war takes place. It's a ferocious war between two wolves. One is evil, full of anger, envy, pain, discontent, avarice, and arrogance. It feels resentment and guilt. It lies and cheats, is filled with pride, ego, and a sense of inferiority," the old man says. His grandson listened intently. "The other wolf is good. It's full of joy, peace, love, hope, serenity, humility, kindness, empathy, generosity, faith, and compassion. The same kind of battle takes place within you and every individual."

The child reflected and turned his face toward the old man. "Which one will win?" he asked.

The old man smiled gently and said, "The one that you will feed."

Consciously Feeding the Good Wolf

Putting out anger with anger is like trying to put out fire with fire. Don't yell back. When you feel angry, step out of the place where the feeling overtook you. Drink a glass of cold water to cool you. Move into another place. Anger results from frustration brought on by unsatisfied desires. Work to overcome the desire and let go of it. In this way it may be possible to conquer the anger and not let it overrun you. Exploding with rage uses a great amount of energy and depletes valuable life force and vitality. Work to replace anger with love and desire with compassion.

Feeding the good wolf requires a concerted effort. Identify the people and places where you find yourself getting angry. Step back inside and reflect. Examine your desires and feelings. Are they linked to fears and insecurities? Are you hoping that someone will change behavior? While it's not likely we can change or control someone else, it's possible to exercise self-control. Face what lies beneath the anger and conquer it with discipline and love for yourself. Which wolf will you choose to feed today? Make efforts to become aware of which enemies hurt you most. Devise a plan on how you intend to combat them, and then practice it. Which antidote will you use to cure them?

28

Cultivate Your Allies

The allies of love, peace, truth, nonviolence, and right action protect against the enemies. Love when shared is like a candle flame that never diminishes. Peace is our true nature like the vast sky above the clouds and rain. Truth identifies the Oneness of all things and connects us with the eternal and unchanging. Non-violence brings us to treat others and the world as an extension of ourselves. Right action, doing the right thing at the right time, brings peace of mind and a sense of satisfaction with a quiet conscience.

These allies help to combat the enemies we encounter—lust, greed, hatred, anger, jealousy, and envy. These enemies cannot stand for long when confronted with the light of our allies, but winning the battle depends on individual effort. The Buddha referred to a similar set of allies called the "eightfold path that leads to the end of suffering." It includes right understanding, right thought, right speech, right action, right livelihood, right effort, right mindfulness, and right concentration.

The *I Ching*, the Chinese book of change and transformation, offers up this advice about building character:

If evil is branded it thinks of weapons, and if we do it the favor of fighting against it blow for blow, we lose in the end because thus we ourselves get entangled in hatred and passion. Therefore it is important to begin at home, to be on guard in our own persons against the faults we have branded. In this way, finding no opponent, the sharp edges of weapons of evil become dulled. For the same reasons we should not combat our own faults directly. As long as we wrestle with them, they continue victorious. Finally, the best way to fight evil is to make energetic progress in the good.

Befriending Your Allies

Instead of fighting and struggling with inner enemies, put the focus on building up alliances with love, kindness, and other allies. Work to build and strengthen them with gentle effort. If you feel angry, build fortitude by strengthening patience and a sense of sacrifice. If envy eats away at you, work to deepen your contacts with compassion. *Seva*, or selfless service to others as practiced in the Indian tradition, is a good way to overcome most all of the enemies. Helping others in need cultivates the terrain of the heart and allows the allies to grow faster.

29

Change Your Mind

Shakespeare wrote, "Oh fool, why do you want to change the world? Change thyself and there will be one fool less." You may not be able to control the situation you're in, but you can change your perspective. Ask yourself, what am I learning? How can I make a positive difference? We (as the "indweller" or witness) enjoy power over our thoughts when we choose to step out of the rushing river of inner dialogue onto the riverbank to observe. The mental chatter may degrade and denigrate. It often criticizes, complains, worries, and frets. Watch it, then change it. Instead of letting it run you down with the broken record of repeated attacks on you and others, counter it.

One day in the tiny mountain village where I lived in Switzerland, I accidentally knocked a glass off of the kitchen counter and heard a voice in my mind say, "Why'd you do that, silly?" It had happened thousands of times before—that voice chattered on, putting me down and constantly criticizing. But this time I consciously noticed. I caught it out and challenged it. In the mental reproach, I recognized a harsh relative's voice from childhood still running through my head. That record had been playing for a long time in my subconscious. That voice, that demon from the past, wore me down and drained my self-confidence. But this time I consciously caught hold of the words and responded. "No I'm not silly. It was an accident. It's not a big deal. I intend to be more present next time."

That voice, which had become an integral part of my mental chatter, halted in a stunned shock. My mind paused in a long moment and a breath of fresh air and a ray of light came pouring in. A sense of spaciousness and relief took over where oppression had held fast before. I knew it was a monumental occasion. That same voice came back several times like an unwanted visitor, but each time I noted it and consciously responded until it soon totally disappeared.

This rooted out one of the humiliating demons of the past that had continued to haunt me. That one small instance of catching the voice from the past marked a period of momentous change. With that voice gone, my self-confidence grew tenfold. I also noticed other "voices"—an old boyfriend who criticized my appearance, a well-meaning relative who did more harm than good, and my own insecurity and fear. They'd lingered on for years, but with this powerful tool, I booted them out.

The Mechanics

Tens of thousands of words chatter through our heads on a daily basis. Stepping back and observing the mind long enough to catch the inner chatter and to change it will lead to big transformation. While sitting silently, driving, chopping vegetables for a meal, or taking a shower, make a note of the mental chatter. Observe the preoccupations, images, and words flowing past in a torrent. Don't engage in the chatter, just observe. We imagine we are this mental chatter until we stand back in silence on the riverbank and watch the debris float past. Stay on the riverbank out of the current for as long as you can. When you get dragged in, become aware of it and make the effort to step out again and become the witness. If you catch out one of those haunting voices of self-criticism, destruction, and negativity, make a decision to change it. Consciously take note and replace the negative words and thoughts with positive ones.

30

Let Go of Attachments

Attachments to people, particular outcomes, or to having desires fulfilled will cause distress, anxiety, and pain. If we bind our happiness to what happens in the world, we'll live on an emotional rollercoaster. Detachment is an important part of spiritual practice and a means of finding peace. But letting go of attachments does not mean acting indifferent or unfeeling. It means doing what you can and surrendering the rest to divine will. Teachers at spiritual retreats often tell the traditional story of two monks to illustrate. The two monks, an aged one and a young one, are walking back to their monastery. On the path they come upon a river where a beautiful woman asks for help in crossing the water. She asks the young man first, "Sir, will you please help me to cross this river?"

"No," he says. "I have taken vows of chastity. I will not touch a woman."

She turns to the old man and pleads for help. "Sir, I cannot cross alone. Will you help me?" The old monk agrees, picks her up, and carries her to the other side. The two monks continue on their way, but the young monk broods and fumes.

Hours later when the sun is setting and the woman is far behind, the young monk blurts out, "I can't believe you picked up that woman. It's against everything we stand for." The old man laughs and laughs.

"Is that still on your mind? I put her down hours ago. But you, you're still carrying her around." By carrying around useless and worrisome concerns, we waste energy. Keep the focus on God and self-inquiry rather than on others.

In India, the monkey represents attachment. To trap a monkey, people place a banana in a jar. When the monkey reaches in to grab it he makes a fist and traps himself. To be free all he needs to do is open his fist and let go of the banana, but he can't let go because he wants it so much. In a similar way, the mind attaches to objects and traps us. We think we will not be happy unless we achieve one outcome or possess one thing or another. But it's so simple to get out of the trap by just opening the mind and letting go of attachments that may hold you back and create waves of misery. It's the fast, easy way to be free and gain deeper peace of mind, and all that's necessary is making a simple decision to do it.

Infinity ∞ Practice: Dissolving Ties That Bind

No relationship, possession, job, or family member will last forever. Only the relationship to your inner Self will endure.

Learning how to let go of ties that bind is essential to the spiritual journey. The mathematical symbol for infinity looks like this:

∞

Picture the shape as energy circulating eternally. Begin this practice by imagining yourself sitting in one circle of the infinity symbol while a person or situation you wish to detach from sits facing you in the other side. Envision the scene filled with white light. The energy courses around you as you sit or stand in the center of one side. It circles around clockwise and flows around the other who occupies the opposite side. Take note of your feelings about the person. Note any bonds that appear between you. What do they look like?

Remove the bonds, chords, chains, or whatever attaches you to the other. Set them in front of you. Also put your negative feelings of desire, neediness, revenge, jealousy, or other sentiments in the same space, along with any clothes or items that connect you to the other. Imagine lighting an ethereal fire that consumes and transforms both the feelings and bonds. Cut the energy into two separate circles now so that one is circling only you in a clockwise direction, and the other is circling only the other person. Let go of the vision of the other leaving him or her in God's careful hands. Feel liberated and light as your wounds and aches are healed by the divine. This may need to be repeated periodically over a period of time to fully accomplish the task of detachment.

My preferred way of letting go is to write out or draw a picture of what I wish to release and then burn the paper in a fireplace or outdoor fire pit. The flames turn the pages and words to ash. It's a powerful symbolic act of dissolving ties. Remember that letting go of attachments is not the same as saying "I don't care." Releasing attachments doesn't necessarily mean no longer spending time with a friend or whoever may be the source of the attachment. In a very real sense, it means letting go of chains that bind us to others' likes and dislikes, sadness and happiness, or opinions about what we should do. It means moving the connection from the gut or tribal level that can pull us down, and consciously raising the energy to the level of the heart and transforming this energy of attachment into unconditional love.

Detachment is an attitude of releasing fears, desires, and false identities that mask the inner divinity. It's arrived at through asking questions like, "Who am I?"; "Where did I come from?"; and "Where am I going?" We are perceived in three ways: the one we think we are, the one others think we are, and the one we truly are—the *atma* or divine Self. Detachment ultimately strips away the many delusions and masks and brings us in touch with our true reality. It can be arrived at by a process of "not that." Through a process of inquiry one may wonder, "Am I the body? The body will be discarded like an old dress but I continue, so I'm not that. Am I the mind? The mind too fades and is not eternal, so I am not that. I am atma, the eternal soul. I am love." Try on this new identity and see how reassuring it feels.

31

Practice Mindful Eating

At the monastery on the island of Saint Honorat, a boat ride away from the hectic coast of Cannes, the Cistercian monks gather for each meal in a stone hall and begin with a prayer. Visitors join in at separate tables, but share in the collective silence. The meal consists of wine and food produced mostly on the island by the monks' labor. The repast becomes another opportunity to contemplate the divine through the food on the table. Though the fare is simple, the sacred atmosphere augmented by prayers of gratitude nourishes the spirit, soothes the mind, and feeds the body so that upon leaving the table a deep feeling of contentment and satisfaction prevails. Eating is a sacred act of worship.

While much attention is given to the food we eat, the way we eat also impacts health. Eating food in a rush or without paying proper attention can cause digestive disturbances and leave one feeling unsatisfied. But taking a moment to pause before a meal to appreciate the beauty, scent, and colors of the food, and feel gratitude for the hands that made it, will broaden your perspective. In monasteries and convents, food is treated with reverence, and mealtimes remain as much a part of worship as mass. The frame of mind in which food is received contributes to its beneficial effects on the body.

Mindful eating begins with making conscious choices about what you eat, how, and when. At meals, make awakened decisions. Most of the time we know what we need to eat, the appropriate quantity, and also what needs to be left out of the diet. But how often do we listen and act on this inner wisdom? Nourish the body temple with healthy, fresh foods that contribute to well-being and leave you feeling light and full of vitality.

While eating, instead of letting the mind wander, focus full attention on the process. Stop eating while watching television, reading, or doing other things. Simply eat. Smell the delicious scents. Visually appreciate the way your meal looks. Notice the saliva that fills the mouth. Lift the fork. Chew. Feel the texture of the food. Swallow. Again bring awareness to the luscious nourishment in front of you. Become conscious of lifting the fork, opening the mouth, and chewing. Notice as you chew slowly how the taste transforms as it moves across your tongue's palate. Don't cram more food in. Swallow before taking another bite. Then start the process over again. In addition to being a good practice in one-pointed concentration, mindful eating also makes the meal more satisfying and fulfilling.

Food is God. Revere it and respect it as it transforms and becomes the body temple and gives life energy and vitality. The quality of time we spend while eating will change how we feel. It's also ideal to make eating a scheduled act rather than a continual, habitual nibbling of empty calories that weigh down and pollute the body temple. Eat consciously—eliminate distractions of television, books and newspapers, and even conversation. If this exercise feels too mindboggling to try alone, mind-body clinics, like Duke Integrative Medicine in Durham, North Carolina, offer courses to teach mindful eating practices for health and weight loss.

32

Decide to Be Happy

Abraham Lincoln lived in a time when his job as president took a great toll on his health, and he is described by some as clinically depressed. Despite hardships created by the strain of the Civil War and the loss of a dear son who brought him solace, Lincoln told jokes and kept his eye on levity. Humor became his life preserver, and he said that folks are about as happy as they make their minds up to be. He brightened situations by turning potentially difficult moments into comedy. Once when a woman sat down on his elegant, silk top hat and became embarrassed, Lincoln said, "You should have asked me before trying it on. I could have told you it wouldn't fit."

Keeping the mind focused on the bright side of life increases longevity, improves mental state of being, and will make your soul sing. Despite severe trials and handicaps, some people choose to smile their way through life and garner the joy rather than complain about the pains. A donor to an Indian orphanage remarked that he had so many riches, but still admired and even envied the joy he saw in the smiling faces of the orphaned children who greeted him at the orphanage. In his office he hung a large portrait of a particularly touching and beautiful girl confined to a wheelchair. Her eyes glowed and her smile beamed with radiance. He never heard her moan or complain, though her situation would have given her plenty of reasons to lament.

Saint Francis of Assisi was renowned in part for his miracle of being joyful. Despite extreme poverty; stigmata on his hands, feet, and side; and a painful, debilitating illness, Saint Francis's fellow companions remarked on his joyful demeanor during his difficult life. The monks were astounded at his ability to compose lyrics and sing the glory of all of God's creation even as he lay dying.

He reportedly sang the "Canticle of Brother Sun and Sister Moon and Stars," an ode he had composed to the beauty of nature, and he asked his friars to sing it every day as well. "In that way he forgot the intensity of his sufferings and pains by considering the glory of the Lord," according to *The Legend of Perugia*. He encouraged the monks to sing with him even on his death bed when he added a tribute to "Sister Death." Song uplifted his spirit, he said, and the pain of his bleeding stomach and illness diminished. "How can he display such great joy when he is going to die?" one of the monks asked. "Shouldn't he think of death?" Instead Saint Francis chose joy and focused on the divine.

Indian saint Ramakrishna also suffered from painful throat cancer at the end of his life. Despite the pain, his devotees admired his joy and ecstasy. "I notice that when my mind is united with God the suffering of the body is left aside," he said. He perceived God in everything and everyone around him from his disciples to prostitutes.

Keeping the mind fixed in the ethereal air of the divine, it's possible to transcend the pain and let our true nature of bliss arise. This is how pain, suffering, and difficulty can help us in spiritual practice. When we suffer, our minds seek shelter in divine solace because nothing else can assuage the pain. For this reason, one of Krishna's devotees prayed for constant challenges and problems in life to keep her mind constantly fixed on God.

We often remove happiness from spiritual pursuits by taking ourselves too seriously, but the great teachers consider joy and a sense of humor to be essential. "There is no way to happiness, happiness is the way," the Buddha said. Renowned Indian teacher Sathya Sai Baba said, "There is no happiness greater than contentment."

Decide to be happy today. Find the little things that make your heart sing. Feel gratitude and extend compassion to others. If you cannot be happy, then seek out contentment. Some ways to choose joy include:

- Keep a positive attitude.
- Have a spiritual practice and maintain it. A study by Duke University showed that people with serious medical illnesses who had strong religious convictions and participated in spiritual activities remained

less likely to fall into depression and when depression struck, they came out of it faster.

- Be playful and curious like a child.
- Be of service to others in your neighborhood, home, and community.

33

Master Money

Money is a great servant and a terrible master. Money represents your time, energy, and resources, as well as the time, energy, and resources of others. Reflect before you spend it. Is something necessary? Will it contribute to your peace of mind? How will you feel about this spending decision in three months or a year? The richest person is the one with the least desires. Use your wisdom to make good decisions that will benefit you and others in the long run. Let yourself remain the master and don't become a slave to credit cards, debt, and desires.

Sometimes we feel a compulsion to buy something to fill up an inner void. How long does the buzz from the new purchase really last? Fill your inner emptiness with spiritual thoughts instead. Though it has often been called "the root of all evil," money itself is not evil. But greed, envy, and the human emotions associated with it can bring hard lessons. Spending money with wisdom means reflecting on needs versus desires and on quality of life versus quantity. When you spend money, you're spending your time and resources (or someone else's). The hard-earned dollars represent minutes of your physical life. The next time you plan to make a buy, think, "Is it worth it? Is it worth the time and energy I put in to getting the dollars to pay for this?"

The Swiss remain some of the most economically conservative people in the world and yet they enjoy one of the highest standards of living and quality of life. They recycle, they're very conscious of quality versus quantity, and they save for tough times. They're not big on credit. They also have great national pride and will buy products that are Swiss-made over imported and support local manufacturers and farmers. The Swiss are also big on creating charitable foundations to support causes.

With these ideas in mind, it's worthwhile considering your values and your priorities and how they coincide with your choices as to where and how to spend, save, or invest money. When you spend or conserve money based on your spiritual objectives, your perspective changes. Let your spiritual wealth grow in inner measure.

Money Energy Practice

Many people think of money as good or bad. Some have said that it's the root of all evil. But it's really the ideas around it, how it is used, and desire and greed for it that give money particular characteristics. By equating money with stored energy it changes the perspective. Some energy (or money) you will need now and some later on. Examine how you use this energy and your attitudes about it.

Start by keeping a note of all expenses for one month. Go deeper and consider what motivates you to spend it. Do you rush out in a moment of insecurity and buy something to shore up confidence? Are you miserly or do you make purchases to boost social status? Do you hoard it? After a month of keeping a record and watching where and why you spend, consider what's really important. Note how you intend to use money in service to your spiritual aims. Will you save for a retreat? Contribute to a special cause or food bank? Or help a friend or family member? By planning ahead and setting intentions, you will become more aware and conscious each time you use cash or a credit card. I like to keep an image of a divine form in my wallet that I see each time I open it to make a purchase. This serves as a reminder that money is divine and to use it with wisdom.

The *Tao te Ching* says, "When rich prosper while farmers lose their land; when government officials spend money on weapons instead of cures; when the upper class is extravagant and irresponsible while the poor have nowhere to turn—all this is robbery and chaos. It is not in keeping with the Tao (the way)." Use money responsibly and wisely and you will make the world a better place.

34

Bring the Mind Home

A student asked a Zen teacher about his practice. "When I'm hungry I eat; when I'm tired I sleep," the teacher said.

The student looked at him perplexed. "But that is what everyone does," he said.

"No," the teacher answered. "When they eat they do not eat, but their mind wanders out to visit many things and remains distracted. When they sleep they dream of a million and one things. This is why they are not like me." This story from renowned Zen scholar, Dr. D. T. Suzuki, describes an essential practice of presence in his classic, *An Introduction to Zen Buddhism*.

"When you eat, eat. When you walk, walk." This is a practical way to bring the mind home. It means being completely present in all actions. Don't let the mind be distracted or drawn out by other concerns in the past or future. Avoid multitasking, like eating dinner with a friend, text messaging, and watching television all at the same time. Stay fully in the present, conscious of the one act you're performing at the moment. Focus on the food—the taste, the smell. Don't rely on a newspaper or other distractions to occupy your mind. Do one thing at a time. Concentrate. In this way, life itself becomes a meditation and awareness expands.

Practicing one-pointed concentration will bring a greater sense of calm and slow life down to a natural human pace. It will also provide expanded moments to be aware of the divine. By doing this one practice, concentration and memory will improve.

When I first heard this teaching after a weekend with Tibetan lama Sogyal Rinpoche at a mountain retreat in France, I felt inspired to come home and be present. On Monday at lunch, I sat at my kitchen table looking out the window and consciously ate one spoonful of tomato soup at a time. As I moved into the moment, all I felt was pain. Tears poured down my cheeks and splashed into the tomato soup. I stayed in the present and wept uncontrollably, as hurt from so many unhealed wounds pierced the moment. Before, when I'd let my mind focus on the newspaper while lunching and kept it constantly moving with a lot of activities, I'd not felt the ache beneath the surface. "What's so great about being in the present?" I said aloud and continued to cry. When I became fully present, I felt all of the pain that I'd stored so neatly and tightly inside suddenly gush up like a newly tapped well. I'd not even noticed it before, because I'd kept it so well under control and my mind constantly busy.

This sounds like a horrible experience. But once the pain surfaced and the tears came out, the wounds healed and then I started to feel the contentment and joy of being in the present. It took a long time to get there, but before living in the present, the pain had been a constant invisible, gnawing companion hovering just beneath the surface. I felt its constant presence and carried it around, only I'd not confronted it.

When You Eat, Eat

What do you do to avoid being in the present? Bring your mind home. Don't leave it at the office. This Buddhist saying, "When you eat, eat," aptly describes the process. The mind is usually out wandering around the world getting itself into all kinds of things that waste time. Gently coax it to come back to whatever you're doing at the moment. Create your own saying like, "When you drink green tea, drink green tea." Using the breath and filling the lungs can bring the mind home. Changing hands when you eat and using the nondominant hand will force you to concentrate on lifting each forkful of food with attention. Consider other ways appropriate to your situation to help you be fully present in the moment. The process may allow both hidden pain and unknown joy to surface. It brings one back in touch with the feelings.

Bring the mind fully into the body and become aware of the muscles, shoulders, feet, legs, torso, hands, eyes, jaw, etc. Keep the attention in the body for a few moments. How does your body feel? Do you have any aches or tensions? This exercise also moves the mind into the here and now. Let surface what needs to surface. It takes less energy to let it rise and release it than to keep it pinned down beneath the surface. Think of how much energy it would take to keep a balloon filled with helium under water. Let it go. Burst it or let the air out. You'll gain renewed vitality.

35

Travel with Purpose, but Enjoy the Journey

Before air travel became common, people traveled by sailing ship across the Atlantic. In the 1800s, the voyage took an average of fifty-three days from Norway to New York. The destination and the excitement of who one might meet made the journey interesting and intriguing. Travel represented adventure and possibility. Today, though a flight may take only six to eight hours, most of us would rather ignore the actual travel and just be "beamed" to the next destination. We just want to get to the goal.

We often have the same attitudes about life. We get lost in aiming and striving to reach the goal and forget that the journey, the process of getting there, and being present during the trip are just as essential. The desire to reach the target brings frustration, anger, and anxiety. But the journey through life to each of the big successes is made of a million tiny increments that include attitude, effort, and perseverance. The setbacks and how we address them can add to the sweetness of the triumphs. While setting goals helps guide the way, only focusing on that final destination means missing out on enjoying the companionship of a lot of good people, seeing the sights at places not on the designated itinerary, and discovering special restaurants in hidden castles along the way.

A good spiritual practice is to do one's best, devote the work and effort to God, and leave the fruits of your actions to the divine. We can do our part and make the necessary efforts, but the final results remain in divine hands. This practice of surrender leaves the worry and successes or failures to God. Life is a long circuitous journey that leads us over mountains, into valleys, and to the sea. We tend to look at the next goal, the next thing to achieve on our list without enjoying the journey. We want to get to our objective without bothering much about the in-between. By moving inward to consider the spiritual perspective, life becomes a meaningful moment. It's all here—the past, present, and future—right now. The things we have now we'd only dreamed of before. The things we'll become and strive to do will grow out of the quality of who we are, what we think, and how we live today. Take a moment to sit back, relax, and enjoy the process. Right now everything is okay. Take pleasure in it.

36

Cultivate Equanimity

Even-mindedness or equanimity makes life smooth and seamless. One farmer showed his neighbors a good example. He worked as a peasant who plowed the fields with his only horse. One day he found that it had run away. His neighbors lamented, "Oh, poor man. Life is nothing but misery. How will you have a crop with no horse? You and your family will starve!"

The farmer said, "We'll see." The horse returned a few days later with a beautiful lively mare, so now the farmer owned two horses.

His neighbors rejoiced, "You're so lucky. Now you'll be rich and prosper."

The farmer kept a steady outlook. "We'll see," he said.

During the summer his son rode the mare and she threw him off. The son broke his leg. "Oh," the neighbors cried. "Now you'll have less help with the farm. The crops may spoil without his help at the harvest. What a terrible fate!"

The farmer again said simply, "We'll see." Soon army recruiters came to the village to draft the farmer's son. When they saw his broken leg they left him alone.

"You're so fortunate," the neighbors cried seeing the farmer's good luck.

But again, the farmer unmoved by the ups and downs said, "We'll see."

Maintaining even-mindedness helps to keep perspective by not letting the emotions raise us too high or sink us too low into the pit of despair. When you experience the ups and downs inevitable in each day, remember the farmer. Step back and take the events with a philosophical, detached view. Take a deep breath and let the waves of emotion slide by without overwhelming you or dragging you down.

Make a practice of stepping back to observe the emotions. Don't block or stop the rising feelings, but just watch them as they shift throughout the day. In a single day they will rise into levels of joy as someone announces acceptance of your project and then dip into moments of despair as you worry about losing your job. Emotions will shift from a word from a colleague or friend, an event at home or in the office, or simply the natural rising of moods as thoughts drift by. By observing your emotions rise and subside, you can remain anchored in the natural state of peace beneath the shifting tide. You will remain on an even keel and be in a good place to cultivate equanimity. This will keep you from being dragged high and low by the waves of external events, internal chatter, and sentiments.

IV

*Relationships
and Sharing*

37

Make Love with Your Partner

Sexual union is holy and pure when performed with the right partner, in the right way, at the right time, and with the right intention. By holding the intent to make it holy, lovemaking can become a practice infused with spirituality. When associated with spirituality, many people think of Tantra. Some teachers misuse Tantric philosophy, mislead students, and put them at risk. Be very wary of anyone playing with your sexual energy and your spiritual aspirations. It's like playing with fire in a drought-stricken forest.

Tantra is a system of Hindu religious philosophy linked closely to the ancient Indian texts, the Vedas. It views the ultimate reality as pure consciousness or pure being. *Maya*, or the grand illusion of life, functions on the relative plane of physical existence through the play of creation, preservation, and destruction. Indulging in physical pleasures and attachment to them traps the soul in the lower self. According to Swami Nikhilananda, a student of Sri Ramakrishna, Tantra prescribes a path of sublimation of physical desires in three steps: purification, elevation, and reaffirmation of reality as pure awareness or consciousness. Its practices require the strict guidance of an experienced, wise teacher, and Ramakrishna strongly discouraged spiritual aspirants from taking to this "left-handed path."

Tantric practices encourage and incite awakening of the *kundalini* energy, the vital energy coiled at the base of the spinal column. This energy remains relatively dormant until the aspirant is ready for it to awaken. When this energy awakens naturally or through certain practices and is raised, it can move the aspirant into new levels of understanding and consciousness. When turned in a downward or wrong direction it can also harm and destroy. Swami Nikhilananda wrote that mantras, hymns, and sacrifices all play vital roles in the Tantric practices, which are not to be left to the untrained and impure for experimentation. The ultimate aim of Tantric practice is to achieve *moksha*, or liberation from maya and the bonds of physical life, and merge in pure consciousness.

Instead of shunning the weaknesses that may contribute to a spiritual seeker's downfall, the philosophy says to seize them and sublimate them as a means of spiritual liberation. Nikhilananda wrote,

> For a certain type of aspirant called "heroic," the actual drinking of wine and practice of sexual union are prescribed, and the teacher carefully points out that the joy and stimulation arising from these are to be utilized for the uplift of the mind from the physical plane.

He goes on to say that the aspirant offers wine, cereals, meat, and fish to the deity and then partakes of the sacrificial offerings.

The pleasure resulting from them is gradually sublimated. "Sexual union, the disciple is taught, is something sacred, whose purpose is the creation of new life, and it should therefore not be resorted to in an irresponsible manner," Nikhilananda says. He goes on that Tantra never promotes sexual excess or indulgence solely for gratification of carnal desires. It unveils the deeper significance of sexual unity as the Oneness hidden behind the curtain of duality and opposites—yin and yang, male and female. In Tantra, each partner aims to spiritualize the experience and raise herself and her partner to God-consciousness on the path to liberation.

From the Heart

In making love with your partner, elevate him or her to the level of the divine. Perceive the divine feminine or divine masculine in your lover and consider giving joy and pleasure to promote unconditional love and support the other in his spiritual journey. Self or ego is loveless, while selflessness is full of love. The very act of union or merging with another can be symbolic of our act of union with God. Feel the energetic experience throughout the body. Very often we attach to the lover through keeping energy blocked at the root chakra or at the level of the solar plexus. Raise the energy to the heart level on the right side of the body. Do this simply by attuning to the energy flowing naturally through the body. Imagine a flower opening petal by petal in the area of the spiritual heart. Let love flow from this place out to your partner.

Playing with lovemaking is like playing with fire or a double-edged sword. It's when we're at our most vulnerable and naked, both literally and symbolically. But holding an attitude of playfulness can bring a sense of lightness. Often in the Western tradition, sexuality has been treated as dirty. The pendulum reaction swinging to extremes cheapens it through promiscuity. Neither approach gives a healthy response to a natural and beautiful experience. Making the right choices about when, where, and how one shares the jewel of sensuality with another requires discernment and transcending the immediate pull of desires. Chastity and loyalty to one partner protects the body, mind, and spirit and keeps the heart whole.

Open your heart and turn your lovemaking into a sacred union with your partner. Honor and respect your chosen one in this act of divine union. Consider it a symbolic union between the divine masculine and feminine within you. Let your mind focus on being present and elevate the energy to the heart level. Enjoy the precious moment of sharing.

38

Have a Laugh

Doing a spiritual practice doesn't mean you have to become overly serious or dour. Laugh today. It may lengthen your life span, reduce pain and stress, strengthen your immune system, make your life happier, and draw you closer to God. The Dalai Lama is known for his joking and light-heartedness while giving serious talks about spiritual well-being. Many Buddhist monks glow with joy and laugh frequently. Hindu teachers often make jokes about spiritual practices, and some believe God has a sense of humor.

Connect laughing with spiritual pursuits by keeping a sense of humor about yourself and your weaknesses. While doing spiritual work and self-inquiry, keeping a sense of play will help you to recognize mistakes and change course without getting bent out of shape. Don't laugh at someone, but laugh rather at a situation or at yourself. It's hard to get angry and stay angry when good-natured laughter erupts in a room. You might also check out laughter yoga as a practice that promotes laughing combined with breathing for physiological, psychological, and spiritual benefits.

A Chinese story tells of three laughing Taoist masters who instructed others by going to the marketplace and village squares and simply laughing. They laughed in the sun and rain in the heat and cold. The same laughter peeled out in all conditions. It rang out to the ears of the depressed, the greedy, the ecstatic, the envious, and the angry, and opened a space for transformation to occur. When one of the three masters died, they respected their dead friend's wish not to prepare the body or change his clothes, but simply laid his mortal remains on the funeral pyre. When the pyre was lit for the deceased, the dead man's pockets were full of firecrackers that exploded in bursts and whistles. He carried his humor even to the grave. The noise astonished the masters and crowd with delight and the teaching with laughter began again.

Lighten a tense and heavy situation by making an easy joke or poking fun at your own attitudes and actions. In his book *The Healing Power of Humor,* Allen Klein describes a life or death situation. During the Cuban Missile Crisis when negotiations broke down and seemed doomed to fail and end in nuclear war, a Russian told a joke: "What's the difference between communism and capitalism?" he said. No one responded. "Under capitalism man exploits man. Under communism it is the other way around." The ensuing laughter broke the stalemate and helped to move the process toward a peaceful conclusion. Having that good laugh together might have saved thousands of lives.

Laughter unites, builds camaraderie, and spreads lightheartedness. Laugh in a good-natured, sincere way and others will want to join with you rather than fight. Humor tools include using exaggeration to break tension in a situation, joking about your own personal weaknesses, making unexpected creative leaps and associations, and playing.

Play Toys

If you feel challenged to keep a sense of humor, you may want to keep a few props around to help out in tough times. Put on a red clown's nose and look in the mirror, buy some bouncing balls, play with pyramid puzzles, and blow bubbles. Keeping these items around in strategic places for those tough moments can transform your humor when you need it most.

39

Send Light Thoughts

Sacred texts point to the power and importance of thoughts. "Let one therefore keep the mind pure, for what a man thinks that he becomes. This is a mystery of Eternity," says the Chandogya Upanishad. In the Bible, the book of Proverbs says, "Be careful how you think; your life is shaped by your thoughts." And contemporary teacher and healer Edgar Cayce put it yet another way, "For mind is the builder and that which we think upon may become crimes or miracles. For thoughts are things." Whether we're aware of it or not, thoughts produce vibrations. These vibrations can be positive or negative depending on the intent and the content.

Most everyone has had some intuitive experience that keys them into what's going on with someone else. Mothers know the power of thoughts and often know when their child is at risk; they often respond by sending loving thoughts of protection. NASA scientist and educator, Dr. Art-Ong Jumsai, studied the effects of thoughts on plants and noted that they thrived when students thought good things and sent the plants love. But other plants died when sent bad vibes. One student reported severe headaches when he sent hatred and anger to a plant that consequently died.

Some people can perceive the shape of thoughts. In her book *Thought Forms*, theosophist and clairvoyant Anne Besant described the appearance of angry thoughts. She saw them manifest as sharp red daggers ready to stab at others, while compassionate prayers of peace and protection literally flew on wings to soothe those whom they were directed toward. This may also explain why some spoken words cause a sensation of physical pain when we hear them, while others soothe and calm.

Mind and body clinics, like those at Benson-Henry Institute for Mind Body Medicine and Duke Integrative Medicine, recognize the role of the mind in illness and healing. They offer programs to help address illness through mindfulness. Researcher Masura Emoto approaches the influence of thoughts in a different way. He studied the effects of words and thoughts on water and captured the results in photographed crystals that appear in his bestselling book *Messages in Water*. His experiments showed that negative words in most any language produced distorted, fragmented shapes, while words "love" and "gratitude" transformed the crystals into perfect, beautiful structures resembling snowflakes.

Studies show that thoughts produce vibrations that resound throughout the body and can contribute to good or ill health. More and more people are becoming conscious of the influence of their own thoughts as well as those of others. Thoughts can be as easy to read or hear as the words printed in a book, and I believe that they will become legible or audible to a growing percentage of the population, which will make it virtually impossible to hide one's true nature or deceive others.

Whether you realize it or not, your thoughts are shaping how others will react to you. How would you feel if the individuals next to you could perceive your thoughts right now? Would you feel at ease or ashamed? What you think may materialize. Seek to use your thoughts to promote goodwill and peace, to build in a constructive way, and not destroy. Become conscious of your inner chatter today. Use your thoughts to help serve others and spread harmony rather than dissension.

Practice Sending Good Thoughts: Part I

Sit quietly and send good thoughts to someone you love or someone who needs extra support and care right now. Think of an uplifting word or phrase, like "God loves you," and send it with affection and kindness. Practice this with several people over the next days.

Practice Sending Good Thoughts: Part II

Is there a difficult situation that you're in or will encounter soon? Silence the mind for a moment in a serene place.

Imagine yourself, the people involved, and the place where you will meet filled with pure, white light and harmony. Visualize the light flowing in freely and let it fill those you may have difficulty with. If you feel resistance, acknowledge it and let it be filled with light too. If you have a hard time visualizing the light, imagine it's there and add a word or phrase to protect and guide you and all involved in the situation. The phrase may be something like, "Guide us and protect us all when we meet." Practice this several times throughout the day or over a period of time with patience, purity of heart, and perseverance. Watch how the scene transforms when you next meet.

40

Give without Expecting a Return

Legendary giving expects no return and seeks no publicity. Back in the fourth century, a kind old bishop named
Nicholas performed so many good deeds that the Catholic
Church declared him a saint; he became world-renowned
as "Father Christmas." His red bishop's dress closely re-
sembled the costume of *Baba Noel* (Father Christmas) seen
in Europe on December 6th, and his example inspires us
to give charitably during the holidays even today. Saint
Nick, as he came to be called, worked tirelessly to help
serve the poor and needy in his small town of Demre, Turkey. Long after he died, he was canonized.

Revered as the patron saint of judges, children, virgins,
prisoners, and sailors, Saint Nicholas's stories of generosity continue to influence the world view of Christmas as
a time to serve the needy, give gifts, and share. The best
known story of his compassion concerned three sisters
who planned to sell themselves into slavery because their
father had no money for dowries. Legend recounts that
Saint Nick threw bags of gold down the family's chim-
ney to save the girls, and one bag fell in a stocking that
hung there to dry. The gold became their means to marry.

The saint remains popular in both Eastern and Western cultures, and may contribute to world peace through his simple elevated actions that have uplifted people's minds over many centuries.

Mother Teresa of Calcutta also spent her life serving and helping the sick and poor. "Love begins at home," she said in her Noble Prize acceptance speech. "Start to love and serve your family, your neighbors; share with the poor and needy around you: a smile, a word, your time, your friendship, your belongings." In the spirit of Mother Teresa and Saint Nick, do something kind for someone. Offer a hand to a neighbor or give money to someone in need without expecting a return. Bring an extra bagel to work. Smile at someone.

Instead of indulging yourself in another luxury, give a gift to an orphan. Don't tell anyone what you've done. Don't seek publicity. What you do doesn't have to cost anything to have an impact. Do it because it's the right thing and it feels good. By moving your attention to others in need, you'll also begin to appreciate the goodness around you. Be careful to provide what is needed and not necessarily what pleases you.

Some people give to others and keep an account of what they feel is owed back to them by the individual they help. Others give to someone today expecting they'll receive a return from someone else when they need it in the future. Others give just for the joy of giving and devote their actions to the divine. Giving comes from one aspect of God and goes to another aspect of God. God is both the giver and receiver, the action and the gifts. When looked at and experienced in this way, the experience brings great joy to all involved with no sense of debt or indebtedness. Discover the joy of giving wherever you go.

Give It Away

Many places welcome volunteers for charity work. If you're attracted to nature, try volunteering with the park service or the Nature Conservancy. Soup kitchens and reading programs for children welcome volunteers to help. Your giving doesn't have to be organized by a group. If you visit your parent in a retirement community, stop and say hello to another person on the way and have a chat. Time, energy, and attention can be just as valuable (and often more so) than money. Hold the inner attitude of gift giving with no expectation of anything from the other. Consider your giving as an offering of God to God. Explore the many possibilities and enjoy.

41

Serve Up Love with Conscious Cooking

Ever notice how mom's foods nourish and fill you with a sense of satisfaction unlike anything else? Mom bakes a cake, prepares the stew, and chops veggies for the soup thinking with love of those who will eat her food. Her kids get not only the nourishment from vitamins, but also the subtle nourishment that has been transmitted to it through the energy in her hands and heart. Unlike fast food that leaves us hungry again in a few minutes, mom's food continues to nourish and leave a sense of satisfaction that truly fills our hunger.

Foods contain subtle properties. When we eat, we consume not only the gross elements, but we also take in the subtle influences of those who prepare meals. With this in mind, Walter Danzer, founder of the Swiss health foods company Soyana, requires that all foods be prepared in an atmosphere of love and peace. "I first understood the importance and the proof of this mindful practice after a meal out at a restaurant with our employees," Danzer says. "We all practice meditation and are peaceful people. After one meal at a pizzeria, we all woke up with nightmares. If only one of us would have had a nightmare, it would not have been remarkable. But all of us had nightmares."

He realized that something in the way the meal had been prepared by the cook had permeated the food and affected the psyche of everyone at the table. From this moment he knew that holding good intentions and preparing food with love would become essential to his company. Danzer deeply believes that the one who prepares foods will transmit his state of being into the food and affect the one who ultimately consumes it. If the preparer feels aggressive, lustful, or angry, he will sow these feelings into the food he touches. On the other hand, if he feels peaceful, thinks good thoughts, and intends for the food to bring health and well-being to consumers, this will be passed on when the food is taken into the body.

Soyana produces soy and rice milk, vegetarian patties, Essene sprouted grain breads, and other popular health foods. Danzer and his employees schedule regular meditation breaks during the work day to maintain a pure and serene frame of mind. Inspired by teacher Sri Chimnoy, Danzer follows a strict vegetarian diet and is careful about where he eats out in restaurants. His small Swiss company, founded in 1981, continues to serve a loyal following in Switzerland and Germany. It includes "loving consciousness" as a company value and sets a good example for other businesses. Each employee leads an integral, healthy way of life based on meditation, daily exercise, and a vegetarian diet. No religious belief is imposed and it's not in any way a sect. But the company works with principles that will bring food preparation into the spiritualized age. "The inner poise and joy [of employees] flows into the food products and thus strengthens the consumer," says Soyana's statement of company values.

Loving Preparation of a Meal

While food channels give out sumptuous recipes, they often leave out one essential ingredient: love. Instead of buying over the counter, preprocessed and packaged foods for yourself and family, give love by consciously preparing the meals. Clean lettuce while consciously wishing good health to those who will partake; chop tomatoes with the mind focused on nourishing those you love with each careful slice. You may wish to prepare your own sandwich for lunch break or make a soup at home in the evening in lieu of watching television.

If you have guests for a meal at home, give them the loving gift of home-cooked foods that will nourish their bodies, soothe their minds, and satisfy their spirits. It will bring you joy and foster peace. You may also want to prepare foods while chanting a mantra like the Gayatri, or focus on your centering prayer. If you cannot prepare your own foods, then you may still recite the mantra or a prayer requesting that the food be blessed and filled with divine light to bring health and well-being to those who will eat it.

42

Be Wily as a Serpent
and Innocent as a Dove

A treacherous serpent lived in a village and disturbed villagers. When a wise man came to the village, they told him about how the snake would hiss and bite, terrifying old and young alike. The wise man decided to visit the serpent who lived at the edge of town. The serpent greeted him with hissing and threats. "I've come to talk with you," the wise man said. "You've been terrorizing these poor people for some time; now you must quit. Take to a higher path and stop biting them." The serpent listened and imbibed the teacher's words. He vowed he would do what the teacher asked because he wished to change his ways and no longer be hated and feared by everyone.

Now when the snake ventured out during the day, he no longer hissed or bit anyone. Consequently, the children and people of the town beat the snake and flung it around by the tail until it was almost lifeless. When the teacher returned sometime later and asked about the snake, the people said they no longer saw it and thought it might be dead. The wise man sought it out and found the once huge snake lying listless, badly injured, and thin from abuse. "What has happened to you?" the teacher said.

"I've done what you said and stopped biting," the snake said.

"Well that's good," said the teacher. "But you must defend yourself. I said you could not bite. I did not say you could not hiss!"

The image of the serpent arose also when Jesus called together his disciples and prepared to send them into the world. During this treacherous biblical period, anyone who spoke against the established order risked his life. "I am sending you out a sheep among wolves," Jesus said. "Be as cunning as serpents and as innocent as doves." The material-minded world will not easily welcome those dedicated to the spiritual path. Making the decision to walk it means shoring up inner strength and sometimes walking alone against adversity. But living compassionately and with kindness does not mean letting others take advantage of you.

Being loving and soft should not be confused with being weak. Love acts in humility, but anchored in the divine it stands on a firm foundation of strength and power. Be as guileless as a dove and as wily as a serpent. This biblical expression describes a wise spiritual aspirant. Doves shine in innocence and purity. They promote peace. To be guileless means to be sincere, straightforward, honest, and frank. It means lacking in deception. One who is guileless doesn't act out of subterfuge or carry a hidden agenda. And yet we're not meant to be stupid in our compassion and open ourselves to hurtful influences either.

A serpent travels mostly unnoticed through the underbrush. It's wise at getting by in the world without drawing attention. It's a symbol for vitality and can hiss to protect itself without harming anything, but it will also bite in self-defense. Despite the seeming contradiction, a devotee of God must integrate both of these qualities to maintain a healthy and sane life. Some situations require frankness and honesty, while others may require silence to meet difficult situations.

Living the Dove-Serpent Paradox

Throughout the day, hold the image of the dove and serpent. Observe your interactions with people as you aspire to grow in spirit. Do you allow yourself to get into situations where you know you will be hurt? Pay attention to your inner serpent. It can sniff out situations and slip in and out of places without being observed. It often moves under cover and yet it's keenly aware of its environment. Work carefully to realize which qualities of the dove or serpent will serve you best today. The dove flies high and is a universal symbol of peace because of its harmless nature. The serpent is wise and self-sufficient. Bring these elements together in your dealings with the world. How can you apply these qualities in your life?

Native American traditions used animals for guidance. Some animals that they encountered directly or through a vision imparted qualities that they wished to identify with and cultivate. These animals also symbolized weaknesses to overcome. Note creatures that speak to your soul and keep an image or carving at hand to remind you of the characteristics you aim to develop.

43

Think Before You Speak

A careless word can start a war while a kind word may mark the start of a lifelong friendship. Think before you open your mouth to utter a word. Don't let the words fly out carelessly. If every human being would make this effort, it would immediately contribute to better understanding and world peace. Before letting a thoughtless word slip out, think. Is it true? Is it necessary to say this? Is it kind? Will it injure anyone? Going through this check list before uttering a sound will save time, energy, and may spare the feelings of someone you love. It will also make people think more fondly of you. Speaking less sometimes promotes greater peace and understanding. Use your discrimination to determine the right path to take with your words.

In this media-crazed era that provokes dissension and attention through vomiting words, we forget how important and powerful words really are. They can get you fired, change someone's opinion of you, get you married, and save you from a fire if you yell "Help!"—but don't cry wolf. Remember Aesop's fable? A shepherd boy took the village sheep to a mountain pasture and when he grew bored, decided to cry, "Wolf! Wolf!" The villagers ran up to help protect their lambs, but they saw no wolf, only a little boy grinning and laughing at their fright and the stir he caused. They returned to their hearths, and the boy cried out again. Again they came and he laughed and laughed at the big joke. Finally a real wolf came. This time when he cried, "Wolf!" no one showed up. They no longer believed him and thought he was playing another trick. The lambs scattered with fear, and some lost their lives.

Think of words as precious gems not to be strewn about loosely like sand. Being economical with words may save you from seriously hurting someone. The injuries caused by a physical cut will heal, but those caused by the tongue can fester for life. The four errors of the tongue are: uttering false statements, scandalizing, finding fault with others, and excessive speech. Use discrimination to determine the right words. This sounds easy, but when it's really put into practice it brings greater awareness of your impact on others and of how much you speak.

Watch Your Mouth Practice

Today, watch your words. If you're prone to blurting out things without forethought, begin to take a deep breath and pause before saying anything. Don't worry about not getting the space to speak in a conversation. Measure your words. Choose them with care and if you're challenged about what to say, ask the divine within you to guide and speak the words through your heart. Then relax and hold trust and faith.

To change a habit of speaking too quickly and spontaneously requires conscious effort. Fix the attention on your heart and pray for assistance. By listening inside before opening the mouth, you'll know what words to use and the proper tone to employ. Remember, often the best response is peaceful silence.

44

Marry Your Mate

Instead of simply cohabitating, do something spiritually adventurous—marry your mate. When you're just sharing a house, it's easy to move out when anyone has a whim or simply gets angry. Marriage binds people together in a commitment of unity and can create one of the best opportunities to build patience, diminish ego, learn about weaknesses, and grow. When perceived as a spiritual exercise, marriage can help both partners mature. By clarifying aims and intentions, a couple can begin to carry a unified vision of their partnership.

Marriage is a symbol of unity. The wedding ring represents wholeness. When a couple marries, the opposites of male and female unite. In many ways, a marriage in the physical world mirrors working toward an inner marriage of the disparate parts of the psyche with the inner partner or Self. It represents striving to achieve balance. "There are different passages in life. Marriage is one such passage, and it is one of the most important ones there is," says Mata Amritanandamayi Devi, better known simply as Amma. "For a person who lives in the world (i.e., a householder), to be able to live a full, productive life, he or she must pass through the passage of marriage with as much love, intimacy, caring, and commitment as possible. Married life, if it is lived with the proper love and understanding, will help awaken the feminine within a man, and the masculine within a woman. This balance can eventually help both of them reach the final goal of eternal freedom."

In America and most Western countries, we have extremely high and unrealistic expectations of perfection from partners. We want a mate who is perfect and complete from the start. But what if marriage helps us to realize completeness and become more refined? A marriage counselor giving a talk at a spiritual center on communication responded to questions. A concerned father said, "My son married about a year ago and now he and his wife are starting to fight. Should they divorce?"

"No," the wise counselor said. "They're about where they should be. First there's the honeymoon period and then comes the adjustment." To understand and adapt is part of the process, she said. But it's usually not done without some friction. She described marriage like two coarse, rough stones pounding against each other in a tumbler. The friction and abrasive action polishes them and makes them shine. Marriage as a spiritual practice becomes a way of removing ego and expanding and growing the heart. It teaches us about love that transcends the romantic image of candlelit dinners and passionate nights and takes us into love as something that extends to periods of sickness, anxiety, and troubles. Through the trials, this love matures and sweetens. It's a work of patience—maybe even an art.

In the end, marriage of two opposites represents the spiritual paradox of the unity of opposites. In building a life together, the individual loses the little self and surrenders to the higher wisdom Self.

Treat Your Spouse Like Your Best Friend

One way of jointly committing to a spiritual marriage is to define a sort of mission statement. Ideally, both partners will define their own ideas of what their mission or motto might be. They may then reconcile them into one joint statement. Next, each partner might define the values they feel drawn to work on in the relationship—patience, compassion, or listening, for example. Each person will reflect on how this might be accomplished.

The couple may want to define collective aims such as growth, expansion, or understanding. By making these aims conscious, they give direction and build a common foundation for making joint decisions and determining goals. A final step may be to define needs and spend some time communicating on a regular basis. Remember to take great care when you speak. Know that each word may go straight to the heart of your beloved and help to open or close the door to this union. If both partners can keep the best interest of the other in mind, this creates an atmosphere of teamwork and mutual support.

Your partner can become your best friend and coach. He or she will know you better than anyone else, and can gently tell you things that no one else would dare. Make time for regular communication, date nights, hiking, dancing, or whatever you enjoy doing together. If possible, try to go beyond living parallel lives that never touch. There's a joy in relating to your spouse as your best friend.

45

Pay Attention to Synchronicity

Synchronicity, *leelas*, or the divine play turn the spiritual path into a delightful experience full of surprises. Though many attribute the idea of synchronicity, the meaningful occurrence of events in time, to Swiss analyst Carl Jung, the idea of divine sport or play traces back into ancient spiritual history when humanity felt a more immediate connection to God. The word "synchronous" means a "simultaneous occurrence in time." *Syn* relates to similar and *chronos* pertains to time, as in synchronized swimming. When events, images, and occurrences like dreaming of someone and then meeting them that afternoon arise, the divine begins to sport about with us and take us into the divine play of life with its mysteries and mystical occurrences.

The leelas also include miracles. The modern mind relies on science and reason, limiting its perceptions to things it cannot conceive of as unreal, irrational, unimportant, or impossible. But what if miracles occur through universal principles that we are not yet evolved enough to respect and comprehend? How unfortunate to dismiss the possibility of their existence and to imagine that Jesus could not have turned water to wine or healed the sick. The spirit has the ability to transcend and have power over the laws of nature as known to science. Even contemporary yogis and saints use their powers to heal and help others. These powers are not used for selfish gains. Visitors to the holy place at Lourdes and other powerful places also report healings that doctors and scientists cannot explain.

While synchronicity may reflect the plays between the inner world of the unconscious Self and the conscious world, they may also be inspired by and arise from the divine. Images from dreams may appear on postcards or birthday cards at the grocery or coffee shop. A serpent from a dream may be recalled by a very real one in the garden or in the form of a child's toy snake that you might mistake for a real one during the day. A friend or enemy who appeared in a dream may also show up during the day to remind you of work to do or reinforce your confidence that you're heading in the right direction.

Pay attention to these synchronistic events. They're often your heart and spirit trying to get your attention. Wake up and take note of what they might be trying to communicate. Play with the images. Reflect on the friends or enemies who appear. What's the deeper meaning that your heart is trying to get you to comprehend?

Often you'll know an event transcends the coincidental by the way it makes you feel. Does it give you a shiver, an inner knowing, or an "Ah-ha!" experience? Don't brush it off. Take it to heart and let the images and feelings that arise simmer inside. Ask the coincidence what it's trying to tell you. Have a dialogue with it in writing or speaking into a recorder. Place yourself in the image's position and respond for it. If you're writing and you're right handed, switch to the left hand to allow the trigger of the synchronistic event to answer. Play with it and let it work through your imagination.

Continue to make notes of events and images that catch your attention in this way. Explore and have fun. Be open to the possibility of miracles and note when they happen. These events are an indication that God really does have a sense of humor and loves to play, delight, and surprise in myriad ways when we open our awareness to this.

46

Revere Your Mother

Without our moms we would not be here right now. Think about it. Our mothers went through months of carrying us around in their bellies; then they carried us around in their arms, fed us, and changed our diapers until we could walk and take care of ourselves. They teach us self-sacrifice and selfless love, and set examples that influence our lives. Almost no one loves us as much as our moms do. The mother is a goddess of patience, long suffering, nurturing, kindness, and compassion. She watches over and protects. She will often make great sacrifices to make sure we get what we need and want. She embodies the qualities of the Divine Mother.

For those who have good relationships, revering mom may come naturally. If emotional injuries and scars resulted from childhood, making a connection can be difficult. Overcoming the obstacles and making amends is very rewarding and marks a big step toward healing old wounds and letting go of bitterness and grudges. As children we're at the mercy of those around us. Regardless of the family situation, we learn and grow from the lessons—both good and painful. To revere mother and father, sometimes these challenging, conflicting, and complex feelings need to be acknowledged. Once they're recognized, work to let them go and allow the wounds to heal.

If you feel motherless, seek out someone in your life who represents the ideal mother and focus on the qualities you see. Someone along the way has hopefully acted as a mother to you regardless of their gender. Finally, make a conscious effort to identify special moments and things your mother has individually done for you. Moms are often the ones who demonstrate sacrifice and teach us about love. It's helpful to find the goodness in your mother and appreciate what she did to give you life and help you grow.

Take a moment to let your mom, dad, grandparent, or someone you love know how much you appreciate them today. Consider the time and energy they've put into raising you and bringing you into this world and feel sincerely grateful. Many small acts of kindness and care went into growing you. Think of one thing in particular you're thankful for and express it in a phone call, an e-mail, or a letter. Reverence for parents and elders will foster a sense of reverence for the divine. Reverence of your mother will draw you closer to the divine feminine.

Working to Love and Accept

Working to love and accept our mothers unconditionally helps us to embrace the Divine Mother who opens her arms so lovingly to us. It's like a step on the journey as we develop and strengthen the divine feminine within us. If you imagine the archetype of the ideal mother, she may appear in a form different from your birth mother. For many of us, the most ideal way in is through our grandmothers, who often acted as strong yet gentle forces of love and protection.

My grandmother was a powerhouse of love. I still recall her thick, warm arms and comforting breast, her flower print dresses and the sweet love that she gave freely without reserve or condition. For others, Mata Amrita nandamayi Devi or Amma serves as a good example. Born in India, from an early age she perceived everyone as her children. Wherever she travels around the world, people wait in lines to receive her hugs, see her soft gaze, and be welcomed by her encircling arms. She represents the Divine Mother in action as she literally embraces *everyone* who comes to her unconditionally with the love of a perfect mother for her own child.

Find a place to sit quietly in meditation and gently focus on the breath. Begin to contemplate your vision of the mother. Let the qualities associated with her—nurturing, compassion, sustenance, or strength—arise. An image may appear of your ideal. If you're not a visual person, then find a magazine photo, an image of your grandmother, or the goddess that fits your ideal and begin to work with it to imbibe the qualities therein. Keep the image in a place where you will see it and allow your psyche to play. You may also wish to write about the qualities that you adore and consciously begin to cultivate them in yourself.

Seva (Selfless-service) for Elders

Many elderly mothers and fathers end up in retirement homes where they spend days missing family and friends. If you can, make an effort to go regularly to spend some time with an elderly person at their home or in an assisted living community. Some groups organize activities to serve the elderly in these homes. This can be a very rewarding service to perform.

47

Seek More to Understand Than to Be Understood

We yearn to have others understand us. We seek them out and try to explain what we mean, what we feel, and what we want. Anyone pursuing spiritual practice must not expect or demand that others understand and adapt. It is we who must seek to understand and (if possible and appropriate) adapt. We are consciously attempting to work in union with the divine. Others are also moved by the divine—all things and beings are. It's our duty to make the extra effort to keep ego in check, understand difficult situations and people, and promote harmony.

Understanding Others Practice

How is it possible to understand another? Begin to study human nature. Observe yourself and why you do things. Work to comprehend the feelings and position of others. Practice putting yourself in someone else's sneakers and see how it feels from that perspective. By making efforts to understand, you will expand your sense of others and begin to know the most appropriate way to adapt. It will also carry you a step closer to the experience of Oneness.

The best way is not necessarily through words. Use the heart to understand. The wisdom heart knows and gets inspired. If you read Tolstoy, Shakespeare, or Dickens, their understanding of human nature is what makes us laugh and cry. Their greatness lies in loving *all* of their characters. Through their writing, these authors give birth to their creations—and they shower all of it and all of the people in it with love, even the most despicable. Why not experiment with creating different characters that personify both the things you adore and dislike about human nature? Play with understanding others in your life too. Indulge them like your beloved characters or your own children and adapt to the situation.

Explore and examine other cultures. If you have opportunities to travel, this is a good time to look around and observe how people do things in other places. Seek to understand what lies beneath the surface. The divine may be perceived with different characteristics and attributes in different places. Some perceive God as having a human form. Others believe the divine has no form. Others may give the divine other characteristics and attributes. But they may all be conscious of the mysterious power that animates life and is the support and substance of all.

48

Remember the Golden Rule

One thread that unites all wisdom practices is this: "Do unto others as you would have them do unto you." This quote from the Bible is echoed throughout all spiritual traditions. The Buddhists text the *Digha Nikaya*, says, "Be generous, be courteous, be benevolent, treat them as you treat yourself, and be as good as your word."

Confucianism states, "Never do to others what you would not like them to do to you."

Hinduism, as reflected in the *Mahabhrata of Vyasa,* says, "Never should a man do to another what he would not want another to do to him; this is the essence of *dharma* [right action]."

"Not one of you is a believer until he loves for his brother what he loves for himself," says the *Forty Hadith of an-Nawawi*, which presents the fundamental precepts of Islam.

"All things are our relatives; what we do to everything, we do to ourselves," is the basis of many Native American spiritual practices.

Sufis believe it is possible to draw closer to God and more fully embrace the divine presence in this life, and they focus on the consideration of the hearts and feelings of others as essential to Sufi teachings. A saying from Sufism is, "If you haven't the will to gladden someone's heart, then at least beware lest you hurt someone's heart for that is our path."

Hold these words in your heart throughout the day and explore what they mean in action. How will you promote understanding today?

V

Purification

49

Lose Some Baggage

Travelers hate losing luggage, but I learned to love it. One night a young woman in my dreams stood in front of her apartment building. A truck pulled up. "I'm looking for Dee Niles," the driver said.

"That's me," she said and he proceeded to unload a parking lot full of heavy, dirty baggage. "Now you just wait a minute," she said to the driver. "That's not mine. It's dirty and yucky. You take that back right now." But he turned over some of the bag tags and she saw her name printed in big letters. "But I don't want that stuff," she insisted.

"Hey lady it's yours. Accept it," he said.

She walked away but the baggage followed her. Dumfounded and in despair, she returned to the parking lot. "Poor woman," I thought when I awoke. She's got all of that dirty, nasty baggage around. I'm glad that's not me." Then it struck me like a cartoon frying pan clanging against my head. "That *is* me." But I don't have baggage like that, I convinced myself.

But Dee Niles would not go away. She appeared over and over in dreams with a lot of bags, and the excess weight made it impossible to journey anywhere with ease. Inside the bags she found coffee addiction, workaholic behavior, codependency, grudges, and more. As the baggage opened up and I did the work in my waking life to clean it out, some amazing things began to happen. Dee showed up with less luggage in the dreams. But, if I slid back into old ways of thinking and working during the day, she would inevitably try to board a flight that night overburdened with heavy crates.

When I made moves to forgive, have more compassion, and share during daytime activities, the symbolic dream luggage kept diminishing in size, until one night years later a miracle occurred. Dee sat in an airport lounge waiting for her flight. A joyful travel guide glowing with light came to her and said, "Are you ready for the journey?" Dee said, "Oh, yes." And I felt her excitement.

She looked down to pick up her bag, but on the floor was just one small carry-on suit bag. When she peered inside, it contained nothing. Dee smiled. Surprised and happy, she stood to follow her guide and intentionally left the last bag behind. I felt so much joy on waking. I knew that I'd really accomplished something worthwhile by working to lose my baggage on many levels. The end of that series of dreams didn't mean I no longer had inner work to do. Other lessons keep coming in different ways and with different images.

Lose Your Baggage Now

To travel comfortably on the journey through life, it's best to travel light. Have you ever noticed first-time travelers who load absolutely everything into their bags and travel with three, four, five, or more pieces of luggage? Watch how hard it is for them to get anywhere. Now, think of this symbolically. I like rituals to get rid of obstacles and baggage and this is one of my favorites.

On a piece of paper, write down anything and everything that you'd like to eliminate right now. This might be an attachment to an ex, an attitude, a grudge, an addiction, grief, stress, discontent, excessive desires, etc. You may want to draw a piece of luggage on the paper to identify it with a symbolic image. Once you write down what you want to part with, dump it. Tear it up. Rip it apart. Burn it in a safe place. Destroy it in anyway. This sends a powerful and immediate message to your psyche that you're ready to let it go. During the day, work to prove it.

50

Clean Up Your Act

At some point on the spiritual journey we feel a need to purge and cleanse ourselves of past actions, ideas, habits, thoughts, feelings, relationships, material things, or places. Many traditions have ritual ways of purification. One of the most renowned in the Christian tradition is the ritual of baptism—a physical washing away of the old to be symbolically born into a renewed state of being. In Hindu practices, various ways are prescribed for purification: a water bath, a bath in ash, and an air bath. Submersion in the Ganges River that runs through India is believed to wash away all sins. When asked about this, Ramakrishna said that the Ganges indeed purifies, but the sins wait on the river bank and jump back onto the individual when he reemerges if he does not come out with a changed heart.

Buddhist practices consecrate and purify places through the chanting of sacred mantras. Before creating a sand *mandala* or building, or a *stupa* or temple, a priest will perform the rites and rituals that prepare the place for the construction. A Native American practice of smudging includes burning an herb, usually sage, to purify Oneself and the environment. Elders among the Cherokee and other tribes are still called to perform the practice to consecrate festivals and celebrations.

Smudging and Clearing

Smudging, using sage sticks wound with a thin string, has found revival in retreats and meditation centers. Smudge sticks are lit and circled around the area with the intention of clearing out unhelpful influences and purifying oneself. A stick of incense may also be used. Choose the space you wish to purify and light the herbs or incense. You may wish to carry it over a bowl to collect falling ash. Moving in a clockwise direction around the space, offer up the smoke and scents, and pray that they may lift away any impurities in the environment in and around you. Gently and slowly make clockwise circles in the air with the burning herbs or incense. You may also wish to accompany this movement with a chant or a sacred word.

It's ideal to do some form of purification like bathing, showering, and brushing teeth before sitting down to meditate or reflect in your sacred place. A salt water bath or Epsom salts will also cleanse and brighten your state of being. Consider bathing as washing away physical as well as psychic impurities gathered throughout the day. While brushing teeth, imagine clearing the mouth of impure words. Another way of gentle purification is to use an atomizer filled with water and mixed with a few drops of essential oils such as lavender, rose water, neroli, ylang ylang, or frankincense. Spray a little around the room where you plan to meditate and also above your head and down to your toes.

You may also practice purification and penance by giving up something relating to a weakness—alcohol, sex, sweets, coffee, meat, or whatever you choose—for a given period, or permanently.

51

Limit Desires

The richest person is the one with the least desires. Next time you shop, cut out one item that you want but don't really need. This practice is called limiting desires, and it can free you from being a prisoner. By shopping less, you'll save time, money, and energy and simplify your life. Put the extra dollars toward a charitable cause, save for a time when you may need it later, or use it to help someone you love. This is a step toward sacrifice of ego desires.

Human desires are limitless. When one desire is satisfied, another immediately takes its place. If the developing world consumes at the rate of developed countries, some scientists say we will need six more planet Earths to fulfill the growing human demands for material things. But some people make other choices. In a remarkable show of faith, a woman known as "Peace Pilgrim" left her home and all of her belongings, save the clothes on her back, and decided to walk across the United States from coast to coast to spread peace.

She set out "walking until given shelter and fasting until given food," and covered 25,000 miles in the first eleven years. She trusted that she would receive what she needed to sustain her at the right time. Peace Pilgrim walked through snow, slept under overpasses, and found or was given clothes and food she needed from 1953 until her death in 1981.

"I had been led to believe that money and possessions would ensure me a life of happiness and peace of mind," she said when she reflected on the start of her quest, which coincided with the deep chill of the Cold War, the Korean War, and the McCarthy period. "So that was the path I pursued. In the second place, I discovered that making money and spending it foolishly was completely meaningless. I knew that this was not what I was here for ..."she said. She discovered her mission was to sow peace in this time of great fear and insecurity, and she walked alone and penniless without organizational backing. She believed that peace came through deep spiritual connection rather than reliance on material things. Her powerful choices continue to influence the lives of many.

Like Peace Pilgrim, I thought initially that my life's mission meant making money and climbing the corporate and social ladders and that this would eventually make me happy. But more things never filled the emptiness in my heart. When my period of spiritual quest for purpose and meaning began, I dreamed it would be beneficial for me to move to Switzerland because the Riviera would not be a place to find support for spiritual growth. Not knowing how long I would wander before settling down, I gave away most of my possessions—Louis Philippe mahogany tables, Napoleon III marble topped chest, my writing desk, etched crystal glasses, porcelain plates, silver, jewelry, and much more. I left for Switzerland with only what I could put in my car. This act of renunciation left me feeling strangely light. The joy it brought to the face of the friend who received sofas and beds to fill her new home remains imprinted on my heart as worth more than gold.

While not everyone is called to leave behind home and material comforts, keeping their value in perspective helps to maintain a good inner balance. Put a limit on your material desires and preserve the Earth and her precious resources. Turn your yearning "godward," and find your fulfillment inside your spirit and in love instead of in things. Consider the spiritual practice of renunciation. To renounce means "to forgo, to give up, or sacrifice." This powerful practice of limiting desires can help you to assess your priorities and make conscious decisions about where you place your energy and focus. Take a moment today and write out what's truly important to you. Contemplate the effects of your material decisions on your spirit, your family, your community, and the planet. Do your choices feed and nourish your spirit? Absolute freedom is being without desires.

52

Go Vegetarian for One Meal

Cut out beef, chicken, turkey, pork, and fish for one meal. By adopting a vegetarian diet, you can conserve natural resources, spend less money, be kind to animals, lose weight, and feel healthier. The *British Journal of Cancer* reported that in a study of over 60,000 people, vegetarians have a significant reduction in risk of certain cancers, particularly of the blood, stomach, and bladder. Vegetarian diets also protect the environment, reduce pollution, and minimize global climate changes. Raising cows, pigs, chickens, and turkey for food requires greater amounts of land, energy, and water than cultivating vegetables and grains for direct consumption. The byproducts of animal agriculture contribute to pollution of air and waterways. Fish populations are on the decline from over fishing of oceans.

Mahatma Gandhi, a seeker of Truth, adopted a strict vegetarian diet in line with his practice of *ahimsa*, or nonviolence; he believed that using animals for food was an act of cruelty. Famous novelist Leo Tolstoy also advocated this. In Tolstoy's essay on becoming a vegetarian, titled *The First Step*, he described watching some men capture and kill a pig as it squealed helplessly. His cart driver, a coarse man who didn't seem particularly sensitive, responded with horror to the throat cutting, fearful shrieks, and bloody escape before the pig was ultimately recaptured and slaughtered. Tolstoy reported that his cart driver said, "Do men really not have to answer for such things?" The novelist observed that even this uneducated man felt the sting of it. "So strong is humanity's aversion to all killing," wrote Tolstoy.

He remarked on the growth of vegetarianism near the end of the nineteenth century as a sign of humanity's spiritual progress and a way of moving closer to creation of heaven on earth. "If a man's aspirations towards a righteous life are serious ... his first act of abstinence is from animal food, because, not to mention the excitement of the passions produced by such food, it is plainly immoral, as it requires an act contrary to moral feeling, i.e., killing—and is called forth only by greed."

Like Tolstoy, the Hindu religion perceives that the passions or sentiments of fear and anxiety in the slaughtered animals will affect the psyche of the one who consumes them. If you love dogs and cats, why not also share this love with an even larger family? If all is ultimately One, then treating animals with respect and care is a vital spiritual practice. The current habit of slaughtering animals to put on the table causes them great fear and pain. If one prays for the peace and happiness of all sentient beings, then the injury and pain of a cow, pig, chicken, fish, or any living creature cannot be separated from one's own.

Compassion requires attention to our defenseless companions on earth and realizing they too have families, know fear, and feel pain as well as contentment. Simply changing the name of a dish from "pig" to "pork" will not erase the harm, though it may assuage the conscience. Gentle cows ambling in pastures die to feed people. Chickens live in dirty, cramped conditions. Turkeys' beaks are frequently removed at birth. Some faiths believe that these harmful actions contribute to world disharmony.

Animals are sentient beings who suffer in much the same way that humans do. They have their own destinies. Let it be some happier destiny than ending up on your plate. Turn your vegetarian dining into a weekly habit or gradually go vegetarian altogether. Many people find that experimenting with a vegetarian diet leads them to lighter thoughts and bodies.

How to Do This Practice

Make a difference in the world by forgoing your usual meat or fish dish just once a week and the impact on the environment and your health over a lifetime will add up. You'll make a positive contribution to nature and practice nonviolence to animals. Eliminate animal products for one meal where you would usually eat meat. Be conscious of your good choice and its far-reaching effects. Do this once a month, once a week, once a day, or cut out meat entirely. You will discover tasty alternatives to meat like quinoa, cashews, amaranth, almond butter, tempeh, lentils, pulses, and other dishes. A vegetarian cookbook will offer up a cornucopia of meat alternatives, and traditional Asian cuisines offer a variety of tasty dishes without meat.

If you choose a vegetarian diet, making a gradual shift allows for time to learn about healthy protein alternatives. You may want to cut out red meats and pork, then ease out chicken and turkey, and finally fish. Some people choose to continue to eat eggs and dairy products while others opt for a vegan diet, which excludes these. Make efforts to discover what's appropriate for your body given your circumstances and health. Balance is best.

53

Breathe Easily

Breath awareness moves us into the here and now. It can also help us to remain present and not give in to panic or the rollercoaster of pain. One Christmas Eve, Mary, a business owner and yoga practitioner, waited at an intersection when a big truck ran through a red light and crashed into her car. Trapped in the wreckage, she felt the pain caused by a broken collar bone. From her yoga lessons she remembered to focus on her breath. "Breathe," she repeated to herself. "Breathe." This became her mantra as the emergency crew cut her out of the car and rushed her to the hospital.

Her conscious breathing kept her out of a state of panic and helped her to transcend the pain. She says, "It took away my fear, allowed me to believe that I could get past this, and gave me faith everything would be okay." Breathing helps in everyday situations too. It quickly transforms attitudes and shifts the mind to a transcendent place. By gently concentrating on the breath, we become more self-aware and conscious, more in our bodies and less in our minds. Through awareness of breath, we become better able to control actions and reactions.

Three Breathing Practices

1) Diaphragmatic breathing: Most of us restrict breathing to only a limited upper portion of our lungs. Diaphragmatic breathing can easily and quickly reenergize a body and quiet the mind. Begin this practice by lying down on the floor or a yoga mat. Exhale and empty the lungs completely. Begin breathing and count to six on the in breath, taking two counts to fill the upper lungs, two counts to fill the middle area of the chest, and two counts to fill the lower lungs. When the lower ribcage pushes up, you'll be using the diaphragm muscles at the base of the lungs, filling the entire space with air. Hold the breath for two counts and then exhale for six counts. Using a metronome to click off the counts keeps it steady, but it's not necessary. Playing some gentle music with a rhythm is another way to relax and also keep count.

2) So-ham breath: It's said that the breath makes the sound "so" on the in breath and "ham" on the out breath. By rhythmically repeating the sounds "so" and "ham" mentally along with the breath, this can improve concentration. Focusing on the breath is also a way to enter deeper into meditation. To add a visual connection, focus the mind on the point in the center of the lip just below the nose and let it

stand there like a watchman as the air moves in and out. Simply focusing on "so-ham" gives the mind a place to remain steadfast during meditation.

3) Breathe away tensions: This practice brings a deep sense of relaxation by combining breath with the intention to release stress. Lie down and let the body sink into the yoga mat; allow the floor to support you. Inhale, filling the three areas of the lungs as in the diaphragmatic breathing. On the exhale, release the muscle tensions and tightness in the facial muscles. Let go of the clenched teeth and relax tight muscles in the jaw and forehead. Breathe in vitality, and let all of the muscles relax as you inhale and exhale once more. Move the focus to the torso and again breathe in vitality and exhale tensions in the shoulders, neck, and arms. Surrender more tension with each breath. Repeat the same for all areas of the body, until all of the muscles relax. Return to natural, calm, rhythmic breathing. Breathe in peace and light. Exhale tensions and anxieties.

You may want to coordinate breathing with movement like tai chi, or try a slow, conscious walk across the floor to bring the breath in rhythm with each step. Focusing on the breath can move you into the state of witnessing and help you perceive with greater clarity. It will put you in a better place to make decisions and take action.

54

Declare a News and Reading Fast

A lot of people start the day with the news from television, the Internet, newspapers, or the radio. If they begin in a good mood with an upbeat attitude, the reports of disasters and murders will certainly change the tone of the morning. Television and media search for drama and negativity to provoke strong reactions. Much of what is reported focuses on violence, death, division, destruction, and doom. The media believe bad news sells more papers and attracts more viewers. It fosters fear, anxiety, stress, and despair. Watching too much engenders the feeling that darkness prevails above all. If you continue to consume it day in and day out, your mind adopts that world view.

Shut off the television. Look around. The world really isn't that bad. It's not in chaos. Put down the newspaper and get a different perspective, one that's not tainted by motives to sell you something or influence your opinion. God is everywhere. Good is everywhere. Look for the things you appreciate in life. Find the things that are going right and working well. Starve the negativity and eliminate mental toxins and pollution by doing a news and reading fast for a day.

A news and reading fast for people addicted to television and Internet may be one of the most radically transforming experiences to initiate a spiritual journey. It wasn't until I first cut out all newspapers, television, and books for a week that I realized how addicted I was to words, other people's ideas, and filling my head with nonstop chatter. A news and reading fast becomes a way to observe habits and break them. It also offers the gift of getting to know your own thoughts and feelings about the world untainted by what everyone else is trying to get you to think and feel. It opens a space to think for yourself.

Note each time you automatically want to go pick up a book or turn on the television or Internet. Replace this reaction with something else like a contemplative walk, journal about how you're feeling, or recite a mantra. It's hard to break long-instilled habits. Become aware of how much time is spent (and probably wasted) on television, e-mail, web surfing, and texting. All of these things break up your day, distract the mind, and limit concentration. You'll free up time to meditate, draw a *mandala*, make a quilt, and do other creative projects. It's a great opportunity to discover your talents.

We have so much to be thankful for. If you still feel challenged to find something uplifting around you, shut off the television and do something to make a difference. Volunteer in a soup kitchen. Pick up trash along the sidewalk. Visit a shut-in neighbor. Build and put up a birdfeeder. Tutor a child or help an illiterate adult learn to read. Count your blessings, and do something to make the world a better place. Extend your news fast to a couple of days, a week, or a month and discover how much better you feel. Eventually, with long periods away from the media, you will begin to know yourself and your unique perceptions of the world. It's refreshing to discover yourself in this way. Give it a try and become your own best friend.

55

Sacrifice

Mothers naturally educate their families about sacrifice without even realizing it. My mom usually took the smallest piece of pie for herself leaving the best and largest for dad and her children. This happened with virtually every treat. She waited to be served last and made sure that all others were well taken care of first. In this way, she taught the value of sacrifice and showed her concern of always giving the best to her family and children. Though she never drew attention to her actions, her selflessness remains an inspiration to me, and is imprinted on my heart.

Nature gives examples of sacrifice too. Honeybees give up their lives to the hive to protect it. Generally pacifists, they will defend their colony, their honey, and their queen to the point of sacrificing themselves. If intruders threaten, bees will sting to ward off threats. But unlike for wasps, this act of stinging is the ultimate self-sacrifice. Once they lose their stingers, their death is certain.

Sacrifice also holds another meaning. In the old testament of the Bible, animal sacrifices represented ways to expatiate wrongs. The word "sacrifice" is derived from "sacred" and means to consecrate or to render holy. Today, many Muslims continue the practice of sacrificing a lamb at the end of the period of Ramadan. The traditional sacrifice of animals like bulls and lambs is associated with a deeper symbolic meaning of sacrificing the animal nature that pollutes human nature, like anger, greed, aggression, envy, violence, lust, and hatred.

As you explore the deep meaning of sacrifice today, consider what it means to sacrifice your ego to the higher Self. What will you give up in base desires and aims to nourish the spirit within you?

56

Scents to Elevate the Body, Mind, and Spirit

Across the globe and across cultures, people use incense and essential oils to heal the body, soothe the mind, and elevate the spirit. Many cathedrals and temples use traditional incense derived from olibanum, a sap from the boswellia tree found in the Middle East and long considered precious. Frankincense and myrrh, gifts the three kings delivered to baby Jesus, were considered more prized than gold. Their scents take us back deep into spiritual history and connect us to yearning for the heavens. Sandalwood has long been used in meditation practices to soothe the soul and clarify and relax the mind. Sticks of incense burn in Buddhist and Hindu temples and their smoke wafting skyward becomes symbolic of the mind as thoughts rise toward the divine and drift up to the heavens.

Essences like lavender contain properties that calm and purify. Balsams, cedar, and fir from pure oils can bring a hint of nature with its soothing effects indoors. Rose, jasmine, and gardenia diffuse fragrances of gardens and thoughts of paradise, beauty, and perfection. The spicy scent of clove contains antiseptic properties and was believed to have been used in a formula during the middle ages to protect against plague. It's also used as a mild anesthetic to prevent toothache.

Using Sacred Scents

Though they come from gross elements—that is, distilled from rose petals, tree sap, seeds, bark, etc., the properties of scent remain subtle and fine, like thought and spirit. Various methods can add scent to your sacred space. Diffusers work well for emitting scents in climate controlled spaces and the best ones use pumps that spread the essential oils through the air without destroying the beneficial properties.

Become a bit of an alchemist and delve into a creative adventure by making your own sacred fragrance. Books like *Essence and Alchemy* by Mandy Aftel give good advice on creating your own sacred scents to use in meditation. If you'd like to try the oils, head to a health foods shop. Most of these places have testers that allow you to try a drop of ylang ylang, vetevier, jasmine, and other essential oils. Check for purity. Synthetic oils do not carry the same beneficial properties and may even be toxic. When used regularly in association with spiritual practice, scents help to move you easily back into that desired state of peaceful being.

57

Simplify

Simple means "uncomplicated, uncluttered, humble, not artificial or ornate." It means being modest. Living a simple life means sticking to the essentials, honing it to uncomplicated perfection, and looking for the loveliness in the common and mundane. Birds lead simple lives. They sing, mate, raise families, and die. Humans do the same, but we sew unnecessary complexity into the patchwork. The Buddha's first and perhaps greatest sermon consisted of simply holding up a lotus flower. Only one student understood his message.

Some aspirants on the spiritual path will shed their old roles and possessions and begin to live with one bowl, one cup, one fork, and one spoon. Monks and nuns practice simple living and may ask for alms to support their chosen life. Saint Francis of Assisi turned his back on his merchant family's wealth and lived a most simple life with one robe and nothing else. He ordered his followers to take nothing, save the clothes on their backs, and beg for food in the hills of Italy.

Simplify life by cutting out the unnecessary things and streamlining activities. Much complication comes from chasing after too many things. Benjamin Franklin said, "I conceive that the great part of the miseries of mankind are brought upon them by the false estimates they have made of the value of things." Move your focus from things to the appreciation of what already surrounds you.

Actively consider what you don't need in your life and how to streamline it and make your life simpler and easier. Notice the difference between needs and desires. Experience pleasure and joy in small things—sun on golden leaves, rain falling on blades of grass, a waterfall, the sparkling eyes of a baby, a butterfly that flitters past, a good apple, or sweet peach. Simplicity is considered a virtue in almost every spiritual and religious tradition. Throughout history, most aspirants and saints held fast to God, but cared less about material wealth. "The key to finding a happy balance in modern life is simplicity," says Buddhist Lama, Sogyal Rinpoche. Where do your priorities lay?

Pare It Down

At a certain period in life, it's natural to begin to pare down and sort out what's essential and what's superfluous. Reverse the accumulation trend. Look around in your life at the things you have, ways you spend money, and needs versus wants. If you're planning on big buys, consider the necessity. Do you really need a second house or another car? Do you need another pair of shoes and a new handbag? Do you need a house this size? This doesn't necessarily mean living like a hermit or a monk, but minimizing the need for that new flat screen television can reduce worries, make you less prone to fill your mind with television trash, and reduce your credit card debt.

Become conscious of status anxiety and buys related to it. Very often we make purchases based on insecurity. We feel, "If I own _____ [fill in the blank], then I'll feel happy, secure, and content." But how often and for how long do those things fill up the emptiness? Consider also your daily life and how you live. What activities might be cut out to streamline and simplify? What attitudes and emotions can be discarded? What words and conversations can be minimized and replaced with a simple smile? What things make your life dramatic and complex? Can you eliminate any of these?

Through focusing on uncomplicated pleasures, the beauty of simplicity and the harmony it brings will become more apparent. Make the effort to refine and enjoy the results of a calmer life.

58

Change Starts Inside

A Zen Buddhist monk dressed in an orange robe walked up to a street vendor, placed his hands together piously, and announced in a deep, resounding voice, "Make me One with everything." The vendor popped a wiener in a bun, slapped on onions, chili sauce, ketchup, mustard, and the works, and handed it to the monk. "That'll be five-fifty," he said. The monk handed over a fifty-dollar bill. The vendor served another man. The monk waited. The vendor served a kid. Finally the monk lost composure and said, "Hey, where's my change." The vendor placed his hands together in a venerable salute and said, "Change must come from within."

On a spiritual journey the focus shifts from "How can I make the world change?" to "How can I change myself?" As we begin to realize that our thoughts, words, and actions shape our world, we understand that only by changing these can we improve the environment. "Let there be peace in the world and let it begin with me," is a transformative attitude. Observe your mind today and change one thought from negative to positive.

Change a Habit

Part of creating change comes through awareness and conscious reflection. "Habit rules the unreflecting herd," wrote poet William Wordsworth. We move through days in an automatic way, relying on repetition. Benjamin Franklin concluded that the way to succeed in changing his bad habits was to become aware of them and replace them with good ones that reinforced his guiding values.

Most of us live in a world of habit. And we have at least one habit that runs counter to our spiritual aims. What habits, if any, would you like to break, and what new ones will you acquire for this practice? Work consciously to change it. Watch yourself as you drop this old hindrance that may once have served you. Like an old car that no longer works for you, trade it in for something new and better that will serve you and allow you to grow and go farther.

"For all of our insight, obstinate habits do not disappear until replaced by other habits," wrote Carl Jung. "No amount of confession and no amount of explaining can make the crooked plant grow straight; it must be trained upon the trellis by the gardener's art..." In other words, it takes ardent effort to transform—and the older we are when we start to change our habits, the longer it takes to break them. Scientist Dr. Art Ong Jumsai studied behavioral patterns in his work on human values and education, and estimates that for someone who is eighteen, it takes about four months to change a habit. For an individual of thirty, it takes eleven months; for someone of forty the period doubles, and it can take twenty-two months to replace an old habit with a new one. At age sixty, it may take as much as one hundred months or over eight years to change a habit.

But it's never too late. In his quest for perfection of character, Benjamin Franklin wrote in his autobiography, "I concluded, at length, that the mere speculative conviction that it was our interest to be completely virtuous, was not sufficient to prevent our slipping; and that the contrary habits must be broken, and good ones established, before we can have any dependence on a steady, uniform rectitude of conduct."

59

Surrender for Serenity

We can't control many things. When the plane departs an hour late and you miss the connecting flight, surrender. This doesn't mean to give in to hopelessness. It means to let go of what you cannot change. The Serenity Prayer, used in many twelve-step programs, marks a high sense of surrender and is a good reminder of a healthy attitude to hold. "God grant me the serenity to accept the things I cannot change; courage to change the things I can; and wisdom to know the difference."

Lao Tzu put it another way as a reminder of how yielding can be the most powerful position. "That the yielding conquers the resistant and the soft conquers the hard is a fact known by all persons, yet utilized by none."

Another word for surrender is acceptance. One of the toughest things in life may be to accept. After years of practicing surrender to divine will, I moved from the beautiful Riviera and Swiss Alps to Charlotte, North Carolina, and married. I felt deeply this was the right thing to do. I knew it with my heart, but my head protested. Why did I have to leave these beautiful places that I love so much? Why? Like with the loss of any dear thing, I moved through denial, anger, and despair. I felt angry with God, though the God in me had prompted the move!

I'd done fine with the idea of acceptance and surrender when things went my way. But when I couldn't have all I wanted in the way I wanted, I protested. It has taken time to surrender and accept leaving behind these places that fill my heart. I don't know if I have a practice to give to you to help with this. It's an everyday prayer. "Thy will be done. Thy will be done. Your will, not the will of my little ego. Let that be the one." When I look back at all of the places I've lived and the many experiences and people I've met, I'm sure that Divine Invisible Hand has guided every step. I am one with it and not separate.

That caring, loving Love has mapped the way all along, and I trust that it is doing so now too. I have come to a place of trust and acceptance. Surrender is associated with faith, and faith means holding confidence that something is right, even if you don't know why. Explore what surrender and acceptance mean to you through gentle contemplation and reflection on times in your life where you were at a crossroads and took the right way. Ever wonder how you came to meet up with your mate, find the right job, and get to where you are today?

60

Stepping Beyond Sex

Sexual energies can be contained and used entirely for merging with the divine. This may seem either revolutionary or antiquated, but not everyone chooses to place their energies in finding a mate, reproducing, or making love for pleasure. Chastity may be a conscious choice. Also, as a body grows older it becomes less adapted to sexual activity. As hormones change, interest in sex wanes and it's good to wean the mind away from body consciousness, move deeper inward, and attach to the spirit. Periods of abstinence may also provide ways to step back and reflect on your attitudes about sexuality and how you use it in relating to others.

If you consciously choose this path, hold it with conviction. There's nothing wrong with you. Society throws sexuality at us nonstop and encourages the mind to turn to it from the earliest age into late retirement. Ads for certain drugs make it sound as if one is unusual by not choosing sexual activity even into old age. But ascetics and aspirants have chosen abstinence for determined periods, or life-long, and devoted their time entirely to developing God-consciousness. If you feel called to this path, respect what your heart desires and move in the direction of your yearning without embarrassment or boasting.

In different cultures, the relationship to the divine varies. Some cultures perceive God as formless and nameless. For others, God is the Father; others see God as the Mother. Some perceive God as the Lover. Zeus seduced Leida in Greece. In India, Krishna, the Hindu god of love, cavorted with the *gopikas*, the cowherd girls, and wooed them with divine music. The milkmaids surrendered all of their thoughts and being to their God in divine ecstasy. Taking the attitude of God as the Lover is one way that can bring sweetness and satisfaction. While a mate may leave, one can never be separated from this omnipresent, divine Lover.

VI

Discovering God

61

Embrace the Divine Feminine

Many European churches rose up over the foundations of temples to the Mother Goddess and replaced her cult with worship of masculine figures. Before the male-dominated religions took over, both male and female deities were revered and the goddess was particularly courted and adored for her mystical power of giving birth to the universe, the crops, and animals. In Egypt, the goddess Nut still adorns temple walls and burial chambers. She's stretched out with her body arched over the earth, her hands touching the ground; her torso shelters thousands of humans under her protection. In Egyptian legend, she gave birth to the sun at dawn every day and swallowed him up again at night.

Nut represented the sky filled with stars and the natural cycle of life. She embodied the inexplicable, mystical, and creative feminine power that gives life to the stars and earth and moves them through the sky. As cultures changed over millennia, the goddess and her qualities of compassion, goodness, nurturing, protection, and creativity gave way to the male approach, dominated by a need to conquer, exploit, vanquish, and explain life through science, studies, and reason. Things that could not be explained rationally to this male-dominated world were considered either fraudulent or simply nonexistent. The goddess slipped beyond the grasp of anyone who believed that intuition, creativity, caring, and mystical experience, and the soul held no real place in the world.

In many Native American traditions and ancient cultures, the Earth Goddess or Earth Mother still prevails as a guiding principle. She gives life, sustains it, and keeps us nourished and whole. In India, the gods find themselves almost always in the presence of the goddess. The masculine expression of divine power cannot exist without the mother creator. Shiva appears with Shakit or Parvathi, Krishna with Radha, and Rama with Sita. One requires the other in equal measure to exist and compliment it. In China, the yin-yang principle of opposites expresses this as well, with yin representing the female force and yang representing the male.

The feminine aspect of the divine is beginning to experience a much-needed revival to balance out the excessive pull of the masculine forces. Women seek out the mystery of the Black Madonnas on trips to European cathedrals to deepen their growing connection to the feminine principle of divinity. Others explore Greek goddesses like ancient Gaia, the original mother nature; Sophia, the goddess of wisdom; Diana, known for strength and chastity; and Hestia, goddess of the hearth and home.

Even in the Bible where the feminine roles have been diminished by interpreters, clergy, and emperors, some women displayed wisdom and intelligence and serve as good role models. Deborah, a prophetess and warrior in the Old Testament, led her people out of bondage and foresaw their victory. Mary Magdalene became a symbol of deep devotion and transformation. Mother Mary links back to the Mother Earth goddess and the mystical power of giving life to man.

The powerful Indian goddesses represent the feminine in a multitude of ways, helping us to identify some of these characteristics in ourselves. Durga, who rides a lion, represents the divine warrior. Saraswati, the graceful goddess of wisdom, beauty, music, and the arts, sweetly encourages the creative process. The five-headed Gayatri subdues the five senses and brings in light.

Personal Explorations

Explore some goddesses in Greek mythology, Indian spiritual traditions, the Torah, Celtic history, or any other tradition and begin to find the ones that speak to you. Study the women in the Bible and find or imagine their qualities. Learn their stories and try to read beyond what the male interpreters wrote. Look at the images of these goddesses and women and contemplate them. Often their forms, as manifested in painting and sculpture, communicate with the psyche and open the dialogue with the soul better than any written word. Find a card, poster, or artwork to keep in your sacred space to remind you of this goddess. Write about the qualities of the goddess and learn her stories. What characteristics does she hold that you would like to develop?

Begin to meditate on the feminine aspect of the divine and develop the qualities you perceive in the goddess. For most of us, particularly in American culture, the masculine qualities of action, assertiveness, and willfulness are well developed, but these need to be balanced with softness, receptivity, surrender, and the creative beauty of the goddess. Regardless of the gender we're born with, both men and women contain the dual male and female principles and qualities. The masculine dominates, exerts, and acts. It's often hard, unbending, structured, and aggressive. The female receives, nurtures, and flows. It gives birth to new ideas while the masculine side is required to put them into action. Jung wrote of the *animus*, or male soul qualities in women, and the *anima* in men. Each seeks balanced expression. When both aspects work in equilibrium within us, there's a feeling of health, wholeness, and harmony. The feminine does not need to dominate, but it takes its place as an equal alongside the masculine.

Consider the properties of the feminine and masculine or yin and yang energies as they manifest within you. The masculine (or yang) is the executive, the actor, and doer with properties of bravery, toughness, brawn, and physical strength. The feminine (or yin) is receptive, creative, gentle, and compassionate. When these two energies are brought together like the god and goddess, Shiva and Parvithi, the perfect god-man or Subrahmanyam is born and serves humanity.

Many books detail the stories of goddesses. Find the goddesses, devas, or women of sacred texts who speak to you and explore them through writing, drawing, collage, and imaging you are that one. You may want to dress up as your goddess and buy or make a set of goddess cards to inspire you. I use a deck of playing cards or five-by-seven-inch index cards, cut out or make images, and then glue them to the cards using rubber cement. Place the goddesses' names, images, and words that summarize their most prominent qualities on each card. Play with them by pulling one out of a deck at random to discover which one will guide your day.

62

Soar on Wings of Selfless Service

Selfless service leads to connection and compassion. I had heard of two state-of-the-art hospitals in India that treat all patients for free. People referred to them as "temples of healing," but I needed to see them firsthand to believe they existed. So I contacted the director and arranged a visit. On the walkway to the entrance of the one in Andhra Pradesh, a series of signs greet the visitor. "Love all. Serve all." "Help ever, hurt never." "Service to man is service to God." In the lobby, a spirit of healing pervaded, and I felt moved to tears by the beauty of this marble hall decorated with a Venetian chandelier donated by one of its patrons.

Doctors and qualified medical staff travel from across the globe to volunteer here and many say they find themselves transformed by the gift of love and a new vision of health care as a spiritual service rather than a profit-making venture. Totally funded by unsolicited donations, these hospitals, inaugurated by the prime minister of India, provide all health care at no charge. Thousands of families, sick because they are poor and poor because they are sick, would otherwise be unable to receive treatment, and therefore, remain in a cycle of poverty. The hospitals have performed over 10,000 cardiac surgeries and thousands of neurosurgeries. They serve people regardless of caste, ethnic background, religion, or social and economic status.

The hospital director graciously allowed me to visit the Bangalore site as well. Prithvi Pani, a cardiac patient there, gave her impressions in the hospital's newsletter, *Mano Hriday*. She said, "Although I have profound faith in God, the moment I entered this divine medical centre, I began to admire [the founder, Sathya Sai] Baba for his selfless service to humankind through his philosophy of 'Love all, serve all.' Every person admitted to this Institute, however poor or rich, is taken care of without discrimination." One of the doctors at the institute protested to Sai Baba, saying, "Why should we give care to the rich even when they can afford it?" Sai Baba responded, "Since illness does not discriminate between rich and poor, why should we?"

Sathya Sai Baba believes that health care, access to education, and water are rights of all people and should be free. In addition to spreading his philosophy of selfless service through providing free health care at the hospitals and medical camps in the United States and worldwide, Sai Baba also provides free education from kindergarten to doctorate levels and builds the much needed infrastructure to bring fresh water to areas where the population once walked miles for a drink. He asks for nothing in return, but gives for the joy of it. He says that love alone draws the necessary funds, volunteers, and resources.

Even on a small scale, selfless service can transform hearts and minds. It is our duty to serve society. Society has given us schooling and a place to grow and prosper. Every small action counts, and through performing selfless service you will benefit more than the recipient through the joy of helping. Make an effort to serve others with devotion. The God we revere is in the hearts of those we help—the poor, weak, sick, aged, and downtrodden. Feel how the power of helping others expands your heart. Remember the service you render is a gift from the God in you to the God residing in the other.

Putting It into Practice

Some people believe they need to quit their jobs to work for charitable organizations in order to find meaning and purpose. Serving others selflessly doesn't have to mean working in a soup kitchen or picking up trash along the road. Doing your job and doing it well is enough. Every day we have the opportunity to serve people. Through work, we serve others. Do your job well and correctly. Put in the time required. This is service in itself. Consider what your duties are and the attitude you hold at work. Ever notice how a smiling receptionist affects the atmosphere of an establishment? His or her welcome can color the rest of your morning with feelings of warmth and kindness. You can make a huge difference regardless of your job simply by loving the work you do, holding a constructive frame of mind, and bringing in positive creative energy.

Service to family and friends is another way to add meaning and purpose to life. By doing our duty toward them, we can feel a deep sense of satisfaction. Take pleasure in serving someone a cup of coffee, opening a door, or going that extra step to help out. It's said that hands that serve are holier than lips that pray. How will you be of service today?

Want more of an assignment? Every workplace or home has a spot that everyone uses—and most ignore. It might be the trash bin, the bathroom, or the coffee machine. In one office, everyone used the photocopier, but put in only enough blank paper to make their ten or twenty copies. In a household, one mother complained that she was the only one who took time to replace the toilet paper. No one else bothered. In some offices, the coffee machines and break areas need special attention to maintain a sense of harmony. If it's appropriate, make an effort to fill the photocopier, add new toilet paper, or make fresh coffee. It's a service to others and it only takes a moment. You'll set a good example and practice humility. Most importantly, you'll create a harmonious and functional environment.

63

Listen

Throughout the day, instead of clamoring to be heard, listen. Put down what you're doing and lend an ear. Pay attention to your colleagues. Listen to your spouse and family. Really concentrate on what they're saying. Listen in a one-pointed, conscious way—not with a wandering mind. Focus on the words and tone. Look into the speaker's eyes. Connect.

Listening is an art that requires practice. It's best done by concentrating and setting aside the ego's desires. Instead of thinking about what you want to say or how to respond, become receptive. This is a feminine quality that benefits both women and men to develop more. For many people the natural tendency to want to speak of oneself interferes with the act of listening and giving space to others. Use this day to sacrifice a little piece of your ego and simply listen to what others are saying, without needing to put yourself on display.

Listen also to yourself and what's going on inside. Listen to your body and where you're holding tensions and strain. Consciously breathe in and relax the muscles, letting go of tensions with each out breath. Note the whispers of your soul; it speaks in the still, small voice that echoes up from the chamber of your heart. Seek out the silent places that don't make demands on your five senses so you can hear its murmuring.

By listening, you'll naturally talk less and conserve more energy. You'll also be more attuned to your intuition and human nature. Your wisdom will grow.

64

Look Beyond Appearances

Things and people are not always what they seem. "Seen through the eyes of love, all beings are beautiful, all deeds are dedicated, all thoughts are beneficial, and the world is one vast family," says Sathya Sai Baba. Look at that person you're having troubles with through the eyes of love. Can you see God there beneath the surface teaching you patience and perseverance?

Sometimes we take abrupt manners and curt words as offenses. But the man who just barked at you may be going through a difficult divorce; the woman who looks stern may be hiding the pain of losing her mother or facing breast cancer. Someone's anger may be an expression of frustration or fear related to illness or pain. By being present and aware, you can look beneath these outer eruptions and even help to move others into a more elevated and healing place. If you feel blocked or bothered, pray that you may be used as an instrument to serve and speak the words or send the love needed to help soothe and heal.

In ancient times, Astavakra, a young man with his spine bent in eight places, came to the court of King Janaka to participate in a competition of learned scholars. He waited at the kingdom gates for several days hoping to be let in. Due to his deformed body, the guards would not let him enter until a man who'd seen Astavkara waiting patiently intervened with the king on his behalf. Finally, the young crippled man was led into the assembly of great spiritual scholars and given his turn to speak in the contest and a chance to win honors. But as he moved to the center stage to address the assembly they burst into laughter at his stooped form. Once the laughter subsided, Astavakra laughed at them in return. One of the scholars said, "We have reason to laugh at you, but why are you laughing at us?"

Astavakra said, "I had thought I had joined a group of great spiritual scholars, but I see I am only among a bunch of cobblers."

"You're even more of a fool than we thought," another scholar said. "Why would you call *us* cobblers?"

"Because like men who choose leather skins for shoes, you judge someone only by the quality of his skin," Astavakara said. King Janaka was duly impressed and he gave Astavakra permission to proceed in the competition. In the end, Astavakra won the highest honors.

Go deep today and look beyond the surface to the heart of the individual before you. Make the effort to meet eye to eye and listen heart to heart. That grumpy cashier or colleague may have just found out her mother was ill, or worse.

65

Drink In Words of Wisdom

Few things inspire a soul more than reading about the journeys of others on their quest for enlightenment. Stories of Jesus, Buddha, Mother Mary, and all of the great teachers give us courage and help us to understand that even for them, the path was not always smooth or easy. Spending time reading about them and reading texts from their teachings uplifts the heart in tough times and is like staying in good company of saints and the holy. The mind and heart merge in the pure source beyond the words.

It's also beautiful when one who knows and connects with the words in a profound way reads the texts aloud and fills the air with the sacred vibrations. If you have a favorite sacred text, keep it on hand to read during pauses and downtime during the day. On the metro, in a traffic jam, waiting for an interview, at a doctor's office, before going to bed, or first thing in the morning, drinking in a few lines can reenergize you and bring courage and inspiration. Reflect on the words you read throughout the day.

Opening a book at random can sometimes give answers to the questions we hold at heart and provide sustenance for the momentary challenge. These words will act as soul food to nourish and support your spirit. While the rest of the world may be stuck in the daily traffic of material concerns, the sacred words will keep you grounded in the ocean of spirit. Reading spiritual words from wise teachers is the next best thing to spending time in their presence. Their good influence will work through you if you fill your mind with their sacred meaning.

Reading with Heart

This practice will help you focus inward during challenging times. Choose a phrase, a quote, or a paragraph for the day. Read it with concentration and one-pointedness. Close the book and try to recall the essentials you'd like to remember for the day. You may want to go back and refresh your memory by reading it at lunchtime and again before bed. Inspirational words from sacred texts echo in the heart and provide sound guidance and support throughout the day.

66

Dance with God

Mystic Sufis whirl in ecstasy to merge in God. The whirling dances of the Mevlevi dervishes originated with the mystic Sufi poet, Rumi. It's said that Rumi's dance emerged spontaneously when he walked through the market's gold working area and responded to the rhythmic hammering of goldsmiths shaping jewels. He began to spin in harmony with the ringing hammers and achieved the divine rapture of surrender. Spinning so intensely and with great discipline, he remained centered and merged in the allness of life. Through the dance his ego dissolved and he fused with the universe. The Sufi dances become a doorway to the divine experience. Watching the trance-like dance state of the dervishes can move spectators into this deep place too. Rumi, as translated by Coleman Barks, wrote:

Dance, when you're broken open.
Dance, if you've torn the bandage off.
Dance, in the middle of the fighting.
Dance in your blood.
Dance, when you're perfectly free.

Dancing has long opened doors to divine ecstasy. The United Society of Believers in Christ's Second Appearing danced ecstatically for God and became known as the Shakers. Hindu dancers stamp their feet and spin out stories of Shiva, the cosmic dancer, as acts of devotion. Shiva's dance and beating of the drum pounds out the rhythmic heartbeat of life. His dance, as represented in stories and statues, represents the movement of existence as the planets turn and the mystical play of life unfolds. Native Americans continue to use dances like the Hopi hoop dance to show gratitude to the rains, fields, nature, and Mother Earth.

Your Turn

Planets orbit in perfect timing and motion. They know where they're supposed to be and how to get there. Physical movement, when devoted to the divine and aimed at touching God, can use the body temple as a means of worship. Turn on your favorite music and dance. Pick a song or sounds that lift and elevate you and turn your face toward the divine in whatever form you imagine. Find your natural rhythm. Let divine energy move through you and use your body temple as an instrument. Remain focused inwardly at your center and experience the ecstasy in movement. Find a private place where you'll not be disturbed and let your heart fly.

If you'd like to express the divine feminine principle, learn to belly dance. This ancient Middle Eastern dance invites women to embrace their bodies, dress in exquisite clothing, and move their energy to higher levels. A good instructor can make it invigorating and playful. It's easy to learn a few steps like the basic Egyptian and hip hits. Add in snake arms and shoulder shimmies, mix it with a drum beat, and celebrate being the goddess. With a coin scarf and zills (finger cymbals), the joyous sounds will lift your spirits.

Dances in community may also unite and bring a collective sense of harmony. Getting a group of people to take steps together and move in tune and rhythm to one song is deeply symbolic. Some people organize peace dances and spiritual rituals that include dances to weave together groups and promote tranquility. Dances around the May pole, square dances, and dances of devotion to God in one form or another bring hearts and minds into a unified movement and aim. If you'd like to learn some community dances, Dances of Universal Peace groups, founded by Zen and Sufi teacher Samuel L. Lewis in the 1960s, can be found around the country. The groups weave together forms of dance from various traditions with the aim of fostering inner and world peace.

67

Pray to Attune

While sitting quietly one dark evening alone in the Swiss Alps, it struck me why prayer is so important. No matter how alone and remote we may be from the world, when we're thinking of God, God is aware of us. Prayer brings us into accord, a state of attunement, or at Oneness with divine presence. When I was introduced to prayer as a child, it meant memorizing and reciting a verse in a rote manner. "Now I lay me down to sleep. I pray the Lord my soul to keep. If I should die before I wake, I pray the Lord my soul to take." The words came out mechanically without feeling or understanding and became a performance for eager parents. This is the kindergarten level of prayer. It's an introduction to something that's beyond the comprehension and capacity of the consciousness of the moment.

Later I graduated to using prayer to ask for things and results—protection for a loved one, good results on a test, or the right mate. This approach connects with the origin of the word *preier*, which comes from Old French and means to beg or petition. I used prayer often when I felt in need, worried, stressed about a situation, or lonely and tired. It remained mostly at a mental level where my mind sought ease and comfort relating to material things. This form of prayer has been around probably since the beginning of mankind.

A story from Indian tradition represents this type of prayer. In India it's not uncommon for seekers to take to the ascetic path and live their lives only on alms. It's considered honorable and beneficial to give them food to support their spiritual journey. One of these beggars visited a rich man's house to ask for food. The servant asked him to please wait in the hallway while the master finished his prayers. From the hall the beggar heard the rich master lament to God. "Give me more, please," he prayed. "Dear God, I need more money to cover my debts. I need a bigger palace. Can't you see this one is too small? Please, God." The old beggar stood up to leave and the servant stopped him. "Why are you departing now?" she said. "Here I have found a bigger beggar than myself," the beggar replied.

It wasn't until real moments of suffering and pain arrived that my prayers started to come from the heart. Despite self-consciousness about praying, I felt that when spoken from the heart the prayers flew straight to their source. This kind of prayer moves the one who prays into a direct connection with the divine. It's not about asking, but rather about listening and receiving. At its best, it brings us to remember and move into divine presence or attune to God. Attuning draws up the image of piano chords being tuned and vibrating in unison. A master tuner strikes the chords to know their sound and when they're out of tune he adjusts them to create a resonance. Imagine prayer like this—as a way to move into accord with divine forces and rise up like notes in beautiful harmony.

One of my favorite prayers comes from Saint Francis of Assisi. His prayer is noble, selfless, and good:

> Lord, make me an instrument of thy peace.
> Where there is hatred, let me sow love;
> Where there is injury, pardon;
> Where there is doubt, faith;
> Where there is despair, hope;
> Where there is darkness, light;
> Where there is sadness, joy.
> O divine Master, grant that I may not so much seek
> To be consoled as to console,
> To be understood as to understand,
> To be loved as to love;
> For it is in giving that we receive;
> It is in pardoning that we are pardoned;
> It is in dying to self that we are born to eternal life.

In the quiet, alone and silent, in deep communion, the divine presence is closer than a mother, more concerned and loving than any other, and sweeter than an affectionate lover. Sometimes, hardened in our material seeking, we find it hard to feel the subtle wonder. Trust and keep practicing, listening, and yearning with a pure heart.

Inclined to Pray

Sometimes it takes real pain and suffering to drive us deep into the heart. When the heart breaks open, the prayers fly home unhindered. In your prayer practice, move deep within and let your words surface from this profound source of wisdom. Let your prayer be filled with devotion, meaning, love, and sweetness. The divine within and around will respond and you may feel enveloped in a soft energy of love akin to warm arms.

A prayer of surrender relieves burdens and worries. Consider what is worth praying for. Be careful about the requests. God has a sense of humor and may deliver what's requested in unexpected ways. One friend who prayed to speak less caught laryngitis and could not talk for weeks. Another devotee prayed always to have problems in this life for fear she would forget God in periods of comfort and ease.

Regardless of how you pray, it's a good idea to ask that divine will prevail. It often knows better than the limited consciousness what's best. You may wish to write out a prayer that inspires you or create a new one. Tibetan Buddhists use prayer flags and prayer wheels to waft and spin prayers out into the ether. The colorful flags, often imprinted with *"Om Mane Padme Hum"* (meaning "Om, jewel in the lotus"), send auspicious blessings into the atmosphere as they hang on mountain tops and in places where the wind flaps and stirs them. Prayer wheels use a similar method. A sacred text written on or in them spins and the movement sends the words of auspicious blessings into the environment.

If you're inspired by these, create your own prayer flags. Find some fabric or paper and write or embroider your prayer of peace, gratitude, or whatever inspires you on the fabric or paper. Attach the flags to a chord and hang them in your sacred space, in your garden, or someplace where they will purify the environment. Prayer from a pure heart combined with devotion will rise to the heart of the divine.

68

Find the Teacher Inside

Many people seek spiritual teachers or gurus for direction and answers. The best place to search for the ideal teacher is within. Inside each of us is the *sadguru* or *sathguru*. *Sat* means "true" in Sanskrit, and *guru* means "teacher," so the *satguru* refers to the "inner" or "true teacher." This is the best teacher, the one who always directs and guides us with our well-being at heart. This teacher is no less than the divine Self, that divine spark of light that is the essence of each soul. It knows all, is all, and knows that you are God—only you have not yet realized it. Pay attention and this teacher will guide you in dreams, in daily life, through the nudging of your conscience, your intuition and synchronicity, and through your heart.

Sometimes teachers we hear of or meet through texts and in person reflect aspects of our inner divinity. But teachers can be at different levels and appear for different reasons. Jesus and his life example may be an inspiration and overarching archetype for you, while many other teachers may appear in other forms along the way. Teachers can manifest outwardly in many shapes and forms depending on the need of the moment. A friend, enemy, lover, guru, spiritual teacher, animal, nature, or story in a sacred text all serve as teachers at different points in the journey. They act like signposts on a roadside or guides along the way.

Much like a Parisian on a street corner in Paris can help you get to the Eiffel Tower or the Seine River, a teacher steeped in spiritual wisdom who knows the map of his own soul can help indicate reference points along the way. But teachers are only as good as their experience and integrity. The best teachers will know through practical, personal experience and live in a sacred inner place that depends on Self-satisfaction rather than worldly approval.

When you consider a spiritual teacher, consider first if she has any experience. Some teachers know all about the theories, but lack first hand practice and wisdom born of experience. Imagine you'd like to learn to swim and two teachers present themselves. The first is a professor who teaches the art of swimming; he gives great lectures on the physics of buoyancy, but has never been to the ocean or tried to swim in a pool. He has knowledge, but no practice. The second teacher is a lifeguard who swims every day; he knows the pull of the currents and gives lessons adapted to the needs of different students. Which one will you call on for guidance, especially when you're drowning?

The teachers who manifest in the world and gurus and saints who you're attracted to are reflections of your own inner nature. In India it is common to bow at the feet of the teacher or guru. This act represents a prostration of the ego to the higher Self, the act of subjugation of the lower senses to the higher wisdom. In a dream, I sat waiting for a revered teacher to pass along the path so I might give devotion and receive his blessings. I held both hands together in prayerful respect. The man, a thin teacher dressed in a dhoti looking very much like Mahatma Gandhi, walked down the path and I waited to prostrate and touch his feet. But when he arrived in front of me, he knelt on the ground and touched my feet. I begged him to stop. He gently smiled. When I awoke I understood that the love and beauty of the divine I revered in him was a reflection of the divine in me.

Make efforts to identify who your teachers are today. Pay attention to them, both inner and outer. Note the lessons you garner and thank those who bring even painful experiences for helping you to grow. Trust your inner teacher to guide you to the lessons. Use discrimination in determining the teachers allowed into your life. Keep a proper skepticism about those who demand large sums of money to guide you to spiritual enlightenment, and be wary of those who seek to have power over you and take your independence and self-reliance. Any teacher who mixes spiritual guidance with sexual advances should set off alarm bells. A true teacher is one who guides you to Self-sufficiency and reliance on your inner wisdom. A wise teacher or guru in human form at the highest level will act as an outer representation of your own divinity and help you to realize it.

It sometimes seems easier to have someone tell us what to do. We want to relinquish our decision making to another person and not take responsibility or learn. As difficult as it may seem, learn to rely on your inner guidance to find the way. Study the example of the teachers you've chosen and then find your own path by walking it. Listen to the inner voice of guidance that whispers from the heart and learn to trust it. In many ways this is a process of trial and error. But by following basic spiritual precepts, like do not harm oneself and others, do not speak unkindly, do not steal, etc., you'll not go wrong.

69

Deify Time

Kali, the goddess with a necklace of human heads, shocks the Western mind. Unaccustomed to seeing death and decay, our hearts tremble with fear as her terrible image reminds us of the nature of life, which inevitably leads to death of the physical body and destruction of all things material. The name "Kali" relates to the Sanskrit word, *kala*, which means "time." This goddess, like the Greek god Chronos (also pertaining to time) who eats his children as they are born, reminds us that our bodies and all in the material realm fall under the rule of days, hours, and minutes.

Time has always been revered as mysterious and unyielding. Divine personifications of time like Chronos and Kali display time's unyielding power. While time may be considered an illusion by some faiths, we are spiritual beings connected to awareness and growth through the body, which lives in a world based on time. The body is like a clock—through time's passing, our bodies grow from tiny babies to tall, strong adults; then hair turns grey, skin wrinkles, and parts wear out. As the body ages, it reminds us of the precious moments of life given to us to learn and grow while we can.

Don't waste time. Using time well and appropriately is a virtue. But sometimes busyness is simply a way to occupy ourselves with activity and avoid experiencing the Self and hearing the still quiet whisperings of the soul. We're afraid to stop, sit quietly, and take stock of what's really going on beneath the surface and all around us. The real work is waiting to be done when we turn inside and listen.

We cannot escape the play of time. Pay attention to how you use time and realize it is your most precious resource. Make a note as you walk through the day. Where can I stop wasting time? How can I move into more of a focus on the eternal and permanent? When can I make space to sit quietly and listen to my heart?

70

Light the Lamp of Devotion

In India, a sweet-faced, ageless-looking woman stood by an ancient banyan tree with an altar constructed around its base and prepared to worship it. In India, worshiping nature in the form of trees or animals becomes a way of revering God in all things. The woman dressed in a white cotton sari trimmed with gold embroidery laid out thirteen small clay pots on the edge of the wall that surrounded the tree. She chanted prayers and one by one filled each pot with oil, then with a wick. Each movement, each word was filled with a sense of perfect presence. Though she must have done this ritual innumerable times before, she performed each act carefully, mindfully, and with great devotion. Her movements and being emanated simplicity and love.

Some people milled about watching her unselfconscious worship of God in the tree. Observing her expansiveness transported me into a space of eternity where all is conscious bliss. The scene transported me back into biblical times, to the feet of Jesus and those attending to him with oil filled lamps. Her love for the tree moved me into a space of timelessness and deep peace. When she completed her worship, the woman took her *prasad,* the food offering she'd made to God, and offered it to the God present in each person standing about the tree shrine. Her devotion and luminous smile elevated those open to her subtle gift. The gift of that moment in eternity remains with me. It was her humble devotion and pure heart that carried me on wings to a higher place.

Mary Magdalene devoted herself to Jesus and humbly washed his feet and dried them with her hair. Mother Teresa devoted her life to God in the form of India's poor, ill, and needy. In current society, devotion is misunderstood and often considered to be denigrating or humiliating. It may even be considered hero worship when looked at through the mind's eye. But when experienced with the depths of the heart, devotion to God makes the heart soar. It uplifts and offers sweetness like the scent from the petals of a freshly opened flower.

Some people practice devotion to God in the form of their children, while some practice this through the divine in their pets. Devotion to God in a spiritual teacher, a parent, or other revered person can lead to a worshipful state. Devotion includes feelings of affection, ardor, love, loyalty, and dedication. It elevates the one who gives it. Practice devotion by seeing the divine in a parent, child, or pet. It will inspire you to open your heart to the highest level of the divine, the One that will never betray, change, or leave you.

As a practice, this may take the form of singing, dancing with God, meditating on the sacred form of the divine that you choose, or selfless service to those in need. It may mean carefully and consciously preparing a meal for your family with full awareness of the divine principle while chanting a centering prayer or mantra to bring in good, healthy vibrations. Consider how to best bring devotion into your work and life.

What's Your Devotion?

In Western culture, we value individuality so intensely that we may consider devotion to something higher than ourselves as difficult to comprehend. Devotion is a beautiful, subtle emotion. Experiment with where you feel it. What or who do you feel devoted to? How would you like to develop deeper devotion? You may want to become more familiar with this elevating emotion by spending time with people who have cultivated this. A visit to a monastery or convent can stir feelings of devotion. Listening to stirring songs of devotion from Buddhist monks to their masters, or other forms of sacred singing can as well. Reading texts by or about people passionate about God also opens the door—Saint John, Saint Teresa of Avila, Saint Francis of Assisi, Ramakrishna, Rama, and more. In Thai temples or Indian shrines, devotees bring offerings to God and bow down. The experience of bowing down to the image of the divine is a way of acknowledging power of the inner divine over the physical world and the ego. As you begin to explore this, find the pathways that feel most right for you. Participating in chants and devotional singing can also allow the heart to soar to newfound levels of adoration.

71

Earn Spiritual Insurance

After several years of serious spiritual practice, I believed that because I was on the right path, life's ups and downs would automatically come to an end. Everything would smooth out and the journey would be easy and delightful. With God on my side, how could I experience any calamity? Then, I lost my job. My French husband moved out and I was living alone in a foreign country. At around the same time, I fell ill with an extremely painful poisoning caused by heavy metals from some dental fillings that a dentist had removed.

The poisoning occurred just as I was in the process of moving out of my luxurious Riviera apartment into a more humble place. I lay on a rough cot (my bed had already been moved out) and I lamented to God. "I'm doing the right things now. I'm working on compassion, cleaning up my act, throwing out hatred and envy. I'm meditating, praying, and thinking of you most all of the time. Why am I afflicted with these difficulties? It seems my life is harder now than before when I didn't think of you."

As I lay in the darkness reflecting on this, I remembered Ramakrishna, the India saint who died in 1886. Despite his great devotion and love, he suffered a debilitating, painful throat cancer and died at middle age. But not once did he turn his back on his beloved goddess, Kali. Instead, his mind stayed in union with her. His constant contemplation of the divine moved him into periods of ecstasy where the pain seemed to dissipate. Ramakrishna's devotees marveled at how his experience of the divine transcended physical pain.

I also thought of Jesus carrying his cross. Despite his compassion and sweetness and the many people he healed, rabble rousers threw stones, insulted him, and ultimately nailed him to the cross. If even these elevated souls have no guarantee against suffering, then what's the point of spiritual practice? Why am I doing this? I wondered. Despair set in, and then after some time I realized as I lay in the dark night that spiritual insurance comes from turning inward and clinging to the eternal; my suffering seemed like a tool to move me deeper inside and closer to reality.

The pain lessened as I moved the focus deeper inside and I trusted that regardless of the outcome all would be right and okay. The end result would be divine will. My spiritual insurance policy lay in the comfort gained from realizing I am not alone. A regular meditation practice and prayer help to fortify the mind, body, and spirit and act as training for challenging times. It's like making deposits to a spiritual bank account. Only the return will be much greater than imagined if you make regular investments of time, energy, and attention.

Car and life insurance is paid for on a monthly basis even though it's not anticipated they will be used. But when a need arises, those who've paid in are covered if they've taken the contract and paid in the proper amount. Spiritual insurance works in a similar way. By investing time in a spiritual practice like prayer or meditation, the body, mind, and spirit collect the benefits and these accumulate. When challenges arise, the spiritual insurance pays off in the form of soothing and anchoring the mind on solid ground.

In your practice today, turn your mind to the divine mysteries and accept. Accept and embrace the paradoxes and pain that are a natural part of life. Let your thoughts be anchored in the goodness of life. No matter what the difficulties, cling to the divine form you adore and let it draw you closer to the core of your Self, the divine spark of light within you.

If you feel pain or anxiety, acknowledge it. Look at it without turning away. Take a deeper step inside and move the focus to your spiritual heart and picture the image of the divine you adore residing here. Rest in this inner place with your beloved divine form for as long as you need. Converse with him or her. Share your anxiety and fear and let Everywhere Spirit fill you with comfort and joy. If pain or emotional suffering tries to draw you out, again acknowledge its presence and again move back to the image of the divine in your heart. This practice brings peace and renewal. When you're ready or when you need to, come back to the ordinary world and continue with your duties. But continue to move back into to this place of refuge again and again as necessary throughout the day.

72

Ask What God Would Do

If you're stuck in a tough decision and don't know which way to go, ask yourself, "What would God do?" Sit quietly and contemplate this, or if you're in a meeting or other challenging place open up a space in your heart for a response. Be willing to receive the ideas and messages that pop in. Sometimes they may be very clear images and impressions, and sometimes the response can manifest as an impulse or feeling. If you cannot "hear" or understand what decisions to make or what to do, pray for God to work through you. Be prepared to accept and surrender to divine will. This is a very powerful practice and can produce miracles. Where we want to explode and vent anger, the God within can and will speak peacefully and wisely—if we surrender to that essence.

Focus on your question for twenty minutes with your heart intent on the divine and answers will be at hand.

VII

*At Work and
In the World*

73

Use the Compass of Guiding Values

A compass will let you know if you're on track. The pointer indicates where you are in relation to the magnetic poles. If you're muddled in a dark forest, the compass and knowing how to use it can get you on track and save your life. Values work with the same power. Whether conscious or not, everyone lives by some values. Most of us allow ourselves to be guided by values from outside sources. They come from media, advertising, friends, colleagues, peers, and family. When guiding values become conscious and internalized, they act like a compass and direct decisions, actions, and thoughts.

In his autobiography, Benjamin Franklin ambitiously listed thirteen values, including frugality, order, silence, moderation to industry, sincerity, and chastity. He defined each. Sincerity to him meant, "Use no hurtful deceit; think innocently and justly; and if you speak, speak accordingly." He made a chart where he listed each one with its definition and determined to practice one value a week. He graded his progress (or lack of it) on the chart. At the end of thirteen weeks he started from the top and worked his way through again. He aimed to actively build his character by consciously focusing on his values and using them as strong building blocks for a solid foundation.

Values supply the basis for the codes established by various religions. They've helped to construct solid societies and allowed for kindness and compassion to prevail over battling hordes. Principles like "thou shall not kill" and "do not steal" establish precepts that guide conduct, attitudes, and laws. In the Jain religion, forgiveness, humility, straightforwardness, purity, truthfulness, self-restraint, austerity, renunciation, non-attachment, and chastity are their ten guiding precepts.

Values grow the spirit. I suspect we generally pick the ones we need and want to learn the most about. A few years ago, two values puzzled me: unconditional love and surrender. I suspected I didn't really understand the meaning of love at all. During most of my life I'd confused it with desire, lust, like, attraction, interest, a distraction from boredom, and a mix of other emotions. I wanted to know what it meant to have a relationship based on unconditional love, work with unconditional love, live, breathe, eat, play, and do everything with it. Surrender felt intimately connected to love.

I suspected that Love, with a capital L, didn't mean going around kissing everyone I might meet. Working with love didn't mean I needed to kiss and hug colleagues and what passed for love in films had more to do with romance and eroticism than with the real, unconditional thing I yearned for. So if it wasn't those things, I wondered, what was Love? When the student seeks, she'll find. I put the questions out to the universe and my answers arrived in unexpected moments of synchronicity.

On a trip to India a sign stood out in a canteen at the ashram I visited. It said, "Love is neither sentiment nor emotion. Love is energy." Those words resonated with a deep chord of truth that touched my body, mind, and spirit. That felt right. I knew intuitively that I felt energized when I loved my work and worked with love. I knew, too, that something happened when real love came into relationships. It transcended a sense of desire and moved into the realm of selflessness. But how would I know for sure when love was present in my doing and being?

I opened the Bible at random. Many people who've married in the Christian faith already know this passage and I had heard it before. But when I found it this time it resounded like a gong ringing out unobstructed through clear mountain air and provided another piece of the puzzle. "Love is patient. Love is kind. It does not envy, it does not boast, it is not proud. It is not rude, it is not self-seeking, it is not easily angered; it keeps no record of wrongs. Love does not delight in evil but rejoices in the truth. It always protects, always trusts, always perseveres. Love never fails."—I Cor. 13:4.

I turned it into a formula to help it make sense to my rational mind:

Patience + Kindness + Trust + Protection
+ Perseverance + Truth − Rudeness − Boasting
− Self-seeking − Pride − Envy = Love

I realized that when I relied on patience, perseverance, and kindness, and kept ego out of the equation by not boasting or being proud, love had a chance to prevail in my work and life. A journal where I kept notes on self-observations helped me to grow in understanding how to practice it.

Many good organizations use these values to guide them as well. Swiss company, Weleda, founded in 1921 by Rudolf Steiner, practiced green principles as part of its fundamental guiding values long before it became trendy. With the motto, "Out of respect for man and nature," the company continues to create natural beauty and health products using raw materials from organic and biodynamic sources and agriculture. The management team proceeds in the same vein as its founder, maintaining a view of the human being as fundamentally spiritual. Their defined values intend to guide the group culture and get the team moving in the same direction, provide a basis for sound decision making, and create a sense of clarity. Expressed values can also guide families and solidify marriages. When they're expressed as guiding ideals, they can help to make unified decisions.

Values may evolve and change, but by working with them consistently you will grow. For this practice, consciously list your values. (A nonexclusive list of values is included below.) Ideally, choose two or three. Define what each one means to you. Write out how you intend to practice them. Keep the list close at hand to remind you of your choices and review your progress regularly. What one guiding value are you drawn to explore today?

If you choose to use values to guide a group, give everyone a chance to identify the values they feel brought you together and will best guide future directions and decisions. Once each individual has identified these on their own, let them be revealed anonymously or not (defined in advance) to the group. Compare your collective choices and determine the values that best describe your collective priorities. Name, define, and determine how they might be put into action.

Some Guiding Values

Right Action	**Peace**	**Truth**
modesty	calm	accuracy
self-reliance	attention	curiosity
cleanliness	concentration	discernment
good behavior	contentment	fairness
helpfulness	dignity	fearlessness
courage	discipline	honesty
dependability	equality	integrity
duty	faithfulness	intuition
efficiency	focus	justice
ingenuity	gratitude	optimism
initiative	happiness	purity
perseverance	harmony	reason
punctuality	humility	self-analysis
resourcefulness	inner silence	self-awareness
responsibility	optimism	sincerity
respect for all	patience	spirit of enquiry
sacrifice	reflection	trust
simplicity	self-acceptance	truthfulness
correct use of	self-control	synthesis
resources	self-discipline	determination
gratitude	self-esteem	unity of thoughts,
unity of thoughts,	self-respect	words, and deeds
words, and deeds	surrender	quest for knowledge
correct use of time	understanding	self-confidence
	virtue	

Continued on next page

Some Guiding Values continued

Love
acceptance
affection
care
compassion
consideration
dedication
devotion
empathy
forbearance
forgiveness
friendship
generosity
gentleness
humanness
interdependence
kindness
patience
reverence
patriotism
sacrifice
selflessness
service
sharing
thoughtfulness
tolerance
trust

Nonviolence
benevolence
compassion
concern for others
consideration
cooperation
forbearance
forgiveness
good behavior
happiness
loyalty
morality
universal love
citizenship
equality
harmlessness
perseverance
unity
appreciation of others
respect for property
national awareness
social justice
fellowship of
humankind
service to others
appreciation of other
cultures and
religions

74

Act on Your Guiding Values

Take one guiding value that is dear to your heart and practice it thoroughly. It might be compassion, courage, patience, or any other value that appeals to you. Explore what it means in depth, and put it to work. At the end of the day, examine how you succeeded and how you would like to do it differently next time. Don't beat yourself up if you didn't reach the pinnacle of success in practicing it. Simply determine to do better and do it. If you succeed to your satisfaction, don't let it feed the ego. Simply offer it to the divine within you and let it go. Plan to practice again later. Repeating this practice will expand your understanding of the values you choose to work with. You may also find that tests arise directly related to your values. Welcome and embrace them as lessons for your spiritual life. As you meet the challenges, watch yourself expand and grow.

In contemporary culture, a popular convenient attitude professes that values are relative and flexible. But some basic precepts and principles form the foundations for living a good, spiritual life:

- Do not harm yourself or others in the broadest sense of the word.

- Love, love, love yourself and others.

- Pay attention to your conscience and obey it.

- Do not steal or take from others without asking permission.

- Employ respect in all of your dealings.

- Be honest and keep your word.

Many more exist. These precepts act like seeds of goodness that will grow good actions and create foundations for a healthy society. If you cultivate them, like a farmer in the field, the results will show like bountiful crops to harvest.

If you've already chosen your values, pick one and practice it today and for the next weeks. Explore what your value means and how it applies in daily life tests. Opportunities to work with it will naturally appear. Now that you're working consciously to practice it, pay attention to the choices you make and see that they're in line with your highest aims. Many people and businesses report that their guiding values become like a compass to direct them through crises and help them make the best decisions during trying times. Make a note of how your practice grows and transforms.

Values Study Circle

The journey seems shorter in the company of a friend. If you'd like to stick to working on your values but worry about having the tenacity and courage, why not initiate a spiritual study group that focuses on fostering human values? Bring together some like-minded friends and set the aim of transforming your life through spiritual practice. Set up the group in a circle and encourage each individual to bring a quote that summarizes their value(s).

Share your values mutually and touch base on how you're practicing them. While in the circle, make it a practice to allow only one person to speak at a time while others listen without comment. Using a speaking stone or ball designates who will speak. Only the person holding the designated item can talk. It's ideal to respect a defined amount of time for the entire meeting as well as for each individual's time sharing in the circle. A lot can be communicated in two minutes.

75

Walk the Talk

A mother came to Mahatma Gandhi to beg him to tell her son to stop eating sweets because they were bad for his health. She traveled a long distance. When she finally met Gandhi, she said, "My son eats too many sweets. He will not listen to me when I tell him to stop. But he will do what you tell him. Please ask my son to stop eating sweets." He listened patiently to her request.

"You must come back in three days," Gandhi said.

Puzzled, she walked away taking her son. In three days, she once again made the long journey and asked him to please tell her son not to eat sweets. "Please son, for the sake of your health and the pleasure of your mother, stop eating sweets," Gandhi said.

The son listened and when Gandhi finished his discourse, the mother said, "But Gandhi, why couldn't you have simply asked him before?"

"I ate sweets too, but since your request I stopped. I could not ask him to do something that I myself would not do," he said. The mother and son went away deeply moved by the integrity and sincerity of this teacher.

While "practice what you preach" may sound cliché, it's packed with wisdom. To gain respect from family, friends, and colleagues, it's essential to do what we advise others to practice. Children waste no time in calling out teachers, parents, and friends who tell them to act one way but don't follow their own advice. When we speak to friends or address colleagues, they will also examine our lives and check in to see if we indeed have the integrity that we require of them.

By backing up words with real experience, our lives become examples that can carry great power. If we ask our children to speak the truth, but tell them to lie to someone and say we're not at home when a phone rings and we don't want to be bothered, then what example do we pass on to them? If you're the boss and you expect people to arrive at the office on time, then set the example.

76

Care for the Body Temple

The body is the temple of the divine. It houses the soul and is the place where we can meet and merge with God. Give due care to the body temple. Keep it clean by nourishing it with pure foods, good thoughts, and healthy exercise. Peace Pilgrim, a woman who dedicated her life to promoting peace by walking across the country, said, "I don't eat junk food and I don't think junk thoughts." In this way she expressed her respect for her body, mind, and spirit.

Everything that is put into the body—be it food, drinks, words consumed through reading, or images taken in through cinema and television—will influence this precious edifice in which we dwell. Our care of it will maintain it. Care for the body temple by eating less. Most of us overeat. Become familiar with your body's needs and take care to provide it with adequate nourishment, but don't overburden it with too much food. If you eat out where meals are often copious, mark off half and save it for later. The body houses the soul. It is the vehicle that takes us through life and allows us embodied experiences. It's the house in which we experience the presence of God. It's our duty to care for it in appropriate measure and feed it foods that will maintain and support spiritual thinking and activity. Protect your temple and keep it clean, vital, and healthy.

Each body is different and needs attention accordingly. Some guidelines that help me include: Reduce sweets, especially from processed sugars. These create an acid terrain in the body that contributes to illness. When the craving for sweets strikes, substituting dried and fresh fruits for candies is a healthier option. Drink plenty of water. Cut back on carbonated drinks. Especially for women, these carbonated colas influence calcium absorption and bone density and can contribute to osteoporosis, according to a Tufts University study. In addition, diet drinks that use artificial sweeteners produce effects that can dull and diminish the body. Coffee, tea, alcohol, and caffeinated drinks in large amounts can be detrimental to the system, contribute unnecessarily to stress, and disturb the digestive tract.

Some of the best foods include natural raw veggies, salads, broccoli and lentil sprouts, and fruits. Yogurts and other fermented dairy products that contain active cultures, often in the form of *lactobacillus acidophilus* and *bifidobacterium bifidum,* support a healthy digestive system. Check to make sure the brands you chose contain active cultures. Nobel Prize winner Elie Metchnikoff investigated the longevity of Bulgarians and concluded that the presence of lactobacilli in large numbers in human intestinal flora was a major factor in successful prevention and treatment of disease.

Almonds are considered one of the best health foods around. With a list of some twenty-five vitamins and minerals in such a small package, they pack a powerful health punch as guilt-free snacks. The local farmers' market can be the best place to hunt for the freshest, seasonal foods grown locally. Seasonal foods support the body in meeting demands of the seasons. In addition to supporting local farms, locally grown veggies and fruits contribute to combating allergies. Ideally, aim to reduce or eliminate the consumption of foods made in a microwave. Microwaves change the structure of the molecules, and studies show that the foods become less nutritious.

Be careful to stay in balance and not become overly obsessed with the body. Keep it fit and toned through stretching and adequate exercise, but don't become overly occupied with appearance. Learn to age gracefully by accepting the natural process of time and the radiance of your inner divine will shine through. You may seek out glowing grandmothers and wise elders who will inspire you to be yourself through their examples of vitality. They can give you the courage to no longer conform to the overbearing ads of plastic surgeons wishing to play on your fears of mortality and insecurity. When grounded soundly in divine Love, God, Allah, Great Spirit, Christ-consciousness, Tao, or whatever name you choose for the divine, no fear or insecurity will enter your heart. You'll feel joyful and free!

Find the divine in the mirror and cultivate your inner goodness; the radiance will shine in your eyes and illuminate your face. When the body falls ill, begin to examine the messages it may hold for you. The body gives warning signs and subtle signals to let us know that an attitude or behavior is unhealthy. A refusal to let go of a situation or surrender control may result in a rash on the knuckles of the hand that grasps too tightly. For me, painful knees represented cutting myself off from the ground and blocking energy in the upper part of my body and head. An ulcer brought up the need to calm my mind and stop internalizing so much. Several issues related to the reproductive system indicated a need to embrace, love, and respect the feminine.

Illness can give messages. If we pay attention to the mind, body, spirit connection and move deep inside to explore the issues and attitudes behind the physical symptoms, we may receive insights that will contribute to healing. Discovering the underlying source of an illness may open the doors to profound transformation and healing on more than the physical level. Use the practice of self-inquiry and you may even dialogue with the part of you that's unwell to discover the source. For the dialogue, take pen and paper and write out the question relating to your illness. You may want to ask your hand, knee, or whatever is ailing what message it needs you to hear and understand. Let the body answer. Using the nondominant hand to write out the response will open a way into receiving the response. Play with the process and listen to your spirit, your inner wisdom. Don't be afraid to ask what you can do to heal.

77

Don't Speak Unkindly of Others, Especially in Their Absence

This spiritual practice is easy when we become mindful of speech. Don't speak unkindly of anyone in their absence. Or, as my grandmother said, "If you can't say anything nice about somebody, then don't say anything at all." If you have something to report or complain about, do it in the presence of all parties involved. In the presence of the person you're having difficulty with, speak softly and gently. Don't judge, accuse, or assume. Keep an open heart filled with love. Whether the issue is about a colleague, sibling, parent, friend, or someone else, bring them into the conversation if you wish to pursue it. Make it open, but remember to speak in a way that invites understanding and promotes comprehension, peacefulness, and compassion. Don't talk behind someone's back. Don't build up alliances and try to convert people to your point of view about a situation.

This practice requires checking the tongue and keeping it under control. It demands that you reserve judgment and not contribute to confusion and dissension by sharing your presumptions and negative perceptions with others.

By keeping unfriendly words at bay, it will improve the work and home environments, prevent misunderstandings, and promote harmony. In other words, don't waste time and energy by spreading rumors. Get to the root of the misunderstandings by first examining your own feelings and motives. Ask yourself, "Am I jealous?" "Am I envious and angry and do I want to get even?" Purify your feelings and later come to those involved with the intention of promoting harmony and resolution.

This is not easy. Your openness may not be reciprocated. With your wisdom heart and knowledge, approach these delicate situations with the highest spiritual intent—to promote unity—and pray for help. If you do not feel you can master your emotions, pray for your divine Self to work and act through you. Your intention will help to guide the outcome and it may be revealed on a spiritual level in the long term rather than in a short-term resolution. Be patient and let the work unfold.

78

Do the Right Thing

The sense of duty guides actions in a profound way. *Dharma*, or duty, means more than doing the right thing at work. It means doing the right thing in all areas of one's life, including professional, personal, and spiritual. It is applied according to the station in life, role, time, and place. When we know our duties, then doing what's required becomes evident, though not always easy.

Ages ago, Arjuna, a brave, powerful Indian warrior at the height of his glory, moved onto the Kurushektra battlefield about to engage in a fight to regain his kingdom. He was driven in a chariot by his friend Krishna, a Hindu god, Arjuna looked into the faces of his dear friends, revered teachers, and family on the opposing side and imagined the carnage to come. His knees weakened and his courage fled. "What am I doing here, Krishna?" Arjuna cried. "Life is so cruel! I cannot kill these people who have been so near and dear to me." Arjuna slumped in the chariot, a glimmer of tears in his eyes.

Krishna turned to him, and able to know their fates far into the future, said, "You have been trained for this moment. If you do not do your duty and go into battle, you will be forever remembered as a coward." Pointing to the enemy side Krishna continued, "These people will die tomorrow anyway whether you take part in the battle or not. Take courage and go do your duty."

In this story from the *Bhagavad Gita*, or "Song of God," the battle becomes a metaphor for the struggle that takes place within us; it's a battle to defeat desires, greed, and selfish tendencies. As the story continues, Krishna reveals the divine secret that the *atma*, or soul, cannot be slain and remains immortal and unaffected by the death of the body. In Jack Hawley's interpretation of *The Bhagavad Gita*, Krishna says,

> One's personal duty in life should be viewed as one's responsibility to his or her highest Self. ... This ultrahigh level of duty carries with it the requirement that one *never* does anything that is contrary to this True Self Within. And even if you consider [duty] more narrowly, from the stand point of being true to your profession, you should not hesitate to fight. For a warrior, war against evil, greed, cruelty, hate, and jealously is the highest duty.

Krishna's discourse isn't for or against war, or about killing. It's a treatise on doing the right thing or following one's dharma, the Sanskrit word for duty or right action.

Contemplate Your Dharma

Take a moment to consider your duty on various levels—personal, professional, spiritual, and familial. Contemplate these and note what you feel are your key duties in each area. Have you committed to raising children? Your duties may include feeding, clothing, teaching, and loving them. Have you committed to a marriage? To running a project for a charitable organization? To taking a job or completing a book? Observe yourself for a day, a week, or a year and note how your sense of duty aligns with your actions. Pay close heed to the nudging of your conscience. It's the voice of the True Self Within keeping you in tune with the song of your soul. Note when you hesitate and feel conflicts between what the True Self Within perceives as the correct choice and the pull of the ego self that is drawn to pleasing and bending to the will of others.

Duty changes with age and station in life; become conscious of your current responsibilities and take note. In traditional Hindu society, stages and roles of life corresponded to duties. The celibate student was initiated into spiritual practice. The householder's life revolved around the home and maintaining a family. The renunciant gave up material desires and devoted life entirely to the spiritual path at around the age of fifty. The ascetic monk or *sannyasa* chose a spiritual life and retained little interest in worldly activities. Acknowledge your stage in the life cycle. It's very painful to watch people who have not graduated to the appropriate stage in life. Some women fight aging and identification with the body which destroys their happiness. They wish to always remain in the phase of the seductress, always attractive and appealing to the opposite sex. Gaining spiritual maturity means letting go of body identification and moving into attachment to the inner world of the spirit. What steps will you take to move you in this direction today?

79

See the World as Mirror

A taxi driver picked up a man at the airport and drove him into the city. "I'm thinking about moving here," the man said. "What are the people like?" The driver's small dog in the front seat lifted its ears.

"Well, what are people like where you come from?" the driver asked. The passenger rubbed his chin.

"Well they're greedy and quarrelsome. They complain a lot and seem lazy. Generally a bad lot, I'd say."

"Well, that's pretty much what you'll find here," the driver said. Later another passenger climbed in and asked the same question.

"Hey, I may move here. What are people like in this area?"

The driver said, "What are people like where you're from?"

"Oh, they tend to be generous and polite. They're community oriented and pretty likeable for the most part."

"Sounds like a good bunch," the driver said. "That's pretty much what you'll find here too." Once the passenger left, the little dog perked up.

"You seem to have told them two different things. I don't understand," the dog said scratching its ear. The driver patted the dog.

"Well the world's pretty much like a mirror," the driver said. "The guy who sees all black where he lives will see all in black wherever he goes. The guy who looks for goodness will find it here too. It's all in the heart of the seeker. The world is just a mirror."

Dreams can function like a mirror also and help us to gain insight to our character and see things that the ego refuses and denies. The characters and people that appear often represent aspects of the dreamer. In a series of dreams, a mate I'd parted ways with kept showing up. "I wish he'd go away," I kept thinking. "I haven't seen him in years." I noticed he showed up when I bought new clothes to bolster ego or when I boasted or tried to attract attention to make me feel worthy. Finally it struck me that despite his outer bravado, he was the most insecure person I'd ever known.

When he showed up in dreams, the scenes revealed how insecurity got in the way of sincerity and reminded me to build Self-confidence and overcome the anxiety and fears of not being good enough. An ex-boss also showed up in dreams. This harsh, erratic man lacked self-confidence in his job, which sometimes brought him to react in unkind and even harmful ways. When this trait seeped into my work, he appeared in dreams to help me become aware of it. As I reflected on their characteristics, I realized that both of these people represented my own deep insecurity and that I needed to work to boost confidence.

The world around us reflects back our expectations, characteristics, weaknesses, and strengths in the same way. Those we dislike strongly may represent some aspect of ourselves that we dislike. Those we like and feel attracted to often reflect back our own qualities of strength, gentleness, or generosity. Unless we know ourselves very well, we get trapped in the likes and dislikes and cannot see clearly. We get caught up in the emotions without understanding what's behind them.

A man in a foreign country anticipated and perceived only discrimination against him because of his nationality. He lamented his plight, how he did not get the best job, the kindest treatment, and so forth. Though he lived in a good place and participated in a vibrant community of nationals and people from an international community, in his heart he expected and searched for prejudice so intently that this is all he saw—pervasively. Those glasses he wore colored his views and changed his countenance.

Since he anticipated rejection, refusal, and denial with such certainty, it often came exactly according to his imagination. He even initiated the rejection, closing doors and refusing others before they had a chance to deny him. What if the man expected acceptance, generosity, and integrity? What if he gained confidence and learned to smile at people instead of glower? What if he learned to love, tolerate, accept, and persevere—and expect the best of human nature? His world would change dramatically.

The mirror of the world reflects back to us the aspects of character, animal nature, divinity, and demon that we carry within ourselves. This is what makes archetypes powerful tools to help us understand. In the hero's journey, all of the characters we meet on the adventure through life reflect aspects of the hero. The mother represents the inner mother—a universal symbol of nurturing, caring, life-giving, and sustenance. The mentor becomes the supportive teacher who helps us to find our way and discover our inner source of Self-confidence. The enemies represent aspects of ourselves that we war with, while the allies symbolize our strengths. This is true of characters in stories and fairytales, just as it is in daily life. Through careful self-observation, it's possible to examine enemies at work or home, find out what causes the animosity, and explore what part of ourselves we need to love, accept, and work more on to overcome.

One way to begin to play with and deepen self-understanding is to list the people we most like and dislike. Take a moment to do this now. Next, write beside each one the qualities that attract or repel you the most. Don't think too intently about this. Write quickly and spontaneously record the first things that pop in. It's good to do this in a quiet, spacious place where you can play and breathe freely. Once you finish, go back and look at the people and what you've written. Can you identify any of the qualities in your friends and foes that you also see in yourself? Come back to the list in a week and then again several weeks later and then months later. Keep your list in a place that you return to periodically. When you come back to it, again think on the people and what you've written about them. Do any of their qualities reflect what you see in yourself? What qualities would you like to build to overcome the weaknesses you identify? What strengths do you appreciate about yourself?

Outer situations reflect what is going on inside of us. People we meet reflect the inner. Eventually all merges, and the veil of illusion between "me" and "others" falls away. But until then, continue to explore those characteristics and qualities that you find. Work to strengthen the good qualities and shine light on the negative ones to diminish them and burn them away. Make efforts to become conscious of the bad qualities and eliminate them. This is some of the hardest work a human being may do—it's also the most rewarding.

80

Work as Love Made Visible

When work becomes spiritual practice, it opens the doors to constant awareness of the divine in a direct and practical way. It can elevate the one who works and become a means of letting the divine invisible hand work through the mind, body, and spirit. In offering the fruits of one's labors to the divine, work reduces the ego and the individual realizes that she is not the doer, but simply an instrument of divine will acting out her part in the world play. "Through performing work selflessly with no attachment to the outcome and doing it as an act of devotion to the Divine, you attain fulfillment and spiritual perfection," writes Jack Hawley, author and consultant to many U.S. companies. "The notion that work and worship are separate activities is common but incorrect. Live your life and do your work in attitude of adoration of the Divine."

Often in our small-mindedness we imagine that we are the achievers, which inflates ego. But can the mind achieve anything without the breath that animates the body? Can the body without a spirit perform any acts? Alone it's just a corpse. If one perceives that all is done through the divine energy that flows through each individual, the heart grows and expands while the sense of the ego-self diminishes and humility takes the lead. This is a liberating way to experience any task. It also calls in divine energy and brings support and strength that surpasses limited human abilities.

Love is another aspect of work as worship. While we may not be able to do the work we love, it is possible to shift attitude and love the work we have to do. A tall, handsome young man at the local zoo sang and smiled while doing his job. He invited customers into his area with warmth and made announcements about his menagerie with joy. What important job would make someone so happy? He ran the carousel! He took tokens from moms and grandparents and encouraged the timid kids to enjoy their chosen animal to ride. While many people might find this kind of job demeaning and complain incessantly about it, his smile and warmth made that section of the zoo a little paradise. His attitude and kind-heartedness became unexpected gifts to everyone receptive to them.

"Love the Job You've Got" Practice

Remember the excitement of getting that new job? The mind treated it as a gift, an opportunity when you first started out. Reconnect with the initial excitement and find little pleasures in your job. Look for the good you can do by keeping a good outlook. Feel grateful for your occupation.

Kahlil Gibran in *The Prophet* wrote that "work is love made visible." Think about it. What you do is a way of making the love within you visible. Gibran continued that if you don't work with love you will sow bitterness, indifference, and negativity into the fruits of your labor. It's better to beg, he wrote, than to work without love. Love is energy. Turn work into a spiritual practice by working with love and performing the task well. No need to join the Peace Corps or volunteer at a soup kitchen to do a good service. Doing your job well and conscientiously in itself is a service to humanity and will give meaning to your life.

Some of us feel a powerful draw away from the world and toward seclusion and isolation. We wish to remove ourselves from the world and pursue spiritual practices in a sort of hermitage, isolated from the cares and troubles of everyday life. But the soul is tested and tried in service to humanity. "You must work in the world," writes Mamma Rosa Quattrini of San Damiano in *Messages of the Virgin*. "I will give you all of my help, but your responsibility and duty are to work for a better world." That work begins inside the individual heart.

"Work affects the soul profoundly," writes Thomas Moore in *Care of the Soul*. "Workers assume that their tasks, too are purely secular, but even ordinary jobs such as carpentry, and secretarial services, relate to the soul as much as to the function." The Shakers, a religious group that started in England and blossomed in America, took the practice of work as worship and elevated it to a new level. The United Society of Believers in Christ's Second Appearing, or the Shakers as they came to be known, developed as a movement in the late 1700s. They lived austere lives of renunciation and work, elevating it to a level of worship. Their founder, Mother Ann, ordered them to "Put your hands to work and your hearts to God," The most eloquent witness to the Shaker spirit of labor is in their furniture. A chair or a simple box made by the Shakers will be worth a good sum of money because of the energy and care invested in it. Thomas Merton in *Mystics and Zen Masters* wrote,

> There is in the work of the Shakers, a beauty that is unrivaled because of its genuine spiritual purity—a quality for which there is no adequate explanation, but which can be accounted for in part by the doctrine of the Shakers themselves and their monastic view of manual work as an essential part of the Christian life.

The Shakers devoted great energy to their labor and had a passion for order, cleanliness, simplicity, practicality, economy, and community. The Millennial Laws that guided conduct in this tight-knit group declared that, "Believers may not, in any case, manufacture for sale any article or articles which are superfluously wrought, and which would tend to feed the pride and vanity of man."

Merton viewed the mind of the Shaker as directed not only to the good of the work or to his personal advantage, but to something that transcended and included "both a kind of wholeness and order and worship that filled the whole day and the whole life of the working community."

Choosing a Divine Presence to Guide Your Work

In medieval times, each job had a patron god or saint who watched over and protected those engaged in labor of wine-making, baking, farming, and more. Saint Honoré, born in Amiens, France, is the patron saint of bakers and is often depicted with the bakers' peel, the long-handled wooden paddle used for reaching into ovens. Demeter is seen as the goddess of agriculture and good harvests. Imhotep is an ancient patron of architecture and construction, and the man behind the construction of the step pyramid at Saqqara, Egypt. Considered the first known architect, he was deified after his death. Explore who might hold ideals that embody the desired qualities to develop in your work and find or create an image, object, story, or poem to keep in your workplace and inspire you to reach elevated heights.

81

Get Physical

A car requires regular maintenance and good fuel to keep it going. The body is like a car. It's the vehicle that houses the soul, and to keep it from getting rusty and worn, the body requires a maintenance routine that includes healthy foods, plenty of water, adequate sleep, and regular physical activity. Being spiritual doesn't mean neglecting the body.

Neglecting to take care of the body, in the minds of some, became a way of salvation. In medieval times some monks and teachers believed that punishing the body with extreme fasting and flagellation would pave the way to a higher spiritual path. Saint Teresa of Avila said that women in particular had a tendency to visit these extremes and warned against it. Today, we need to give appropriate care to this precious temple of the soul and yet not exaggerate or become obsessed with it. Like a vehicle, the body will age and bear the wears and tears of life. It's part of the process and how we deal with this gracefully becomes one of the many gifts of walking a spiritual path. A few basics will keep it in good running order.

Operating Manual

- Stretch it out. In spiritual practices, it's essential to
  keep the energy flowing up and down the spine.
  Keeping the spine supple will promote health and
  help the energy to circulate through the body. For
  inspiration, think of how a cat stretches. Stand up,
  place your hands on your knees, and curl the back
  slowly up and down like a cat. The *kundalini* energy, the vital energy that animates the body, lies
  at the base of the spine and rises during meditation. Stretching and bending help energy to flow
  smoothly and keep the body vital and vibrant.
  Gentle yoga classes may be beneficial. Maintaining
  the body temple in form will help keep the mind
  healthy and sound. Regular, gentle exercise is part of
  this routine.

  A simple head and neck exercise helps and can be
  done most anywhere. Bend the head three times forward, three times to the right, three times left, and
  three times to the back. Don't force it and be sure
  to stop if you feel any pain. Next drop your head to
  your chest and circle the head three times right and
  then to the left three times. This gentle stretch immediately loosens the muscles and helps the energy
  to flow freely. It sometimes clears up headaches. Try
  this several times a day while taking a break from
  the routine. You may also want to practice integrated

awareness through movement using tai chi or *chigong* (or *qigong*) and other meditative movement practices. Real meditation comes when the silence and awareness of the sitting practice moves into waking experience and is fully integrated with conscious action.

- Drink plenty of water. Everybody needs plenty of water to hydrate, purify, and help eliminations. This sounds like a no-brainer, but most people still don't drink enough H_2O. This doesn't mean liquids like coffee, tea, or soft drinks—just *water*.

- Clothe it in naturals. Wearing clothing made from natural fabrics that don't bind or restrict can do wonders for a body. Silks and cottons, especially organically grown, feel soft and caressing and they work in harmony with a body's energy and the environment. Polyester and other synthetic and petroleum-based fabrics may contribute to irritation and stress. Wools and cashmere are best worn with a barrier between the skin and sweater to protect sensitive skin. Experiment to feel what works best for your body.

- Eat less. Eating less will lighten the body and lengthen life span. Choosing fresh, vibrant, low-calorie foods like sprouts and salads will help to keep it fit and provide healthy nourishment.

82

Keep Your Word

Words contain power. They carry weight that can heal or kill. Weigh your words, and when you give them, keep them if they're positive and they will lead to doing the right thing. This will eliminate confusion and garner respect for you as a trustworthy individual.

An argumentative man showed up at an ashram as the teacher gave a discourse on the power of speech. This is ridiculous, thought the student. He yelled out from the crowd to the guru, "That's not true. Words have no power to change anything."

The teacher dissented. "They do," he said. To prove it he turned to some strong men near him and said, "Take that man out of here."

As he was being escorted out, the student suddenly realized the truth in the teaching and felt remorse for his foolishness. "I'm sorry," he uttered. "I've been rash and ignorant. I see you are right. With words we can change many things. Please forgive me teacher." The teacher asked the guards to release the student and allowed him to stay. Again words changed the direction of the situation.

In another situation, a woman in a small village had a child of mixed ethnic background. When the child grew up to be a man, someone who drank too much at a village festival insulted the young man by calling him degrading names and announcing he should go away. The young man took offense and pressed charges and the older man was condemned to pay a fine for his unkind words.

Watch how your own words shape your thoughts as well as the thoughts and actions of others. By keeping your good word, you will garner the respect and trust of others. "A good word is a good tree its roots are firm, and its branches are in heaven; it gives its produce every season by the leave of its Lord. And the likeness of a corrupt word is as a corrupt tree uprooted from the earth, having no establishment." These words from the Islamic texts *Ibrahim Sura* remind us of the fruits that our words bear in the long term.

Verbal and Written Contracts

Giving one's word, promising, or vowing to do something, whether verbally or in writing, represents a sacred contract. Though words are greatly devalued by their overuse, they still hold power to commit. People make plans and organize days around someone who's given her word that she'll be present and active for an event. A reputation can be built and destroyed on a few false words. When contracts are signed regarding loans or other interactions, both parties have duties and obligations. If these go unfulfilled, society suffers from the broken faith and unpaid debts. This results in havoc and confusion and affects many people. Keeping your word counts. Reflect on your relationship with words and how you use them. Do you say you'll be somewhere and then show up half an hour late or not at all? Do you tell someone that you'll buy a gift, get tickets for a concert, or send money to a child and then not follow through? It's best to use words sparingly and even remain silent until you aim to fully act on keeping your word.

83

Look for Good

At retreats, teachers like to tell a story about Jesus's capacity to look for the good. Jesus walked with disciples down a road, and up ahead the disciples saw a dead dog. Some of them rushed ahead and debated about what to do. They wanted to cover it over and hide it so Jesus would not see its ugliness, but they found no leaves and had no time to bury the carcass. When Jesus approached, he noticed the decaying animal. "Look at those lovely white teeth," he said pointing to it. I imagine his deep repose and a slight smile as he spoke in a soft playful tone.

The people who accompanied him must have felt a sense of puzzlement and shock. *How could he see anything good about that corpse?* they must have wondered. But the teeth truly were beautiful and perfect. Similar stories are told also of the Buddha and Allah, who replace Jesus as the protagonist, and this emphasizes the universal quality and character of divinity to look for goodness in unlikely places.

Today, magnify the good and diminish the negative. Train the mind to look for the good—the God—in each individual and event. The mind has a natural tendency to seek out what's wrong and bad. It wanders toward the depths and seeks out the coarse and unrefined. It complains and criticizes. It's the nature of the mind to move downward toward baseness. Elevate it by searching for and finding the good in others and in challenging situations. You'll soon find goodness in yourself too.

Strike a careful balance and watch out for denial. Make an effort to see the whole picture in all of its various shades and tones from black to white with all of the shades that color the spectrum in between. Take power over the five senses and move the focus and perception "godward," or inward instead of outward.

This one simple practice can transform a life simply by the power of changing perspective. Begin to note your inner dialogue and how you speak of the world. A woman at a retreat spoke about how everyone where she came from had been cruel, harsh backbiters. She complained loudly and moaned that she found it difficult to find any friends in the new city where she lived. Unless she changes her focus to look for kindness and goodness, she will most likely find the same "backbiters" again simply because this is what she focused on.

God is said to be omnipresent residing in all things, beings, and places. Can you find the loveliness in the decay? Can you see the beauty inherent in the moment? Can you be grateful for a situation that may seem difficult? Sometimes it seems like trying to find a needle in a stack of hay, but it is there. The omniscient, all-pervading divine is right here in every breath, word, and action. Seek and you will find it.

84

Satsang:
Enjoying Company of
Spiritually Minded Companions

It's very difficult to hold to a spiritual path and ideals without seeking the company of like minded seekers. *Satsang*, or enjoying spiritual companionship, is prescribed by ancient Buddhists and Hindu traditions as a way to maintain footing on the right path. During the journey, walking alone can be challenging. But having a spiritual group or friend by your side to help lift you up when you fall and encourage you in the right way can mark the difference between success and failure. When we make mistakes, sometimes we need to know that someone else will call us out and remind us of our commitment. When we fall into despair and feel isolated and abandoned, it's encouraging to have a strong arm to help us up and a ready hand to lift us to higher ground.

The people we spend time with will influence our thoughts and actions. By choosing those who also aspire to Oneness, the learning can be shared and reinforced. Consider the companions around you right now. What common threads bind you? Do you feel they influence you to become a better person or do they drag you down into activities and debates that waste time, energy, and money? Choose your friends carefully. They can make all the difference in the world in how you succeed on your journey.

VIII

Inner Transformation

85

Raise Vibrations with a Mantra or Centering Prayer

Peace is our true nature, but we must make efforts to culti-vate it. A one-word mantra or centering prayer can soothe the agitated mind and keep it focused so you can feel your inner peace beneath the turbulence. The mantra, or use of sacred sound to uplift the spirit, comes from spiritual traditions around the world, including Hinduism, Bud-dhism, and Catholicism. The vibrations of sound hold in-fluences that help elevate the atmosphere. One of the most renowned mantras is the word "Om," pronounced "aum." It is represented in sound and form. The Om symbol, ॐ, represents the different levels of consciousness in waking, dream, and deep sleep states.

The curved line above represents the veil of *maya*, which means illusion or the transitory world. The point above it is symbolic of merging with the divine in one-pointed concen-tration. Om is considered a sacred sound and symbol in both the Hindu and Buddhist traditions, and when recited three times it harmonizes the body, mind, and spirit. It represents the essential energy of the universe and is considered the only mantra necessary for someone seeking a sacred mantra. Repeating it twenty-one times with the mind focused on the form and sound will help to raise the spirit. *Malas*, or prayer beads, help to keep track of the numbers.

Practiced and preached by Thomas Keating, a Trappist monk, centering prayer is a Westernized version of the practice. It becomes a form of meditation with the single word as a focal point of concentration. Keating says that centering prayer is like two friends sitting in silence,and just being in the other's presence. The one who prays invites in the Friend (God) and prepares to receive. For the centering prayer, choose a word that is sacred to you. It might be "Love," "Om," "Peace," "Thank You," Truth," or "*Shanti*" (Sanskrit for "peace"). Learn the deeper meaning of the word you choose and let it unfold and blossom in you. In your interior silence, repeat the word with heart. You may also wish to repeat it aloud and feel the sound as it vibrates against your skin. When the mind wanders, bring it back to the word and continue to repeat it.

Repetition of the name of the divine is a profoundly transformative spiritual practice when done with faith. For example, Ave Maria (Hail Mary) recited by Catholics or *Om Namah Shivaya* (I bow to Shiva) heard in Shiva temples increases the positive vibrations and emanate throughout the environment. Any divine name you choose can transform by bringing you into contact with a powerful divine essence. This repetition of the divine name is also a form of prayer of protection, which brings in light to chase away darkness. Names and forms are many, but God is one. Some may choose Mary, Buddha, Allah, Jesus, Shiva, Durga, Yahweh, Wakan Tanka, Everywhere Spirit, Father, Abba (Father), or Sai (Mother). Repeat the name silently to yourself. If you have an image associated with the name, keep it at hand in a visible place. Allow it to arise and remain constant. Let the sound echo through your mind. Cling to this name and let it reveal its deeper essence. This can be done at home, in the office, or in a challenging situation. No one needs to know of your silent practice except you.

Using the chosen name, repeat it continually to anchor the mind and dwell in divine presence. When the mind slips away from the name, focus on the image. When it slips from the image, move back to the name. In order to develop one-pointed focus, remain loyal to the name and image dearest to you and do not change on a whim. Through repetition of the name, the mind merges in the spirit of it.

A spiritual parable reveals the aim of the mantra or centering prayer. A man received a genie to grant all of his wishes. The gift giver warned the man that the genie would do his bidding, but he must constantly keep the genie busy with new tasks or the genie would destroy him. The man agreed and asked the genie to build him a new house, plant his fields, and give him many gifts until he had no more work for the genie. The genie started to turn on his master, but the master pointed to a pole and said, "You must climb up and down this pole until I call for you again." The genie climbed up and down and remained occupied until the master called. The mind is a genie. One word prayer and mantras keep it busy while you draw closer to the stillness of your inner divinity.

86

Getting through the Dark Night of the Soul

Life journeys can sometimes be difficult. When faced with uncertainty, death, or other major changes, we sometimes fall into depression and lose our taste for life. We can also lose faith in God and suffer from a sense of despair and separation. This period of doubt that challenges the soul is characterized as "the dark night of the soul" by the mystic Saint John of the Cross. Saint John wrote the book of the same title while imprisoned in a tiny cell in Spain in 1577. In the book he described the passages of the soul, from its awakening from darkness and confusion about its reality and identity to its ultimate merging or receiving of lightness from the divine. Saint John, a contemporary of Saint Teresa of Avila, suffered in poverty as a child. Later he worked in a hospital where he saw terrible anguish, and finally he found himself a prisoner at the hands of members of his own religious order who opposed reforms he'd initiated.

Living in the suffocating, dank, dark cell, but believing intensely in God and divine power, Saint John experienced mystical visions, and his extraordinary life and writing continue to speak to people today. His life of poverty and persecution could have produced a bitter cynic. Instead, it gave birth to a compassionate mystic who lived by beliefs that "Where there is no love, put love—and you will find love," and not to use violence or intimidation for, "Who has ever seen people persuaded to love God by harshness?" His map of the soul's journey continues to resonate with us as we experience the passage into feeling separate and cut off from God and our faith is tested. It aptly depicts those troubling and trying moments where we feel we've moved into a dark place out of contact and beyond the boundaries of God's reach.

Viktor Frankl, an Austrian Jew, experienced his dark night in a Nazi concentration camp and used the experience to help others. "If a prisoner felt that he could no longer endure the realities of camp life, he found a way out in his mental life—an invaluable opportunity to dwell in the spiritual domain, the one that the SS were unable to destroy. Spiritual life strengthened the prisoner, helped him adapt, and thereby improved his chances of survival," Frankl wrote in *Man's Search for Meaning*. He lost his wife and parents in the camps, and yet found meaning in even the most absurd, painful, and dehumanizing situations of life through spiritual connection.

When suffering seems too much to bear and grief and despair flood in threatening to inundate us and pull us under, finding a buoy to grab hold of feels nearly impossible. But it's only a temporary turbulence on the journey.

In the spiritual realm we search for equanimity—a place to anchor in a port of storm where we're protected from the rough seas. An anchor that brings calm is the repetition of the name of the divine. When the mind runs wild with glee or dives into despair with anxiety and depression, by recalling the ephemeral nature of emotions and life and repeating the name of the divine most adorable to you, it's possible to keep from being tossed on the turbulent sea and maintain even mindedness. Building foundations on the divine is a sure way to stand strong through difficult times.

On frequent travels between Antibes, France, and Lugano, Switzerland, long stretches of the highway perched on cliffs and wound through long tunnels that broke through the mountainsides. The experience of the blinding, brilliant Mediterranean light mixed with the plunge into the tunnels lit only by the car's headlights seemed like a symbolic parallel to my experience of the inner journey at the time. My emotional life was marked with moments of brilliant lightness and joy mixed with periods of darkness, despair, feelings of being misunderstood by those around me, and a real sense of loneliness. The periods of brightness contrasted starkly with the blinding darkness inside the tunnels. But it had to be endured to get to my destination. At the end of the road on either side, the lush green mountains waited or the azure sea sparkled. The darkness in the middle was just a necessary passage.

"This Will Not Last" Practice

Remember it will not last. When one of Krishna's devotees afflicted with despair learned that Krishna would depart from his village, the devotee wept bitterly. Knowing he would be separated from the physical form of the God he loved brought great distress. "How can I live without you? I can't keep my mind anchored. I'll be swept into pleasurable highs and then drop into the lowest depths of despair," the devotee cried.

Krishna took a piece of paper, wrote on it, and handed it to the man. "Whenever you feel extreme suffering or joy, take this and read it," Krishna said. The man unfolded the paper and read Krishna's words: "This will not last." It's a reminder that no pain can go unhealed, and no separation or loneliness will be permanent.

Find a passage from a book or a sacred text that speaks to your challenges today. Write it out on a piece of paper and keep it with you throughout the day. Reread it at breaks, lunch, and again before sleeping. Use it as an anchor to keep you from going adrift. Light the lamp of hope in the heart and keep marching on. You'll soon be out of the dark night and back in the light. Remember always that you are not alone.

87

Identify with the Witness

When troubles seem heavy and tears seem endless, turn deep within. In the depths of this vast ocean inside of you is the witness. In the anguish and the suffering, it feels as if a split occurs and we become both the one experiencing the pain, and the one who remains unaffected and knows that all will be fine. When the weeping and pain seem to overwhelm, the witness observes in serene silence. Move in deeper. Merge with the witness. Let the tears flow until they cease. Let the pain break open your heart and soften you. The witness remains ever unaffected by all of these ups and downs. It is ever steady and at peace. This is your true nature, your deepest identity. The witness is the Self.

A film projected onto a white screen does not dirty or stain the screen even though blood and suffering may temporarily appear in the scenes. The screen remains white and pure. So it is with the witness. The sensory world brings tests and trials to soften and enrich us and move us closer to God. Identify with the witness and you will know in the depths of your Self that all is as it is—perfect and sublime. Know that you'll get through the challenges and be strengthened by moving closer to the truth of your being.

In the spiritual realm we search for equanimity. "Your joy is your sorrow unmasked," Kahlil Gibran wrote in *The Prophet*. "Only when you are empty are you at standstill and balanced." When the mind runs wild with glee or dives into despair with anxiety and depression, we can find comfort by recalling the ephemeral nature of emotions and life, keep from being tossed on the turbulent sea, and maintain even mindedness. Remember the transitory nature of things and life, and cling to the underlying eternal essence. Remember, do not put your faith in the outer world, which will constantly change. Put your faith in your Self, the permanent and divine nature that thrives within you.

Calling the Witness

Often pain and anguish are the gifts that drive us to discover the depths of our souls. If you're in pain physically or experiencing mental or emotional anguish, go to a place where you feel comforted—your bed, a cathedral, a park, or some other place where you may be alone. Acknowledge the pain, suffering, and angst. Move inside and bring the focus to the area of the heart on the right side of the chest. This is the seat of the spiritual heart where the Witness resides. Let your awareness remain here in this place of calm away from the storm. Observe the waves of emotion that arise. Let tears flow. Become aware of tensions. Feel anger or whatever presents itself. Let them rise like clouds of fog being burned off by the morning sun. New clouds may appear and some may seem thicker. Let them rise while you remain anchored in your heart, in the light. This practice can radically transform your vision of the world and reduce the power of external events and emotions over your spirit.

88

Put Inner Housekeeping First

Before leaping into selfless service and community volunteer work, set down the soup ladles, put aside the aprons, and consider what kind of inner housekeeping needs to be done. Ever get dreams about cleaning bathrooms, sweeping floors, or wiping windows clean? It may be a sign that it's time to do some inner cleanup. Often we want to immediately leap into action and change the world by charging head on into community work. But if there is to be peace in the world, then it must start at home, in our own hearts and homes, within our families, and then with neighbors and people in the immediate vicinity.

Periods of spiritual transformation require downtime to get your inner house in order and simply be with yourself and reflect. Sometimes they require solitude and distance from the people you love and usually serve. This is a moment where the soul withdraws from the outer world to look inside at what's undone, what needs to be demolished, and what needs to be renovated. Take a moment and explore your inner place. What does it look like? Consider what you need to do to care for your spiritual Self right now. It's okay and necessary to take a step back and assess where you've been, what you want to do differently, and where you want to go.

Next, when the time is right, consider what problems you need to work on with others in the home. Start small. Look around and consider what needs mending and what leaks need repair. Think metaphorically. If there are equivalent things that need to be done in the physical house, this is a good time to complete it. Bring attention to the issues and address them. The tools you need to help you include detachment, meditation, understanding, and prayer. Make efforts to advance spiritually, develop compassion for family members, practice forgiveness, and clean house.

The better you know yourself, the more effectively you will be able to help others. This doesn't mean you have to be perfect before setting off to serve in a soup kitchen or hand out blankets. But if we improve our home life first and attend to those duties and relationships, then we will be better equipped to move into helping out in the community, the state, and the nation.

Consider "homework" or "self-work" as the basis for a solid foundation for all other types of work. By creating a firm foundation of self-knowledge before going out into the world, your inner transformations will create solid ground for doing work that will make the world a better place. Some people flee into activity, whether for business or charity, as a way of avoiding the real inner housecleaning that needs attention. This excessive activity is a form of laziness that promotes inner stagnation of the spirit. Doing some housekeeping, both literally and figuratively, may help you become more effective in serving others on a larger scale later.

Inner Housecleaning List

What work do you need to do to clear out your inner space and prepare for receiving and helping others? Take time to go deep and reflect on things at home that may need special attention first. Make your good inner life and home life solid foundations for future service to society.

Promote World Peace from Home

World peace starts with each individual finding peace and working toward it in her own heart and making efforts to create a terrain of calm and serenity at home. Next, take this out to share with neighbors and the community, and then with the world at large. Finding peace and promoting it requires more than just saying, "I want peace," or "I will be peaceful." It means making conscious, concerted efforts to sacrifice desires for things, be humble, and diminish the ego's raging demons of hatred, anger, envy, jealousy, and greed. The Buddha said, "Peace comes from within. Do not seek it outside."

Lao Tsu said, "Freedom from desire leads to inner peace."

Peace Pilgrim stated, "When you find peace within yourself you become the kind of person who can live at peace with others."

These three combined become a good formula for achieving world peace. It does not matter if the others around you follow your example. It's not possible to change others, but through one's own efforts, patience, and forbearance, the love spreads and transforms hearts.

89

Discover the Rooms of Your Soul

Houses may be one of the best symbols for the soul. In many ways, they describe the difference between interior and exterior, and through dreams and inner vision, they can reveal our interior state of being. Many spiritual teachers have used palaces, houses, and rooms as metaphors to describe inner explorations. Jesus said, "My house holds many mansions." Saint Teresa of Avila meditated on entering the rooms of her interior castle and instructed seekers on what they might find on the inward journey through these rooms. Swiss psychiatrist Carl Jung literally materialized his house of dreams in stone and mortar. He dreamed of the maternal hearth and built it along with a tower on Lake Zurich. He did this over a twenty year period as his dreams revealed the new rooms. The motto carved in stone above the threshold in Latin reads, "*Vocatus atque non vocatus deus aderit*," meaning, "Called or not called, God will be present."

Inner houses reflect the state of the soul and may come in many forms and sizes from glass walled green houses to palaces or broken-down shacks. It's possible to live in a McMansion and dream of a messy shack. I lived in a comfortable apartment when my first dream house appeared. In the dream I arrived at the sidewalk and saw a rundown old place with peeling paint, shutters half off, and rotting floor boards on the porch. No grass grew on the brown lawn and no flowers dared peer out of these untended flower beds. Nothing was maintained. I crossed the threshold and entered inside. The living room contained a worn sofa with stuffing coming out. Old newspapers lay piled on the dirty floors. A police tape roped off the basement and warned me not to descend, and the stairs to the upper story needed repair.

I awoke with a start and immediately began doing inner housecleaning. Inner housecleaning meant replacing irritation with patience. I renovated by replacing anger with compassion and changing self-defeating habits. As my interior space of the soul changed, so did my dream house. The basement became accessible and I saw shadowy demons, but when I eventually ascended into the attic I moved into the light and found myself surrounded by loving beings. The house also became a white marble palace with many rooms to explore, a green house filled with lush tropical plants, and much more.

But one morning I awoke with this dream: I enter into my living area escorted by my guide. It is a mess: chairs overturned, stacks of papers in disarray, and all looks dirty and dingy. In the next scene, I return with my guide (a light-filled, wise part of my Self) and she points out the big changes. Now I'm standing in the same space only this time it is perfectly clean. All of the chairs are set up as if waiting for a symphony. A round table sits in the center of the room with a crystal vase of red roses on top. A shaft of light falls on the flowers and the entire room is light and airy. It's beautiful. After looking around, I turn to my guide and say, "But I liked it better the other way!" I awoke with a shock and banged my hand on my forehead. I must be crazy, I thought. I didn't really like it the other way. I just felt more comfortable in that familiar mess.

Houses are universal symbols of refuge and shelter. As we change and transform, they also change and transform to show us our inner state. Author Clare Cooper Marcus explores this in the other direction by examining how our physical homes reflect the unconscious state of our souls in *House as Mirror of Self*. She uses cases studies to show how the places we live in reflect where we are on our life journey to wholeness.

Renovating Your Inner House of the Soul

Begin to explore your relationship to your inner house through guided visualization. Imagine yourself walking along a path. Breathe in the fresh air. Hear the birds twittering. As you continue to walk down the path, you come upon the gate to your house. Open the gate and cross into this area. Is it a new place or does it feel familiar? Note what the exterior of your house and grounds (if any) look like. Walk to the door, cross the threshold, and enter inside.

Move into the main room and explore the surrounding rooms. Do you have basements and cellars? Do you find upper stories and attics? Explore at your leisure, and then when you're ready, slowly and gently return to the place you left from.

Take a few minutes to write about your interior house. Is it a villa or a mansion? A teepee or a hut? Write continuously without stopping. Make a drawing or collage of your house. If you'd like to explore more, place your writing and drawing on a chair across from you and have a conversation with it. You may want to write out this dialogue. Tell it how you feel about it. Ask it what it would like you to do to maintain it, or if it would like you to explore new areas. Revisit your house periodically and see if anything has changed.

The Chandogya Upanishad says,

> Within the city of Brahman, which is the body, there is the heart, and within the heart there is a little house. This house has the shape of a lotus, and within it dwells that which is to be sought after, inquired about, and realized. What then is that which dwells within this house, the lotus of the heart? ... Even so large as the universe outside is the universe within the lotus of the heart. Within it are heaven and earth, the sun, the moon, the lightning, and all of the stars. Whatever is in the macrocosm is in this microcosm.

This house of the heart leaves a vast space to explore. Enter in. In quiet meditation visualize the interior rooms of your soul. Dare to open new doors. Do you have any renovation or construction work to do? Explore the room of the heart. Venture into this final frontier with courage and overcome any obstacles of fear or hesitation. Is there anything in your interior house that you would like to manifest in the rooms of your physical dwelling? How can you bring together the inner and outer into a more harmonious whole?

Threshold Drawings for Protection

The *kolam*, or threshold drawing, is a beautiful ritual art performed on a daily basis in southern India. Women sweep clean their houses and stoops. Then at dawn they create elaborate designs using rice powder or chalk. It's aimed to bring auspiciousness, bless visitors, and protect the house. If you'd like to experiment with this form of art and ritual for your home, the Internet site *ikolam.com* shows how to layout the dot grids that make up the basis of these intricate designs and gives instruction on how to complete them. These can be a fun and creative way to welcome protection for your inner renovations and invite in and share blessings with good friends. You may also want to name your house, a common practice in Europe, and place a motto over the portal as Jung did.

90

Fast and Slow Down

Fasting marks a period of purification. In countries like France, Italy, and Switzerland where Catholic practices prevail, the period of Lent means sacrificing a much loved food or habit during the forty days before Easter. This idea of fasting or renunciation is intended to move the focus inward and "godward." Influenced by this atmosphere in Antibes, France, I decided to try fasting for twenty-four hours as an experiment. I knew that saints, hermits, and spiritual aspirants across the centuries had used the practice as a way of moving into a deeper realm of spirit. Native Americans prescribe fasting during certain ceremonial dances and vision quests. It's also used by Muslims during the period of Ramadan. The Islamic text, Baqara Sura says, "Fasting is prescribed to you as it was prescribed to those before you that ye may [learn] self-restraint."

On a beautiful spring Sunday I started a fast and replaced espresso and buttery, rich *pain au chocolat* with glasses of water. I set out to walk along the seaside down to the market where scents of freshly baked croissants and steaming coffee curled enticingly through the air. My stomach grumbled, but I held to my commitment to not consume any food or drink anything except water for one full day. Farther up the cobblestone street, the stalls in the covered market displayed beautiful arrays of saffron, turmeric, cinnamon, and lavender. The first strawberries glimmered red, and fresh melon from Sicily and Cavillion smelled tantalizingly sweet. Despite the temptations, I walked past the displays with a detached heart and everything became its sparkling and radiant self rather than something to consume. My mind didn't go out and grasp the things and imagine them on my plate for lunch, but rather I simply appreciated the extraordinary beauty, fragrances, and colors.

Watching the shoppers caught up in grabbing a fresh tomato out of the hands of another or pushing to get ahead in line, I saw where I often had done the same. But fasting, I walked along feeling oddly liberated from the whole game. A lightness and joy came over me as I walked past the vendors of ceramic from Faience and Moustier, past the Asian batik dress shop, past the pasta shop with its luscious array of fresh ravioli and sauces. My heart soared above the red clay tile roof tops and yet remained an actor as part of the scene. My stomach grumbled in protest and demanded food, but my heart said, "You're always fed. Now it's time to nourish me." It was a magnificently liberating experience with no need to think of food, cooking, or consuming for an entire day. I later extended the fast to longer periods as a way of stepping out of the usual constraints of the world.

Fast and Slow Practice

It's called a fast, but in many ways it could be called a "slow" because it offers a chance to slow down and stop being drawn out by the senses. For one meal or one day, fast. Drink only water. This is a natural way to purify the body and clean it out. It's an ancient practice and one that is still useful. Check with your doctor and use your wisdom about the process. Fasting allows for a moment to watch the mind and observe attitudes to food. While fasting, pay attention to the mind's desire to run for food out of habit. Become aware of it. Watch, and when the fast is over, change the habit of eating food unconsciously and simply out of habit instead of hunger.

"A genuine fast cleanses body, mind, and soul," Gandhi wrote. He fasted often and accompanied it with prayer. Fasting one day periodically opens the way to observing one's mind and detaching from the demands of the physical body. It's also considered a healthy way to eliminate toxins by drinking sufficient quantities of water. In a society that wallows in too much food, rarely do we give the digestive system a chance to take a break and rest. Most people tend to nibble continually all day long. A fast of twenty-four hours with only water generally brings more lightness and energy. It helps one to get a perspective on the relationship with food and how eating is often done out of habit or social constraint rather than hunger.

Fasting loosens the fetters of the physical bonds on the spirit and gives an opportunity to step out of the usual rhythms and demands of the world. Choose a day with no social obligations and decide to fast, taking in only water. You may want to choose a time of particular significance, like the celebration of the winter solstice or full moon days. Observe your mind. Observe how your body feels. If you drink large quantities of coffee, tea, or other caffeine drinks, you may experience headaches as the body goes through withdrawal. If you're used to sugar highs from the foods laden with corn syrup and sugars, you may also experience some momentary feelings of lowness as your body adjusts to a natural state without the sugar-induced highs. Before fasting, you may want to check with your doctor if you're taking medication or have concerns.

During the fast, with a detached frame of mind, let the new perspective brought about by the experience grow in your spirit. A fast can bring one deeper into the spiritual realm and facilitate a move naturally away from material concerns. It can also give you extra time to spend contemplating or walking quietly in nature.

91

Chant the Gayatri for Protection

The Gayatri is an Indian goddess of light. With five heads and ten hands, she sits on a lotus. Her placid face remains in balance above the pulls toward laziness or excessive activity. She conquers the five senses and brings in light for transformation. A natural beauty and harmony emanate from her presence. This radiant goddess is revered in India where devotees circle around her chanting the mantra that evokes her presence at dawn.

The Gayatri mantra comes from Vedic texts and brings light for protection and transformation. It helps clarify and remove confusion from the mind. It will uplift a heavy environment and bring in new energy. It's associated with the deity Surya, the sun. This mantra can be used by anyone of any religion, caste, or creed. It is prescribed to be repeated in threes—that is three, six, nine, or more times. After repeating it, chanting "*Shanti, shanti, shanti,*" which means "peace," three times is prescribed to bring in serenity. To be effective, the words should be pronounced correctly. It is ideally chanted at dawn, noon, and dusk, but can be chanted anytime and anywhere. Visit the website www.awakeintheworld.com to hear a recording of the mantra.

The words of the mantra follow:

> *Om*
> *Bhur bhuva svaha*
> *Tat savitur varenyam*
> *Bhargo devaysa dheemahi*
> *Dhi yo yonah prachodayat*
> *Om Shanti, shanti, shanti.*

The meaning can be roughly translated from the Sanskrit as:

> Om [the primordial sound], we meditate upon
> the Spiritual Efflugence of that adorable Supreme
> Divine Reality, the Source of the Physical, the
> Astral and the Heavenly Spheres of Existence.
> May that Supreme Divine Being enlighten our
> intellect so that we may realize the Supreme
> Truth.

It's said the powerful Gayatri mantra was discovered by Sage Viswamitra during the time of Rama, and he used it to create a parallel universe. The mantra bestows protection, improved intelligence, and promotes illumination. This prayer is directed to the Divine Mother. If pronounced incorrectly it may cause confusion. The mantra must be approached with humility and reverence, as a gift of God.

It's said to be given to us as the third eye, which reveals the inner vision so that we may achieve God realization. People who have ethereal vision notice that places where the mantra is chanted are visibly illumined by its vibrations.

92

Who Are You? Check Your ID

"I perceive that we inhabitants of New England live this mean life that we do because our vision does not penetrate the surface of things," wrote Henry David Thoreau during his experiment of living in nature at Walden's Pond. "Soul mistakes its own character, until the truth is revealed to it by some holy teacher, and then it knows itself to be *Brahme* ["God" in Sanskrit]," he wrote. A tiger raised with sheep will think it is a sheep and walk around timid and afraid of other tigers until another tiger befriends it and reveals its true identity. Very often we think of ourselves as the things we possess and the roles we play. We identify ourselves with our cars, homes, clothes, and our bodies. We limit ourselves to thinking we are the lover, mother, brother, or executive. But what happens when we lose these roles?

Mr. Ponce, a man in his eighties, lived alone in a small assisted living community a block from my apartment in Antibes, France. We met one day when he fell in front of my building and from then on our paths crossed regularly on our daily walks. As his health declined he came outdoors less, so I took him fresh French baguettes or new batteries for his hearing aid. Despite the decline in his health, he kept a good morale. One day when his legs were too weak to carry him outside for exercise, we sat inside talking about life and his desires to travel like his grandfather had in the merchant marine. He pointed to a credenza and asked me to open the drawer and remove a stack of photos. In one photo as a man of about forty, he stood tall and strong by his wife at the stone barbecue of his beautiful villa on the French Riviera. In another image he stood as a young man, perhaps in his thirties, along with other important men— the mayor, some businessmen, like himself, and a senator. He pulled out a photo of a car that had been brand new ten years ago. Then he sighed deeply with regret.

"It's all gone," he said. "I'd thought I was my job. Then I retired. I'd thought I was my house and car. But they're gone too. I'd thought I was a husband, but my wife died six years ago and I had to learn to cook and clean. Most of my friends are gone too." He pointed around him. "This is it. This old body, this little room. This is what's left. And even my health is going." He said, "I want to put on my grave stone: 'What I am is what you'll be. What you are is what I was.'" This was his message to me as I sat beside him, young and fit with a sea-view apartment full of beautiful things thinking my body was immortal and my affluent situation would endure forever. All life is transitory. All the material things and relationships that we thought would endure pass. Only the relationship with the immortal Self remains.

"I Am God" Practice

In quiet reflection, settle into the silence as the witness or observer of your life, your actions, and thoughts. The immortal Self remains unaffected by the external play of aging bodies and shifting tides. What do you consider most as your identity? Do you associate yourself with objects, relationships, properties, jobs, projects, or accomplishments? Strip them all away for an instant. These are all very, very small and limiting.

Set all of these outer identities aside for a little while and take a break. Take a step into the core of your Self and capture a sense of who you are beyond the roles you play and the things you possess. Gain insight into the vastness of your soul and carry it with you ever present in your mind. Practice identifying yourself with God. Know yourself to be the Immortal Self that will not die. If the word "God" is too big, use the words "Love," "Peace," "Truth," the "Immortal Self," or some other name that you identify with the Eternal Absolute.

Try the mantras: "I am Brahman."; "I am Love. I am God."; "I or am That." (Or "*Tat Twam Asi*," which means the same in Sanskrit.)

Be sure to remain practical. A young aspirant who received this teaching from his master walked home, head high repeating, "I am God. I am God. I am God." An elephant driver coming down the road, yelled, "Get out of the way. The elephant's gone wild." The young man continued to repeat. "I am God. I am God." He imagined that in his new found identity, he would remain invulnerable. "Get off the road," the elephant driver yelled frantically. The elephant stormed by and the young aspirant with his new mantra stood firm. The elephant knocked the student into the brambles leaving him bruised and bloodied. When he returned to the guru, he asked, "What happened? You taught me that I am God. I don't understand." The teacher said, "You are God—and so is the other. Why did you not listen to the voice of God telling you to get out of the way?"

Remember your true identity today and respect that this is the same identity as others. By relating to people in this way, relationships transform.

93

Nurture Perseverance and Patience

In our fast-food culture of immediate gratification, we forget about the power of perseverance. Most people are not overnight successes, nor do they discover inventions overnight. They journey to fame, renown, and spiritual awareness through long periods of hard work, study, patience, purity of intention, and perseverance. Thomas Edison made as many as 10,000 attempts to create the light bulb. Instead of each attempt being a failure, he perceived it as learning about what didn't work. Discouragement and impossibility did not enter into his mind. What if he would have stopped short at 9,999 tries? We might still be in the dark! Albert Einstein discovered the theory of relativity in a flash, but said it took him ten years to explain it. Abraham Lincoln faced many defeats and hardships before becoming president of the United States. He overcame extreme poverty, lost elections, faced what seemed impossible odds, and finally won election to the highest office in the country.

In the realm of the soul, sticking to the practices is a key to success. Doing meditation once a week, or practicing compassion only when you feel like it will not carry you very far. A man seeking to develop perseverance asked his teacher for help to develop the quality he lacked. The teacher led him to a huge boulder and gave him a small hammer. The teacher pointed to the rock. "Break this into two parts," the teacher said and left the man to his task. At first the man hammered fast and furious and little chips of stone flew away, but after some time his enthusiasm waned and he worked less intently until he finally lost interest altogether. He sat down on the ground in despair thinking he would never break the rock in half. After some time, the teacher returned to check the man's progress only to find his student sitting down with a dejected frown beside the rock. The master picked up the hammer and with one swift, hard blow split the rock in two. The man looked up astonished. "How did you do that?" he said.

"You stopped just one blow short of success," the master said.

What spiritual discipline do you need to continue working on? Make a note and put it into practice. Success will be close at hand when you determine to do it and persevere.

Dig a Well

A man seeking water tried to dig a well. He went around the yard, dug a few feet down, and found no water; then he moved to another spot, dug a few feet, and found no water.

He continued to move about without going deep enough. Some people approach spiritual life this way. They try one teacher and change. They try one spiritual practice for a few days and then change. It's not necessary to do all of the spiritual practices. Find a few that resonate with you and do them every day in a disciplined way. Go deep. Keep digging in the same place, and sooner or later you'll strike water. Don't give up after a few tries and throw your hands up hopelessly in the air. Work hard and get to the source. Soon the water gushes up like a fountain and you can share the benefits with others. Which practice will you choose? Make a plan and stick to it.

94

Journal to Revive Your Soul

Writing holds the power to heal. Hildegard von Bingen, a mystical nun who lived in the twelfth century, wrote, "I saw a very great splendor, in which sounded a very great voice from heaven, saying to me...write what you see and hear...When I did so I rose from my sickness with renewed strength." Hildegard's writing revived her health. Her works included tomes of inspirational spiritual guidance, a study of the healing properties of herbs and plants, and the composition of spiritual songs.

Many seekers across the ages used writing to maintain their contact with God and explore their feelings and experiences. Saint Teresa of Avila wrote perhaps as a way to maintain her sanity during mystical experiences and as a way to share her vision of the interior castle of the soul. Mother Teresa of Calcutta expressed love and doubt about her faith. Blaise Pascal wrote of an evening where he experienced bliss and peace beyond all bounds in a sheer vision of pure light. He concluded that one can know and experience God "not only by reason but more so by the heart." And Saint John of the Cross wrote while he was imprisoned in Spain and his words on the dark night of the soul continue to resound in hearts around the world.

Each of these seekers and saints shared tears and fears with their private journals, revealing doubts, and triumphs as they struggled to develop faith and deepen their connection to God. Their notebooks acted as confidants and friends who listened unconditionally as the authors poured out their hearts. Today, their writings reveal struggles and devotion that enrich us as we confront our personal dark nights of the soul and other life challenges on the path.

Sacralize Your Pen and Paper

Sometimes our best spiritual companion is our notebook. Sitting down to check in on perceptions and feelings through writing can mean the difference between living consciously or continuing to snooze through life. Putting pen to paper with the aim of reconnecting with your spirit and paying attention to the still, quiet whisperings of the heart is a way to perceive what's going on beneath the surface.

When journaling is combined with the act of divine listening in quiet meditation, the pad and pen become ways to enter into creative space where solutions arise naturally and unforced. While the mind may be occupied with a mantra or prayer, answers and understandings arise unprompted, and suddenly pieces of the puzzle come together.

Sometimes insights surface that astonish with their clarity—as if one is standing on top of a mountain peak and the fog suddenly lifts revealing the clear and light landscape. At other times this moment of meditation combined with journaling can be a way to refill the well of creative energy.

I've found the best approach to spiritual journaling is to schedule a set time every day. I begin with a meditation. Opening with a prayer of gratitude or protection helps to set the tone and intention. Go into the meditation without expectation. Be silent. Keep the mind focused on the breath or a single word like "Love" or "Peace." If you find it hard to focus on the word, try writing it over and over again as a written meditation to focus the mind. Remain in this spacious place of quiet. In the beginning, your mind may jump around with agitation. But if you persist in creating this silent space, your spirit will get into the habit and meet you there. Expand the moment to five minutes and then ten. This sounds difficult at first, but if you make the effort, it will be a time that you will eventually look forward to with pleasure. It's a place of refreshment and renewal.

After a few moments of focusing the mind in this way, note any impressions that may arise. It's essential to leave your expectations behind at the door and simply enjoy the time without phones or Internet. Maintain a playful attitude and hold the creative space. Next, write for a few minutes with the intention of checking in with your soul. Ask it what it needs of you to grow. How can you feed and nourish it? You may want to ask what you can do to align yourself more fully with your soul's purpose. Then write. Let it respond to your questions in a simple dialogue, a poem, or free writing. When you're done, put it aside. Later, before bed or upon waking, read what you've written. Put into practice the things that feel in line with your conscience.

Self-Forgiveness and Healing: Write a Letter from God

If you find it difficult to forgive yourself, or struggle with faith, imagine God writing a letter to you. Take pen and paper or sit with your computer and begin to write. Remember God's qualities of infinite love and compassion. God loves all of his creation. Nothing can happen against divine will. God loves all of us unconditionally, regardless of what we have done, what we think, or how we behave. We are children of the divine and there is no more indulgent and loving a mother as the Divine Mother. She forgives all if we make amends and intend to move and work in harmony with her.

Happy writing!

95

Schedule a Regular Self-Examination

A regular self-examination through introspection will help to assess where you are and guide you in the direction you aim to travel on your life journey. Are you in maximum spiritual health? What kinds of soul vitamins do you need to reinforce and nourish your soul? Do you need to become more of a human being and less of a human doing? Do you need more balance in time between the ones, twos, and threes? That is between time alone, time one on one with a friend or partner, and time in groups or community activities?

Is your heart happy? What are you yearning to do that you need to act on? Are you treating your body temple in a respectful way? Do you care for your mind by feeding it with good thoughts and good reading or films? Make this self-inquiry a regular practice. Try it at the end of the day and consider where you've been and what you've done. What would you like to do differently next time? Do a more in-depth inquiry at the end of the year.

Sometimes, take the reflections deeper. Dare to ask the truly meaningful questions: Where have I come from? Where am I going? What's the purpose and meaning of my life?

Ponder these questions thatnswer since the beginning of time. "He who knows others is wise; he who knows himself is enlightened," said Lao-Tzu. Step inside and find out who you are.

96

Prepare for Death

In this world, when people think of preparing for death, they consider writing a will and making sure their burial arrangements are in order. On a spiritual level, preparing for death of the body helps to set a frame of mind and fix it on the spirit. We rarely see death in the West. Occasionally, we may see a bird fallen from the nest in spring or hear of someone's untimely passing. But rarely do we experience the death of an individual while sitting in the room with her holding her hand. The ancient wisdom practices of the Buddhist and Hindu traditions relate that the essential aim in life is to prepare for dying. Every single thought and step leads to this moment and preparation of release from the physical bonds.

In *The Tibetan Book of Living and Dying,* Sogyal Rinpoche reminds us that the state of mind upon death is a key to opening the door to peace. "All of my masters would give this as their advice, for this is the essence of what is needed as you come to die: 'Be free of attachment and aversion. Keep your mind pure. And unite your mind with the Buddha.'" He goes on to say that the ideal way to die is to first have given away everything, both on an inner and external level, so that there is as little yearning, grasping, and attachment of the mind to these worldly things as possible. "So before we die, we should try to free ourselves of attachment to all our possessions, friends, and loved ones," he writes. "We cannot take anything with us, so we should make plans to give away all of our belongings beforehand as gifts or offerings to charity." His work has been used to inspire courage in hospice patients and help them to approach their final days consciously.

Hindu practices teach that training the mind and heart to focus on the divine now will lead to an end of the cycle of birth and death. Where the mind rests at the end of life is where it will return to if the individual is to be reborn. By training it to always focus on God, it can achieve *moksha*, or liberation from the cycle of rebirth.

Every day takes us closer to death of the physical body. When we realize the natural process of life and accept it, we use time and energy more wisely. Reflect on how you will use your time and energy today. Does it take you closer to God and your divine Self? Or does it separate you from the holy? Keep the mind pure and free from desires, and keep the heart connected to the form and name of the divine that you adore. People who have an opportunity to prepare for death of the body through a terminal illness that endures over a period often become very transparent. They make peace with foes, say the things unsaid to family members, and value precious moments in the body in a way that those of us who imagine that we are still immortal do not. They don't take an instant or a breath for granted, but drink in each second of life with added gusto.

Transcending Body Consciousness

Consider the butterfly. In its previous state it lived as a caterpillar, munching leaves, inching around on its belly, and spinning itself into a cocoon. It had to die to the worm life to experience the beauty, joy, and levity of the butterfly's flight. The essence in the caterpillar and butterfly are one and the same—and yet the old had to die for the beautiful new creature to emerge. Death, when prepared for in a mindful way, is an opportunity, not something dreadful to fear.

In this spiritual practice, contemplate death of the physical body. Revisit the light meditation, and during the experience, merge with all things. Remember, "I am in the light, the light is in me. I am the light." The attachment to the body diminishes after a time and you come to identify yourself with the light. In many wisdom traditions, death of the body marks a release of the soul from the mortal coil and a return to its immortal condition. One mantra to help in challenging moments is: "I am not my body. I am not my mind. I am God. I am the Indivisible Supreme Absolute. Fear and worry do not enter here. I am content." This mantra reminds us of the true nature beneath the physical appearance.

IX

Cultivating Oneness

97

Commune with Nature

*"The earth seems to rest in silent meditation; and the
waters and the mountains and the sky and the heavens
seem all to be in meditation."*
—CHANDOGYA UPANISHAD

Get in your car, unlock your bike, or put on your hiking shoes and head out to your favorite place in nature. If you're an urbanite with little experience beyond concrete, make this outing an adventure of discovery. There's something about unruly, unpredictable, fickle nature that can attune us to being right here, now. While the city wears and tears at the nerves and makes constant demands on the senses, nature offers a miracle cure that soothes the ragged, weary soul and gives a sense of confidence that all will work out.

Scientists prove that there's more oxygen where trees grow in abundance and this naturally energizes the body. But there's something more about forests, streams, stones, seas, plains, and deserts—something that brings a sense of awe and even makes a rushing mind ease into a more natural rhythm. There's harmony in the elements; the tones and shades of green, gold, sky blue, pink, and violet calm the eye. Sounds blend together with a host of other songs from the cricket and cicada to the frogs, hawks, turtle doves, and owls calling all with purpose. The earth, solid underfoot, supports every step. Scents of honeysuckle and wild flowers mingle with moss and sap to tantalize the nose. Nature calms the senses.

Change, that natural movement of life that we tend to resist, is the permanent state of the natural world. Though we resist it in our lives, we love it in nature. We are awed when the buds pop out on trees in the spring; when the clouds turn to wisps and then drift away; when the leaves turn brilliant gold, red, and orange and drop off the branches; when a million unique snowflakes fall gently and the sun sets golden pink. We smile in awe and make treks to the forest or mountain tops and streams for a taste of harmony and peace.

In nature we move out of controlled climates and four square walls to places where rivers rush and roll, polishing stones into smooth, round works of art that attest to the passing of time. On the mountain peak the blowing breath of the breeze inspires the human heart to accept change, enjoy it, and experience wonder at the invisible hand that works its constant magic as the spheres turn and day becomes night. The silence, punctuated with gentle rustling of leaves or a hawk's cry, urges us to sharpen our sense and expand, transcend, and fly. A flash of a deer's tail or the sparkle of a trout's scales brings the mind to slip into *satori* wonder and pause. A hawk swooping silently downward rises up with a fat croaking frog dangling from its talons, and even death becomes part of the natural process of life—Generation, Organization, and Destruction: GOD. God is in the details.

Let your gaze become relaxed and open. With a deep breath, allow your brows and forehead to loosen as your mind eases into a gentle attentiveness to the moment. The heart's awareness expands and replaces the constant, narrow-minded goal seeking of the head. But the time draws to a close. The real challenge comes now: to carry this mindfulness with each step back to the car, bike, or train, back to the din and drone of the city, and remember that just below the surface, the silent harmony of nature waits ever present. In one last breath, take a piece of nature with you to carry you through another day.

98

Greet Others with *Namaste:*
See God in All

Namaste means "I bow to the God within you." *Namah* in Sanskrit means "to bow reverentially" and *te* signifies "you." Namah is often used in conjunction with a mantra associated with divinity as in *Namah Parvathi* or *Om Namah Shivaya* ("I bow to Parvathi or I bow to Shiva"). "Namaste" is a common greeting in some parts of Asia where the salutation is often accompanied by the gesture of holding both palms together in front of the heart and bowing to the one to whom it is spoken. It's a reminder of the omniscient and omnipresent God within all. Practice seeing the form of God you love and revere in all human beings.

Ramakrishna experienced the divinity in all directly and immediately, but he almost lost his job as a priest when he fed the ritual food offerings to a cat. One of the priests took the issue in protest to the wealthy woman who owned the courtyard and temples. The priest complained he did not follow the prescribed rituals and that this was a form of sacrilege. Ramakrishna answered that all had become divine consciousness, including a wicked man who passed in front of the temple, a prostitute, and the cat.

"That is why I fed a cat with the food that was to be offered to the Divine Mother. I clearly perceived that all this was the Divine Mother—even the cat," he said. At that point, he no longer needed to go to the temple to move his mind to worship. Instead he adored everything. "I used to worship the deity at the Kali Temple. It was suddenly revealed to me that everything is pure Spirit. The utensils of worship, the altar, the door frame—all pure Spirit. Men, animals, and other living beings—all pure Spirit. Like a madman, I began to shower flowers in all directions. Whatever I saw I worshipped," his disciple recorded in *The Gospel of Sri Ramakrishna*.

Practice Reverence of All through Namaste

Greet others with "Namaste." In your heart, reverentially bow to them and seek out the divine. If it's not appropriate to do this aloud, then greet them in the silence of your heart and mind. Expand this practice by working with light meditation, and imagining the light in all. When encountered with challenging people and situations, recall the light and the greeting "Namaste." Make it a practice of conscious awareness. By becoming aware of the divine in all, this transformative practice changes us as well as others. In the moments of grace and awareness, at a cash register with a gruff attendant, at a hospital with a disgruntled nurse, or at the airport with a curt employee, bring the awareness of the divine into the moment and let it uplift others along with you. Seeing God in all is a quality of the divine.

99

Defragment:
Unify Thoughts, Words, and Actions

If you've ever seen Picasso's portrait of the fractured *Weeping Woman*, the image captures a sense of the fragmented soul. One jagged, oversized eye hangs on a face, seeming to look in a different direction than the other eye; the mouth splits off appearing almost like two mouths on one distorted face. The image reflects a common malaise in modern society—fragmentation. In most of us, it manifests when the mind moves in one direction, the mouth says something that contradicts it, and actions take off in a completely different direction. This inner lack of unity results in a sense of disharmony, unease, and a deep agitation of the spirit.

When we're divided within ourselves, we waste energy and contribute to confusion around us by thinking one thing, saying another, and doing yet another. How can we expect to find peace with so much division? Division weakens, but unity brings compounding strength. A house divided against itself cannot stand. The head pitted against the heart cannot go very far. Begin to do your inner work and make sure that all of you is moving in the same, unified direction toward a positive, uplifting outcome in the direction of wholeness.

Harness the power of unity. If the mind thinks, "I want to write a book. I must write it," but in speech you say, "I can't write. I'm not a writer," and you never schedule time to sit down with a pen and paper or in front of the keyboard, then you will be challenged to obtain a successful outcome. On the other hand, if you think, "I will write," and you say, "I am a writer," and you also sit down to a daily writing practice at five a.m. and learn the process, then the alignment brings great energy and power. Sooner or later a book will emerge.

The Buddha said, "The thought manifests as word. The word manifests as the deed. The deed develops into habit. And the habit hardens into character. So watch the thought and its way with care. And let it spring from love, born out of concern for all beings." Practicing unity of thought, word, and deed is a way to simplify, save your energy, and gain momentum to carry you forward with powerful force. A regular meditation practice or periods of quiet contemplation will help you gain perspective.

Watch yourself, and at the end of the day measure your aim to be unified against how well you achieved the goal. Work to unify body, mind, and spirit. Keep working at it and make it a regular practice. It's a powerful practice of self-observation that will lead you to higher elevations. Another divide occurs when attention splits to different things. We know when we converse with someone who is off thinking about something else. We also know if the mind isn't there and we're not being heard. Yet when energies and mind are concentrated in the same place at the same time, the quality of presence enters in and the relationship improves radically. We act consciously and our lives transform. Memory also improves and we're better able to know exactly what to do and what words may be comforting or how to resolve a problem.

It's very disconcerting when one goes to get a haircut and the hairdresser's mind is out to lunch. Know what I mean? She's clipping on automatic pilot—she's not there and you know it. Kids are very attuned to this quality of presence in their parents. They're likely to call them out and demand complete, one-pointed attention. God's the same way. God wants the full focus on the divine, not some half-hearted approach where the mind's pretending to be in meditation, but is off traveling half way around the world. Through constant integrated awareness, unity becomes the rule rather than the exception.

100

Merge in Silence

Author Aldous Huxley called our modern times, "the age of noise." We hold history's record for physical and mental noise as well as the "noise of desire," he wrote. Rarely can a nook or corner be discovered where television, radio, advertisements, cars, or other vibrations do not disturb. For some people, lack of noise implies boredom, isolation, and separation. But the practice of silence opens up a transcendent place in harmony with nature and puts life into perspective. It's a way of stepping out of the rushing river and standing on the river bank away from worries. Silence brings us into attunement with a deep source of inner stillness.

"Silence is God's first language," wrote sixteenth-century mystic Saint John of the Cross. Exterior silence in the environment promotes interior silence that draws us close to God. God's voice or the still, small voice of the soul can be heard in the depth of silence. Intentional silence is a good way to deepen contact with the inner divine source. With regular practice, it provides the foundation for a steady mind. This is why it is said silence is golden. Practiced for centuries by *yogis* and *yoghinis* (male and female ascetics who master the senses and the mind), monks, and spiritual aspirants, it's a powerful way to remember one's Self and be conscious while others may get lost in the rush.

The Religious Society of Friends, better known as Quakers, make silence a key in their gatherings. As seekers of Truth based on direct experience, they use silence to know the divine within and only speak when they feel prompted by this divine voice. They seek out the presence of God beneath the superficial. In the silence, they affirm that all are equal in possessing "that of God" within and can address the essence of God in others without the need for an authority or minister. Sometimes silence is used when two or more gather outside of worship as a way to invite in divine presence before moving onto discussion.

After a divorce and job loss, quiet time and solitude became part of the process of self-discovery and a way of learning who I was without a partner and who I was beyond the role of a business executive. When I traveled on business, my immediate reaction to an empty hotel room was to turn on the television and occupy the space with noise. It soothed, I thought. Later, when I used the television to fill up a quiet, deserted home, the noise became an attempt to escape from emotions and thoughts hovering beneath the surface. Filling space with sound became a way to avoid facing fears and insecurities and hear the whisperings of my soul. It took some time to become comfortable with my Self in the silence. I practiced a day with no television or music. Later came a day without speaking, and it prepared me for a silent mountain retreat that lasted nearly a month. These days gathered momentum, and in silence I learned to befriend my Self and be a good, supportive companion for my own growth.

The notion that I needed to get to know myself may sound funny or odd since I was with "me" twenty-four hours a day, but I really only saw and paid attention to the tip of the iceberg. In the silence came self-knowledge, as the stuff from down below began to float upward into view. With the self-knowledge came acceptance and self-love. Silence gave the gift of all of these very potent and priceless treasures. Once I befriended myself on those deeper levels, I became better able to love and befriend others too.

The Practice

Take five minutes, an hour, half a day, or a week and keep silent. Do not speak or write during the chosen period. Get off the Internet. Silence, *mounam* in Sanskrit, refers to taking a vow of silence to listen to the deep interior quiet of the heart. This silence is always there latent within us beneath the agitated ocean of the mind. Don't wait for a retreat to try it. Eliminating talking will bring you more in touch with it and soothe the mental agitations.

If you choose to have a silent period and can't retreat, carry your silence into the world. It may require some preparation and possibly a badge or a note to inform family and friends you may meet during the day. Shut off your cell phone. Turn off the music and television and unplug the computer. Still the tongue and stop the pen. Use the quiet time to observe yourself, your mind, and others. Notice sounds, sights, and smells you might normally have overlooked or ignored. In the beginning, if you are not used to silence, you may notice the agitations of the mind. Go deeper. Note how you feel in the quiet of your heart. With practice you will come to look forward to these periods of silence as a retreat. Appreciate the calm interior and the joy of turning inward toward your divine spirit. You may notice that you have more energy after a day without speaking.

If you've never tried it or feel intimidated by quiet time, make a special effort to give it a try. Ease into it and test the waters. Explore what makes you feel uncomfortable. Write about your first experience with silence and watch your reactions on the many levels of body, mind, and spirit. Writing exercises that come out of the periods of silence often give birth to deeply inspired words. I encourage you to move into the silence. Be brave, take heart, and try. It may require some effort, but the gems that you'll find will be more valuable than anything that you'll pick up in a marketplace. The silence is pregnant with possibility.

101

Lighten Up with the *Jyothi* Meditation

A thousand candles lit from a single flame will not diminish the first light. The *jyothi*, or light meditation, ignites the lamp of love in the heart and shares it with others. It's an ancient meditation that helps improve concentration by encouraging the mind to follow the flame of a candle as it moves throughout the body, mind, and spirit, then expands to friends and family, the environment, colleagues, strangers, and even enemies. It broadens the sense of self beyond body consciousness and ego and brings a deep sense of peace. The light meditation uses the light of a flame as the focus for the practice, and leads the one who practices from concentration to mediation, which merges the individual consciousness with the universal consciousness.

If you stand in a dark room and light a single candle, the light becomes a beacon. When that light extends to other wicks around the room, the light begins to overpower the darkness and the first flame is not diminished in any way by what it has shared. The light as a symbol eradicates darkness, ignorance, desire, fear, hatred, and ego. God is light, and when light meets light, your light merges in divine light.

Lighting the Lamp

This practice draws from the ancient Indian spiritual texts called the Vedas. To begin, find a quiet place where you'll not be disturbed. Shut off cell phones, computers, and any background noise. Schedule it at the same time and place every day. Collect your candle and matches. An oil lamp with a steady flame also works well. Keep the spine straight throughout the practice by sitting on the floor or in a straight back chair. A meditation cushion may also be useful if you choose to sit on the floor. A meditation cushion placed on a yoga mat will protect the ankles if floors are hard. Begin the meditation by lighting a candle or lamp. Softly focus on the flame and then close the eyes.

Imagine bringing the flame into the head between the brows. As it enters the head it fills the thoughts with light and brings good thoughts. Where there is light, no darkness can enter. The light moves gently down to the lotus blossom of the heart. As the rays fall on the heart petals, they begin to open and unfold. Bad feelings dissipate. Darkness cannot remain here. Next, move the flame to fill the chest and shoulders, then move the light down both arms and into the hands. Light-filled hands will do good deeds. Next, move the flame to fill the torso, legs, and feet. Feet filled with light will carry you to good places.

Move the flame gently and slowly back into the head and into the eyes and ears. These eyes filled with light will see only good. And ears filled with light will hear the good. As the soft light fills your entire being, your senses take in vibrant, bright, pure sensations. Now move the light out and let it expand into your friends and family. Let it expand to animals and birds, to your enemies, and into all the objects around. Let it purify your habitat and spread to all of the earth until all is illumined by the same light. Basking in this expansive light, repeat to yourself: *I am in the light. The light is in me. I am the light.* Bring the meditation to an end by moving the light back into the heart. Let it remain there to accompany you throughout the day.

This meditation leads to liberation. The light in one's self is found in others. In the jyothi meditation, the body drops away and you are the light. There are three things: the meditator, the chosen form (as in the light), and the process of meditating. When these three merge into one, this is meditation. The light meditation helps to move the seeker through these steps. If you'd like to simply listen as you're guided through the meditation, please visit the website www.awakeintheworld.com.

102

Practice Nonviolence

Maintain peaceful thoughts, words, and actions. This is the practice of nonviolence—do not harm others in thought, speech, or deed. Even a harsh look or an angry word may cause injury to others. Responding with violence to others is ultimately committing injury to oneself. Every action evokes an inevitable reaction. Will you practice tolerance, fortitude, perseverance, and equanimity today or resort to animal-like behavior? Remember to help ever, hurt never. Or as the biblical saying goes, "Do unto others as you would have them do unto you."

Mahatma (meaning "great soul") Gandhi considered the practice of nonviolence and the search for Truth inseparable. "Not to hurt any living thing is no doubt a part of *ahimsa* [nonviolence]. But it is its least expression. The principle of ahimsa is hurt by envy, evil thought, by undue haste, by lying, by hatred, by wishing ill to anybody. It is also violated by holding on to what the world needs," he wrote in *Truth is God*. For Gandhi, greed or hoarding and harmful thoughts became acts of violence as much as physically injuring someone. Gandhi's practice of nonviolence brought down the British rule of his country and inspired nonviolent protests by Dr. Martin Luther King in the American South.

This practice of compassion and nonviolence can be extended to what you eat, how you live, and how you speak of others. Nonviolence is a key principle in spiritual practice. When extended to oneself, others, and the world at large, its effects are far-reaching and profound. Imagine a world where no one spoke unkindly of anyone. Imagine having the foresight to consider how one's actions today may harm or help others and shape events and lives.

Making It Your Reality

Hold this practice of not harming close to your heart and make the effort to practice it in your life. First, watch your thoughts. Pay attention to the inner dialogue, and observe the words and feelings behind it. Are you encouraging to yourself and kind to others? Do those thoughts criticize and denigrate?

How do you treat your body? Do you overburden it with too much weight and little exercise? Do you drink, smoke, or take in substances that will harm it? Do you eat a well-balanced diet? In relation to others, how do you speak and act? Do you wish them ill? Do you rejoice when others are happy and have success?

How do you treat the world? The Earth is there always supporting life through its gift of food, air, water, and fire.

Do you acknowledge and respect it? Do you recycle? If you have lawns, do you cut out chemical pesticides and petrochemical fertilizers? The Jains revere every living thing from the planet Earth to the microbes. They do not consider themselves as above anything or below anything in creation, but rather equal to all. Lord Mahavir, a founder of Jainism born in 599 BCE, preached universal love and emphasized that all living beings, irrespective of their size, shape, and form, and however spiritually developed or under-developed, are equal and deserve love and respect.

When Jains walk they carefully avoid stepping on ants and insects and they often wear surgical masks to protect microbes from being drawn in by their breath and killed. To some this may seem extreme, but even spiders and bugs are sentient beings that feel fear and sense peace. If one gets trapped indoors, if possible place a container or glass over it and slip a piece of paper underneath the glass, creating a temporary portable cage. Carry the glass outside and release the creature.

This mantra wishes peace and bliss to all of creation and all sentient beings: "*Samasta Loka Sukhino Bhavantu; Samasta Loka Suhkino Bhavantu; Samasta Loka Sukhino Bhavantu*," meaning, "May all worlds and all living beings be happy."

103

Embrace Someone of Another Faith

"In reality, there are as many religions as there are individuals," Gandhi wrote. At work, in our neighborhoods, and throughout life, we meet people who celebrate a variety of religious and spiritual practices and beliefs. Often we grow up with the teaching that our tribes, religious beliefs, and God(s) are the right ones and others are all wrong. But what if God and the religious forms that arise take varied forms to please different cultures and fit their needs?

Jelaluddin Rumi was a revered poet who lived in the thirteenth century during a time of violent crusades and conflict. Despite the divisions that created wars for holy lands, Rumi said, "I go into the Muslim mosque and the Jewish synagogue and the Christian church and I see one altar." His enlightened vision saw God in each place. He saw God also in bread baking and lovemaking, not separate from himself. Rumi perceived that someone who placed importance on boxing people into religions and nationalities would cut off the heart from the vision of God. *La'illaha il'Allahu*, or "There's no reality but God; there is only God," (or, more simply stated, "There is no reality but the

Self") sums up his being and body of work. When he died in 1273 in Iran, people from across a vast array of religions gathered for the funeral to pay tribute to his deep wisdom, tolerance, and exuberance for life.

Where minds sequestered God into little spaces belonging to only a select few, for Rumi, God knew no boundaries, did not discriminate, and indeed was not separate from anyone. His words in his Book IV of the *Mathnawi* say, "Some go first and others come long afterwards. God blesses both and all in the line, and replaces what has been consumed, and provides for those who work the soil of helpfulness, and blesses Muhammad and Jesus and every other messenger and prophet." No condemnation filled his words, no division, no discrimination between Christian and Muslim. His view of the world originated in his deep, embodied experience of the divine and his realization of the Truth as omnipresent.

Forms are many, but the God we all celebrate and revere is One. Open your heart; open your mind. Embrace the people who come to mind as worshiping in a different way and accept them and their choices. Many people who do not follow organized religions march to an inner tune with the same God marking the rhythm.

"All are calling on the same God," said Sri Ramakrishna. "It is not good to feel that my religion is true and the other religions are false. All seek the same object. A mother prepares dishes to suit the stomachs of her children. Suppose a mother has five children and a fish is brought for the family. She doesn't cook the same curry for all of them. ... God has made religions to suit different aspirants, times, and countries. All doctrines are only so many paths." Ramakrishna spoke from experience and explored not only the Hindu path, but he adored Jesus and the Christian way, as well as the Islamic path. He found all to lead to the same God. Forms are many; God is One. Indian ruler Akbar is also renowned for his ability to embrace and synthesize not only his traditional Islamic religion, but also Hinduism, Jainism, and Zoroastrianism, and he also met with Jesuits, setting an example for his times in the sixteenth century.

Promote understanding and look for unity instead of division and separation. Embracing those who are different does not weaken the connection to God, but rather reinforces and makes us stronger. Rigid beliefs become brittle and crack while those that expand and allow others in can make us deep and rich in wisdom.

104

Contemplate a *Yantra, Mandala,* or Medicine Wheel

Yantras and mantras hold spiritual significance and transmit subtle properties that help seekers move closer to the divine. Used in Hindu practices, yantras are symbolic representations of a mantra and aid to help focus the mind in meditation. The word "yantra" means "machine or instrument" and it is considered a tool for spiritual practice or upliftment. It is represented in an image that may include a square, circles, a lotus, triangles, and a point at the center. Usually etched on metals like copper, silver, gold, or stone, the yantra is a physical or visual representation of a mantra. A mantra is the name of God and the yantra enhances the power of the mantra and gives it a visual form. By focusing on the yantra, the seeker is conducted to the one single point at the center where all merges. He is able to internalize the message of Oneness through meditating on the image.

Yantras come in many forms. The Shree Sai Chakram yantra contains the symbols of all the world's major religions around the exterior and these each represent pathways into the center. They include the Om symbol representing Hinduism, the cross for Christianity, the flame for Zoroastrians, the Jewish menorah, the Islamic moon and star, and the Buddhist wheel within a twelve sided boundary. Inside, the form of the yantra follows the stages of the spiritual journey. The practices of truth, right action, peace, nonviolence, and love create the names of the petals of a lotus near the center of the image. An inner triangle brings balance and names the three sides as goodness, beauty, and truth. In the center, a single point represents merging with the divine. This yantra represents the unity principle and how all religious paths essentially espouse the same underlying truths and lead to God.

Mandalas, created and used by Buddhist monks, take on deeply spiritual meanings and also provide a powerful experience to the observer. "Mandala" is a Sanskrit word meaning "circle," and it depicts the circle of the soul or Self with steps or doors to move inward. Sand mandalas are like maps of the psyche and make up an essential teaching of Tibetan Buddhists. Like a yantra, the mandala is much more than it appears. As the monk lays out the foundations in geometric design to create the mandala, he learns that the image in sand is a representation of a palace. His aim is to meditate on the process of crossing the threshold into the palace. He must overcome obstacles and demons and move to the center to merge in Buddha-consciousness.

Buddhist monks who create colorful sand mandalas may take a week to tap out the bright colored sands in intricate designs. The Drepung Loseling monks in America create mandalas at museums and sacred sites around the country. After the 9/11 attack on the World Trade Center, the monks created a special healing sand mandala to honor the dead and foster world peace at the Sackler Gallery in Washington, DC. At a Lugano department store, I watched seven Tibetan Buddhist monks on an elevated platform create a vibrantly colored healing sand mandala in honor of Tara, the goddess of compassion, health, longevity, and healing. In a Swiss library, another Buddhist monk spent one week slowly drawing the boundaries and filling in the geometrical design with millions of grains of sand tapped meticulously through metal cones.

In Western culture, we would carefully protect and preserve something that we'd spent so much time generating. But at the end of the process of creation, all of these mandalas were consecrated, chanted over, and then dissolved. At the ceremony of dissolution, the monks sweep the sands together and the brilliant colors merge into a mass of gray. Half of the Tara mandala, believed to be imbued with healing vibrations, was distributed to the crowd in vials. The rest was taken to the lake and poured in to share the healing properties with fish and animals. The mandalas at the library and the Sackler Gallery were swept into brass metal pots and taken to the nearby river where the sands washed them away to the ocean. This final act of dissolution acts as a reminder of the impermanent nature of life.

If you're inspired by the art and beauty of yantras and mandalas, find one that suits you and contemplate it. Focus on the center and remember that Oneness with all is the goal. Mandalas and yantras are beautiful works of art and may be placed in an office or another area where you spend time to help you maintain a spiritual focus throughout the day. Like the Tibetan Buddhists, Carl Jung saw mandalas as images reflecting innate archetypes, patterns built into the soul that guide our journey. "Mandalas reveal images of our spiritual essence, the seed forms that contain the tree of our existence," writes Anthony Lawlor in *A Home for the Soul*.

Make Your Mandala or Medicine Wheel

You may wish to create a mandala of your own. It doesn't require special training, only a desire to experiment, explore, and play. The basic elements include paper, colored pens, crayons, or pencils, and if you'd like to get adventurous, prepare some paints. Draw a circle and begin to fill it up according to your mood, your feelings, and your aims. Do you seek to make a mandala that represents your soul? It may be a map of where you are right now. Find your center and experiment with the colors and forms that attract you. Remove the idea of a right or wrong way and return to your childlike sense of play. It's still there. No one will grade or judge your creation. Free up the space and enjoy the process. Don't stop at one. Continue to create others. If you're inspired, do one a day over a month or create one that reflects a recent dream.

The medicine wheel also uses a circle as its container. Used by Native Americans of the North West and plains, it was originally laid out in stones across a field. Today, it's adapted for work in therapy to help patients find balance. Draw a circle and divide the wheel, a symbol of the continuity of life, into four quadrants that represent the spiritual, physical, emotional, and mental realms. Consider each of these areas of your life and draw or write what fills each area. Consider if the four are balanced. The central point is the most powerful place. You stand in the center.

105

Become Like a Flute

The flute has long been a spiritual symbol. Krishna loved his reed flute and carried it on his belt. One day Radha, his consort and companion, asked him, "Why do you love your flute so?"

Krishna smiled his alluring, playful smile and said, "This flute was first a reed. It withstood the hot sun and monsoon rains. Then it got itself bored out completely until it became entirely empty so that now I may blow my breath through it and make divine music."

The flute was also an image of the human being's relationship to the divine for Sufi poet Rumi. His poetry flowed through him like divine music through a flute. "Who is making this divine music?" he asked as he wrote. He referred to God, of course. Sometimes Rumi let the Invisible Flute Player take over and said, "Let that musician finish this poem." Rumi's poetry arose naturally and mystically because he became an empty flute through which the divine inspiration gently blew its sweet notes.

> God picks-up the reed-flute world and blows.
> Each note is a need coming through one of us,

A passion, a longing-pain.
Remember the lips where the wind-breath
    originated,
And let your note be clear.
Don't try to end it.
Be your note.
I'll show you how it's enough.
Go up on the roof at night
In this city of the soul.
Let *everyone* climb on their roofs
And sing their notes!
Sing loud!

—RUMI

Only by becoming empty and open to the divine that beats out the rhythm of the human heart, will the music of Love move us. Without taking credit for the words, actions, wealth, and progress, all is devoted to God and not separate from God's will. In this emptiness there is not me and you, not us and them, but only divine I, united in breath.

Emptying Out to Make Divine Music

When the ego stops taking credit for all that happens, the illusion of control falls away. Make a daily practice of offering yourself, your thoughts, words, and actions to the divine. Pray for guidance that the small ego self may not interfere and that divine will be done. At the end of each day, offer the good deeds, work, accomplishments, and all that has happened to God. Step into the realization that God is the doer. By offering the action and work to God, as well as the fruits of the actions, God will gain the benefits and the spirit will grow in humility.

106

Conserve Natural Resources

Conserving natural resources is a spiritual practice. When it comes to water, air, foods, and all of Earth's gifts that we consume, we've become so disconnected from the processes related to them, that we no longer realize the effects and consequences of our decisions. It's only in drought periods with city water restrictions that we may begin to consider taking shorter showers and cutting back irrigating lawns and gardens.

If we make Internet purchases and a delivery truck brings it directly to the door, the waste and greenhouse gases from transport will be more significant than if we source something locally. Farmers' markets provide produce from locals; this produce will more likely be fresher, use fewer petrochemical fertilizers and pesticides, and be more environmentally sound than items shipped from across the globe. As for household items and clothes, I love the European attitude of going for quality rather than quantity. In France, Italy, Germany, Switzerland, and much of Europe, people often prefer to spend a little more upfront to have items that are well made and beautiful rather than cheap and in need of replacement in a few months.

By holding an attitude of conservation and preservation, you will naturally begin to look at the bigger picture and think of what you need to buy in a more conscious way. Consider taking shorter showers to conserve precious water and help the environment. Pay attention to waste of food, paper, electricity, gas, and all of the resources used every day. Can you find a shorter route to work? Can you use a bus or subway instead of your car? Is it possible to turn the heat down a couple of degrees and shut off the lights? Could you use LED bulbs to lower electrical usage? You may not think your contribution to conservation will make much of an impact, but every little bit counts. Think of the effects multiplied by seven billion-plus people on this planet. Imagine the effects if everyone lives with respect for our Mother Earth. Do it for your Mother Earth, this magnificent orb that sustains life and nourishes us lifetime after lifetime. Here are two simple steps:

Go Organic

Practice conscious, eco-friendly buying when possible. Purchasing organic products over conventionally grown ones can help the environment by reducing the use of synthetic fertilizers, chemicals, and pesticides. Why is this a spiritual act? When we begin to realize the far-reaching effects of our smallest decisions, like buying organic lettuce, then we take care to make choices that will provide benefits beyond our own wallets and backyards. Taking this broader perspective promotes interconnectedness and expands our sense of community.

Conventional growers use pesticides that can seep into the water tables and become toxic to animals, nature, and human life. Organic farming practices work more in tune with nature through water conservation and the elimination of chemical fertilizers, pesticides, and genetically modified organisms (GMOs). Many organic products exist in supermarkets and health food stores and can be purchased at a small premium over regular fruits, veggies, and other products. Organic cotton clothing and beauty products also make you feel good and move you deeper into harmony with nature.

Recycle

To recycle means literally to "put through the cycle again; to give something another life." Many cities provide recycle bins to collect plastic bottles and paper. Make a contribution by separating recyclables from the trash. It will cut down on the size of waste sites, and only takes a moment by tossing the aluminum cans, milk jugs, and newspapers into the right container as soon as you dispose of them. It's easy. Switzerland, a country with one of the highest standards of living, recycles some 95% of waste. We can too. Do your part. Every small effort counts, and Mother Earth will appreciate it.

107

Seek Truth

A teacher led five blind men to an elephant, placed their hands on it, and asked them to describe it. One held fast to the trunk, another to a thick, leathery leg, another to its side. Another blind man asked them to each describe an elephant for him so he would have some knowledge about it. One man said, "It's like a python." Another man said, "No, that's not it. It's thick and hard like a tree trunk." Another who had touched the tail said, "No it's like a thin rope." Yet another who touched its side argued, "You men didn't encounter the same animal as I. The elephant is no different than a big wall." The teacher with sight stopped their arguments and intervened. "You are all correct," he said. "You all perceived pieces of the whole. But in reality, the elephant is all of these things and more." Only the teacher saw the whole picture and helped them to understand it.

Truth is of two kinds: relative and absolute. Relative truth may be true right now and change later. Absolute Truth is eternal and unchanging. A relative truth might be, "the grass is green." Tomorrow it may turn brown from drought or frost, so this truth is one that changes according to circumstance. Absolute Truth with a capital T points to the permanent. This Truth includes precepts like "God is Love." Grasping the bigger divine Truth is like seeing the whole elephant. When we cultivate sacred vision, it connects the pieces together and gives insights into the Oneness of all life.

When we hear or experience a truth, it resonates within us like a perfect set of harmonious chords and we just know with all of our being that something is right. Listen to what resonates with your deepest sense of life-affirming truth today. Make an attempt to step into a different place and see a bigger piece of the picture. When hiking in the mountains, one usually begins in a low area with a very limited perspective. You might see the parking lot and a house or two. But on the way up the mountain, the surrounding village and valleys come into view. When you arrive at the peak, a vista opens up where it's possible to see for miles in many directions. Imagine an event you'd like to gain some perspective on. Now imagine you're standing at the top of the mountain; examine it from this perspective. From the higher perspective does more understanding dawn?

Explore truth and what it means in practice. Speaking truth is advisable if it does not harm others. Listening to truth from great teachers broadens the mind and inspires the hungry heart. When notions of relative truth become more real, we realize that more than one way or view can be right. By holding the search for truth as an aim, answers will become visible like facets of a jewel. From one side or another, only parts of a diamond may be visible. But from the top, the whole stone with its many facets is revealed. Seek the higher view.

108

E Pluribus Unum: Cultivate Oneness

"Move together; grow together; remain united and share knowledge. Live together in harmony and friendship without giving rise to conflict."
—THE VEDAS

The noble motto *E Pluribus Unum* appears on the ribbon clenched in the eagle's mouth on the U.S. one-dollar bill. Those words are linked intimately to the foundations and aspirations of this country. It's meaning, "From the many, One," transcends the simple idea of unifying states into a government and cuts through divisive politics. It calls for unity in diversity as a guiding principle and resounds with deep spiritual principles. Its truth reaches into the depths of human hearts and has been used as a guiding principle to shape the nation and the hearts and minds of citizens. The saying whispers of the Oneness that is the essential underlying reality of this world.

In today's America, we have a lot of *pluribus* (plurality or diversity in Latin) and not enough *unum* ("oneness" or "unity"). The nation focuses on division and multiplicity rather than on the vast commonalities that unite us. We concentrate on our little tribe, our family related by blood, our immediate community, or our special interest group. Media, religious groups, ethnic groups, and political factions consider their own narrow interests without remembering the fundamental value of unity and sacrifice that built the country and hold this diverse society together. These distinctions of "my community" or "my group" are like walls in the mind—and like the Berlin Wall, they must be torn down to unite the separate parts.

"A human being is part of a whole, called by us the 'Universe,' a part limited in time and space," Albert Einstein wrote. "He experiences himself, his thoughts, and feelings, as something separated from the rest—a kind of optical delusion of his consciousness. This delusion is a kind of prison for us, restricting us to our personal desires and to affection for a few persons nearest us. Our task must be to free ourselves from this prison by widening our circles of compassion to embrace all living creatures and the whole of nature in its beauty."

Abraham Lincoln took a similar view of peoples during his time. When asked as to his opinions regarding the new Irish and German immigrants that were the subject of much debate and abuse at the time, the president answered, "I esteem them no better than other people, nor any worse." He sought equanimity. This is the gift of seeing all with equal eyes.

Physicist David Bohm in *Wholeness and the Implicate Order* writes about wholeness and the mind:

What I am proposing here is that man's general way of thinking of the totality, i.e., his general world view, is crucial for overall order of the human mind itself. If he thinks of the totality as constituted of independent fragments, then that is how his mind will tend to operate, but if he can include everything coherently and harmoniously in an overall whole that is undivided, unbroken and without a border (for every border is a division or break) then his mind will tend to move in a similar way, and from this will flow an orderly action within the whole.

Sun shines on all equally. Trees share their shade with all without discriminating who is good or bad or what color or nation they come from. Jasmine flowers and roses give their sweet scent to all. Practice looking at what unites you with others today. Acknowledge the differences and respect them, then look for the things you have in common. There are more things that connect us than divide us. Focus on what unifies and find common ground with those around you. This will bring understanding and break down mental barriers at work, home, and in the world. Give up pushing politics; stop trying to enforce your likes and dislikes, and instead become aware of judgments to discard. Many views can be truthful and right depending on where one is standing. Move into the deep terrain of the soul. In the eyes of the other is the same spark of the divine that resides within you. Seek it. Acknowledge it in your heart. The mind divides. Spirit unites.

But here is a caveat. Use your wisdom. Identifying and practicing the unity principle does not mean that all are treated identically. Use discernment in this regard. A Supreme Court justice may get on his hands and knees and allow his grandchild to ride on his back, but when he sits on the bench, he will stand upright and play his role with dignity and authority and command respect. Contemplate the connection between unity and your *dharma* or right action. Listen to your common sense and act on it.

Practicing Oneness

1) The *jyothi*, or light meditation, is a good way to expand the heart, break away false mental perceptions, and share light and love with others. It helps to transcend body consciousness and break the bonds of body identification. In the light, the darkness of separation cannot survive. The original sense of the phrase "E Pluribus Unum" was considered related to and inspired by the color spectrum. Pure white light is made up of blue, violet, green, orange, red, and yellow.

When a prism refracts or divides the light the colors are separated out. When they're united, they form one beam of white light, a symbol of purity. Medical intuitive, Edgar Cayce, in his booklet on auras wrote, "The perfect color is white, and this is what we are all striving for. If souls were in perfect balance, then all our color vibrations would blend and we would have an aura of pure white."

2) Let go of attitudes that bring judgment and criticism.

3) Connect with others through the heart more than through words. Make efforts to understand and serve others regardless of their background, social status, ethnic group, or country of origin.

X

*Completion
of the Cycle:
Awake in the World*

On the *mala* of 108 beads, one additional bead, knotted between the circle of 108 and a tassel, hangs at the end. Some say it represents transcendental consciousness or the seat of God. It might also be symbolic of stepping out of the wheel of karma or life that perpetually drags most of us back into the fray and keeps us distant from our souls. This one bead marks the beginning and the end of a series. It is not used to count the mantras or prayers, but remains unaffected and unused, and yet intimately connected like the Witness or Spirit. It brings the count to 109.

One plus *zero* plus *nine* brings us back to one-zero (ten) or simply *One*—a number of wholeness and unity. It represents the height of spiritual attainment, enlightenment, nirvana, the experience of Oneness, and *ananda*, which means supreme joy. This bead acts as a reminder of why we do the practices—to weave the fabric of our lives into a tapestry of joy. When you reach this bead you know you've completed a cycle.

109

The Guiding Bead: Embodied Spirituality in the World

After some time it becomes easy to sit in meditation, recite prayers, sing devotional songs, and write about the spirit in our self-created sacred space at our altar. But all of this really only makes sense when we actively live it every day in the world. A constant and conscious awareness of inner life carries with it increased responsibilities. We can no longer retreat into the excuse of ignorance about the impact of our actions on others, ignore the state of the world, or stand apart with an illusion of superiority. We're drawn in and demanded to get involved in the dirty, messy, sometimes confusing world and still keep our light, meditative mind, open heart, and bring love to those around us even in difficult situations.

When this story began, I had initially moved from the French Riviera to the Swiss Alps after losing my job, going through divorce, and enduring illness. Those three events were my three-alarm wakeup call that initiated a journey to awaken and live in a deeper, more vibrant way. In the Alps high above the world, I'd begun to grow comfortable and content with a routine of weekly fasting, dream work, prayer, meditation, celibacy, and long periods of silence and solitude. I'd imagined that my life would continue to be devoted almost solely to deep spiritual practice in my self-made hermitage, and I felt mostly happy. But just when I thought I knew the direction life would take, a shocking thing happened. A man came into my life and my whole world changed again.

We'd known each other from high school and he came to visit in my little village in the Alps. We married and I moved back to the United States. This marked a new phase, one where life required me to be conscious and awake in a relationship, with family, at work, and in the rush of American life in a big city. I resisted, pouted, and felt angry. *I can't believe you* [meaning my wise, knowing Self] *made me move back to the U.S. There's no space for spiritual practice there*, I repeated and resisted the change. Then it hit me: *There's space for it everywhere, and a very pressing need. I've got to practice all that I've learned and live it awake in the world*. I dreamed that every corner of the city where I live is sacred space, and in meditation I saw that the entire world is permeated in divine consciousness. This was a call to awaken even more.

One teacher said that real meditation begins when we do it actively involved in the daily grind. He didn't mean sitting down and chanting Om on the office carpet; he meant actively bringing in the conscious awareness and presence developed from those deep moments of quiet and being the Witness, integrated yet unaffected like the 109th bead. For me this means living every day by bringing some of that meditative quiet into the world, expanding the heart, broadening the mind, and loving all with tolerance and joy. This is the real test and I call it embodied spirituality.

It's no longer intellectual, theoretical stuff that remains in the mind. It's not relegated to reaching up into high spheres of the spirit away from the earth. It's no longer scheduled only for certain times of day or saved for a sacred place, an altar, or a particular act or ritual. It demands being grounded, centered, and bringing the spiritual directly into everyday living without exceptions. It happens every day, everywhere—at work, at home, in our heads, in our hearts, and through our actions. It draws us closer to the experience of Oneness and dissolves barriers of division and separation.

Most of all, it brings a deep sense of peace, meaning, joy, and fulfillment that far exceeds the temporary pleasures of acquiring material rewards. Embodied spirituality is the treasure inside the chest of life, and though the journey may seem arduous, discovering the gems brings deep satisfaction and ecstasy that transcends and yet includes the body and mind. When you do this work, you will be assured of leaving a legacy of peace and accord, and your whole being will know that your life has been worthwhile.

Embodied Spirituality Practice

Today, be grateful for your chance to live in the world and be conscious of your Spirit. You will meet people who will try to hurt you intentionally or not. You will find yourself losing patience and feeling irritated. People may steal from you. You will be caught in the rush, feel wounded and betrayed, and you'll want to contract and close your heart. But don't.

Instead, wake up. Make efforts to expand and be the example of love in action. Sow patience and peace wherever you can. If you're injured, don't injure in return. If you're insulted, have the presence of spirit to see the hurt in the heart of the one who seeks to harm you and let it go. Practice forbearance, the soulful art of enduring the difficult moments with humility and understanding. Let go of the injury done to you and grow. This is profoundly transformative and a way of acting from divine inspiration.

If you do good, offer it to the divine who is the real doer behind the veil. If someone does good to you, feel gratitude and joy. These are simple, small things that make up the movements and precious moments of our short lives. Life is too brief to fill it with sharp words, anger, disharmony, and thoughts of revenge. Sow seeds of selflessness and do your practices quietly. The peace you carry within you will make a difference and help to soothe the troubled waves of confusion in the world.

For those who desire to live apart, like monks away from the world, this is not the path of our times. It's good to retreat for a season to gain perspective and self-understanding, but we're called to actively participate through our work, volunteering, living, and loving in the world. It's here where we become purified like gold under the jeweler's fire, and our impurities surface and burn away.

Don't put too much faith in the material world, and above all don't ever doubt your inner teacher. You are divine. Act like it, live it, breathe it, be it. Learn what love is and share it. These are the rewarding secrets that will truly enrich your life and help you to live awake in the world.

Gratitude Page
(Acknowledgements)

To write a book requires many years of inner work, work in the world, support from friends and family, reflection, patience, and perseverance. This is an opportunity to express gratitude to all of those people who have helped to bring this book together and offer it up to God embodied in each of you. I'm grateful to Carrie Obry at Llewellyn for her vision and for being midwife to my first book, and to my agent, Krista Goering, for getting it into her hands. I appreciate the help of Tony Showa, Mary Tribble, Walter Danzer, and others in giving permission to tell their stories. I'd also like to extend a special thanks to Coleman Barks for permission to use his poetry translation in this work.

I feel special gratitude for being surrounded with supportive and gifted writers who have offered insight and given guidance. Sarah Susanka read an early draft of this work and responded with enthusiasm and helpful reminders about the scope and direction. Hannelore Hahn, founder of the International Women's Writing Guild (IWWG), supports many women writers through the IWWG and helps to make writing dreams come true. She has been an encouraging muse on the path to completion. I'm grateful also to the people who patiently read preliminary drafts and gave feedback.

Many teachers and friends helped in the process. Carolyn Rivers, founder of the Sophia Institute, provided encouragement and kind words along the way. Special thanks to the study group in Ticino where many of these ideas developed and were tested. I'm deeply grateful to Sri Sathya Sai Baba for his light and guidance on this path of Self-discovery, and to Lama Sogyal Rinpoche who helped to reconnect me with compassion and a sense of what is essential.

Much of writing is everyday stuff and requires endurance and patience. The loving, long-term support and enthusiasm of my husband, Mike, for my work is invaluable in getting the words onto the page. Even when I sometimes see no end, he's there to encourage me to keep going. Special thanks to Nick T., who gave me a place to rest and reflect during the final draft of this work in Val Verzasca. And a very special expression of gratitude to my parents who believed in the end result and offered up regular moral support.

I have deep feelings of gratitude to all of those teachers whose presence I have felt inspired by and lived with during the many hours of this writing and of living the writing: Jesus, Buddha, Astavakara, Krishna, Hanuman, Gayatri, Sarwasti, Allah, Mother Mary, Ramakrishna, Mother Nature, and more. Each one remains a powerful source of energy and wisdom to draw from when needed.

Bibliography

Aftel, Mandy. *Essence & Alchemy: A Book of Perfume.* New York: Bloomsbury, 2002.

Ashliman, D. L., ed. *Aesop's Fables.* By Aesop. New York: Barnes & Noble Classics, 2003.

Besant, Annie, and C.W. Leadbeater. *Thought Forms.* New York: The Theosophical Publishing House, 1925.

Bird Francke, Linda. *On the Road with Francis of Assisi.* New York: Random House, 2006.

Biziou, Barbara. *The Joy of Ritual: Spiritual Recipes to Celebrate Milestones, Ease Transitions, and Make Every Day Sacred.* New York: Cosimo Books, 2006.

Brennan, Barbara Ann. *Hands of Light: A Guide to Healing Through the Human Energy Field.* New York: Bantam Books, 1988.

Burrows, L. *Education in Human Values.* India: Sri Sathya Sai Books and Publications Trust, 1988.

Cameron, Julia. *The Artist's Way: A Spiritual Path to Higher Creativity.* New York: Putnam, 1992.

Campbell, Joseph. *The Hero with a Thousand Faces*. Waukegan: Fontana Press, 1993.

Campbell, Joseph. *Primitive Mythology*. New York: Penguin, 1991.

Cayce, Edgar. *Auras*. Virginia Beach: Association for Research and Enlightenment, 1978.

Chevalier, Jean, and Alain Gheerbrant. *Dictionary of Symbols*. Translated by John Buchanan-Brown. New York: Penguin, 1996.

Cooper Marcus, Clare. *House as a Mirror of Self: Exploring the Deeper Meaning of Home*. Lake Worth: Nicolas Hays, 2006.

Delaney, John J. *Dictionary of Saints*. New York: Doubleday, 1980.

Devi, Mata Amritanandamayi (Amma). *Immortal Light: Amma's Advice to Families*. India: Mata Amritanandamayi Devi, 1994.

Einstein, Albert. *Ideas and Opinions*. Translated by Sonja Bargmann. New York: New York Crown Publishers, 1954.

Frankl, Viktor. "Experiences in a Concentration Camp." In *Man's Search for Meaning*. Translated by Ilse Lach. Boston: Beacon, 1959.

Franklin, Benjamin. *The Private Life of the Late Benjamin Franklin, LL.D. Originally Written by Himself, And Now Translated From The French*. London, 1793. Originally published as *Autobiography of Benjamin Franklin, Memoires De La Vie Privee*. Paris, 1791. Free editions are available online at www.ushistory.org.

Gabbay, Simone. *Nourishing the Body Temple*. Virginia Beach: A.R.E. Press, 1999.

Gandhi, M.K.; compiled by R. K. Prabhu. *Truth is God: Gleanings from the Writings of Mahatma Gandhi Bearing on God, God-realization and the Godly Way*. India: Navajivan Publishing House, 1955

Gawain, Shakti. *Creative Visualization: Use the Power of Your Imagination to Create What You Want in Your Life*. Novato: New World Library, 1995.

Harvey, Andrew. *The Essential Mystics : Selections from the World's Great Wisdom Traditions*. New York: Harper Collins, 1997.

Hawley, Jack. *Reawakening the Spirit in Work: The Power of Dharmic Management*. San Francisco: Berrett-Koehler, 1993.

The Bhagavad Gita: A Walkthrough for Westerners. Translated by Jack Hawley. Madras: East West Books, 2001.

Hegde, Dr. A.S. "Brain, Mind, and Spirituality." *Mano Hriday: The Newsletter of the Sri Sathya Sai Institute of Higher Medical Sciences,* January 2002.

Hislop, Dr. John. *The Power and Potency of the Gayatri Mantra*. Sri Lanka: Sri Sathya Sai Organization, 1978.

The Holy Bible (New International Version). New York: Hodder and Stoughton, 1996.

Howard, Beth, "The Secrets of Resilient People," *AARP Magazine*, November/December 2009, p. 34.

Huxley, Aldous. *Science, Liberty, and Peace*. New York: Fellowship Publications, 1946

Jagadeesan, J., ed. *Reflections of Divinity: The Divine Teachings of Major World Religions*. Malaysia: Sai Youth of the World, 1999.

John of the Cross. *The Dark Night of the Soul*. Translated by Mirabai Starr. New York: Riverhead Trade, 2003.

Jung, Carl G. *Modern Man in Search of a Soul*. San Diego: Ark Paperbacks, 1995.

Kasturi, N., ed. *Sadhana: The Inward Path*. India: Sri Sathya Sai Books and Publications Trust, 1976.

Keating, Thomas. *Foundations for Centering Prayer and the Christian Contemplative Life; Open Mind, Open Heart; Invitation to Love; The Mystery of Christ*. England: Continuum, 2002.

Key, T. J., P. N. Appleby, E. A. Spencer, R. C. Travis, N. E. Allen, M. Thorogood, and J. I. Mann. "Cancer Incidence in British Vegetarians." In *British Journal of Cancer*, 2009, pp. 101, 192–197.

Klein, Allen. *The Healing Power of Humor: Techniques for Getting through Loss, Setbacks, Upsets, Disappointments, Difficulties, Trials, Tribulations, and All That Not-So-Funny Stuff*. New York: Putnam, 1989.

Krystal, Phyllis. *Taming Our Monkey Mind: Insight, Detachment, Identity*. York Beach: Red Wheel/Weiser, 1994.

Lawlor, Anthony. *The Temple in the House: Finding the Sacred in Everyday Architecture*. New York: Putnam, 1994.

Linn, Denise. *Sacred Space: Enhancing the Energy of Your Home and Office*. New York: Random House, 2005.

M, a disciple of Ramakrishna. *The Gospel of Sri Ramakrishna,* Translated by Swami Nikhilananda. New York: Ramakrishna-Vivekananda Center, 1942.

Merton, Thomas. *Mystics and Zen Masters.* New York: Noonday, 1967.

Mitchell, Stephen. *The Tao te Ching.* New York: Harper / Row, 1988.

Moore, Thomas. *Care for the Soul: A Guide for Cultivating Depth and Sacredness in Everyday Life.* New York: Harper Collins, 1992.

Mother Teresa. *Nobel Lectures, Peace 1971-80.* Edited by Tore Frangsmyr and Irwin Abrams. Singapore: World Scientific Publishing, 1997.

Murdock, Maureen. *The Heroine's Journey: Woman's Quest for Wholeness.* Boston: Shambala, 1990.

Myss, Caroline. *Anatomy of the Spirit: The Seven Stages of Power and Healing.* New York: Bantam Books, 1998.

Nikaya, Anguttara. *Anguttara Nikaya: Discourses of the Buddha.* Translated by Nyanaponika Thera. Sri Lanka: Buddhist Publication Society, 1970.

Nuova, Citta, Mons. Filippo Caraffa, ed. *Enciclopedia dei Santi:* Bibliotheca Sanctorum, vol. IX, ed. Rome.

Pani, Prithvi. "Gratitude and Appreciation: A Letter to the Hospital Administrator." *Mano Hriday: The Newsletter of the Sri Sathya Sai Institute of Higher Medical Sciences,* January 2002.

Peace Pilgrim, *Peace Pilgrim: Her Life and Her Work in Her Own Words.* Santa Fe: Ocean Tree Books, 1982.

Pierce, Penney. *The Intuitive Way: A Guide to Living from Inner Wisdom*. Hillsboro: Beyond Words Publishing, 1997.

Random House Webster's Unabridged Dictionary. New York: Random House, 2001.

Rilke, Maria Ranier. *Rilke's Book of Hours: Love Poems to God*. Translated by Anita Barrows and Joanna Macy. New York: Berkley, 1996.

Rinpoche, Sogyal. *The Tibetan Book of Living and Dying*. San Francisco: Harper, 1992.

Rumi, Jalal al-Din. *The Essential Rumi*. Translated by Coleman Barks and John Moyne. New York: Castle Books, 1995.

Sathya, Sai Sri. *Chinna Katha—I: Stories and Parables*. India: Sri Sathya Sai Books and Publications Trust, 1999.

Sathya, Sai Sri. *Chinna Katha—II: Stories and Parables*. India: Sri Sathya Sai Books and Publications Trust, 1999.

Sechrist, Elsie. *Dreams: Your Magic Mirror*. Virginia Beach: A.R.E. Press, 1995.

Sandburg, Carl. *Abraham Lincoln: The Prairie Years and the War Years*. Orlando: Harvest Books, 1954.

Suzuki, D. T. *An Introduction to Zen Buddhism*. New York: Grove Weidenfeld, 1991.

Saint Teresa of Avila. *The Interior Castle*. Translated by Mirabai Starr. New York: Riverhead Books, 2003.

Theodore de Bary, W.M., ed. *Sources of Indian Tradition*. New York: Columbia University Press, 1958.

Thoreau, Henry David. *Walden's Pond*. Austin: Holt, Rinehart, and Winston, 1948.

Tolstoy, Leo. *The First Step*. *Published in Essays and Letters*. Translated by Aylmer Maude. New York: H. Frowde,1909, pp. 82–91.

Tucker, Katherine L., K. Morita, N. Oiao, M. Hannan, L.A. Cupples, and P. Kiel. "Colas, but not other carbonated beverages, are associated with low bone mineral density in older women: The Framingham Osteoporosis Study." *American Journal of Clinical Nutrition* 84, no. 4 (2006): 936–942.

Tzu, Chang. *Basic Writings*. Translated by Burton Watson. New York: Columbia University Press, 1964.

The Upanishads. Translated and edited by Swami Nikhilananda. New York: Harper/Row, 1963.

Vogler, Christopher. *The Writer's Journey: Mythic Structure for Storytellers and Screenwriters*. New York: Boxtree Limited, 1996.

To Write to the Author

If you wish to contact the author or would like more information about this book, please write to the author in care of Llewellyn Worldwide and we will forward your request. Both the author and publisher appreciate hearing from you and learning of your enjoyment of this book and how it has helped you. Llewellyn Worldwide cannot guarantee that every letter written to the author can be answered, but all will be forwarded. Please write to:

Debra Moffitt
c/o Llewellyn Worldwide
2143 Wooddale Drive
Woodbury, MN 55125-2989

Please enclose a self-addressed stamped envelope for reply,
or $1.00 to cover costs. If outside the U.S.A., enclose an
international postal reply coupon.

Many of Llewellyn's authors have websites with additional information and resources. For more information, please visit our website at:

www.llewellyn.com